MW01716646

A QUEST FOR FREEDOM:

AN AFRICAN AMERICAN ODYSSEY

A QUEST For FREEDOM:

AN AFRICAN AMERICAN ODYSSEY

by

MACK KING CARTER

FOUR-G Publishers, Incorporated

1993

A Quest for Freedom

FOUR-G Publishers, Inc.
P.O. Box 2249
Winter Park, FL 32790

FOUR-G Publishers Cataloging-in-Publication Data:

Carter, Mack King, 1947-
A Quest for freedom: an African American odyssey/Mack King Carter.

1. Afro-Americans—History. 2. Racism—Religious Aspects. 3. Afro-Americans— Social conditions. 4. Afro-American —families. 5. Afro-Americans—Education.
I. Title
E185.C36 1993

ISBN 0-962542-38-5

Copies of this book are available from:

Mt. Olive Baptist Church
400 NW 9th Avenue
Fort Lauderdale, FL 33311
954-463-5126

Printed in the United States

DEDICATION

TO OUR GRANDCHILD: BRITTANY NICOLE
"Poppa's Baby"

May her journey across life's tempestuous sea
be less hazardous.

Preface

Why write a book? He/she who does is imperiled because he/she opens himself/herself to the charge of indecent exposure. If literary perversion ensues, penance is required before one can break the threshold of paradise. What is this book about?

This book grows out of a relentless experience of disenfranchisement, where a people is constantly defined, redefined, and categorized by the oppressor. And this oppression has not only been sanctioned sociopolitically, but also theologically. Therefore, this book is a socio-theological analysis of the oppression of African American people.

It is a challenge to the White (Beige) Institutional church to renounce and repent of its attachment to culture and racism. Without equivocating this book looks upon White (Beige) Institutional Christianity to be an enemy to oppressed people, and is therefore an enemy to Jesus of Nazareth. The missing ingredient during the Civil Rights movement 1955-1968 was that there was no organized effort to picket the White (Beige) church. The term "Beige" must replace the term "White" because "White" as a description of Caucasians is a misnomer. However, since the term (Beige) is not yet in vogue, in order to avoid confusion, the term "White" will be used. Because of the longevity of ethnic confusion, the terms "Black" and "African American" will be used interchangeably.

Since the White (Beige) church is married to the dominant culture, it cannot be a factor in the liberation enterprise unless it is completely dismantled or radically transformed by Jesus of Nazareth.

This book is also a challenge to the African American church to become the "Alternative Consciousness." If it fails, it must also be eliminated. If the African American Church can overcome its preoccupation with Pharaoh and his palace, our liberation is at hand.

Beyond all this, this book is an attempt to bring into focus some of the major issues confronting African Americans in the twenty-first century, such as the family, education, economics, politics, and the role of religion and the church. Our musings here cannot be considered as a prescription. Its purpose is to create discussion in order that our people might collectively rise up in creative fashion against the evil of oppression.

The difficulty in communicating in such a work as this, is that the truth must be told. When the naked truth is told, it is very easy to be called a pessimist. However, there can be no hope without truth. I still believe that the African American people could become the leaders of a movement that would subvert what Pharaoh and Caesar have to offer. Only then can the Infinite intersect our finitude.

Mack King Carter
Fort Lauderdale, Florida
1993

Acknowledgments

I sincerely express my gratitude to my wife Patricia Thomas Carter, who, besides being a constant companion, counselor, and critic, has endured the peculiar idiosyncrasies of a prophet, pastor-teacher for two decades.

I am deeply indebted to my late maternal grandmother, Lula Johnson 1881-1960, who faced oppression in its severest form and still embraced the Biblical Christ.

My parents, the late Frank Carter, Sr. 1898-1973, and Modlea Carter, from whose lips I heard stories of survival in this land of disenfranchisement; my brother Frank Carter, Jr.; my late sister Geraldine C. Robinson 1945-1980; and my elder sister Ruth Leamon have made me grateful for the nuclear family experience.

Our daughters, Lisa and Pamela, continue to bless us on our journey towards the freedom that's in the Carpenter from Nazareth.

My full time and part time staff have been loyal and supportive. My executive secretary, Mrs. Gearldine Pettis, who typed both the first and final draft of this manuscript is efficient, skilled, patient, and kind. Also Mrs. Gwen Elliott, who assisted in the typing, read both drafts, offered suggestions, and made helpful corrections, is also talented, efficient, and kind.

Rev. Wayne Lomax, my Assistant Pastor, is like a younger brother and is also my able colleague in ministry. His gifts are tremendous. Mrs. Sonya Fox, a faithful member of our congregation, read and corrected the manuscript. My friend, Dr. Bobby Joe Saucer, made helpful suggestions, and the supporting cast of the Mount Olive Baptist Church must be given credit for loyalty to me during a decade of prophesying for the King.

To all these, and others not mentioned, I shall always be grateful.

I've Known Rivers

I've known rivers:
I've known rivers ancient as the world and
older than the flow of human blood in human veins
My soul has grown deep like the rivers.

I bathed in the Euphrates when dawns were young.
I built my hut near the Congo and it lulled me to sleep.
I looked upon the Nile and raised the pyramids above it.
I heard the singing of the Mississippi when Abe Lincoln
went down to New Orleans, and I've seen its muddy
bosom turn all golden in the sunset.

I've known rivers:
Ancient, dusky rivers.

My soul has grown deep like the rivers.

By Langston Hughes

Contents

Chapter One

Enemies of African American People

Beyond a shadow of a doubt African American people have been historically besieged in America. But it is a grave error to begin a study of African Americans with a study of plantation life from 1619-1865. To do justice, we must begin with Mother Africa, for all peoples are derivatives of Africa. As Countee Cullen said:

> What is Africa to me:
> Copper sun or scarlet sea,
> Jungle star or jungle track,
> Strong bronzed men, or regal black
> Women from whose loins I sprang when the birds of
> Eden sang?

Slavery

The most devastating period in African history was the enslavement of millions of Africans in Central America, South America, the Caribbean, and the United States. All forms of involuntary servitude are morally wrong, but the form that was used in the United States of America was the most bestial. The European slave trade began in 1444 and continued for four hundred plus years. During the period Africa lost above forty million people to this nefarious system of dehumanization. Lerone Bennett, renowned historian, captures the slave scene as follows:

> The slave trade was people living, lying, stealing, murdering and dying. The slave trade was a black man who stepped out of his house for a breath of fresh air and ended up, ten months later, in Georgia with bruises on his back and a brand on his chest.

> The slave trade was a black mother suffocating her newborn baby because she didn't want him to grow up a slave. The slave trade was a bishop sitting on an ivory chair on a wharf in the Congo and extending his fat hand in wholesale baptism of slaves who were rowed beneath them, going in chains to the slave ships. The slave trade was a greedy king raiding his own village to get slaves to buy brandy.
>
> The slave trade was a pious captain holding prayer serves twice a day on his slave ship and later writing the famous hymn, "How sweet the Name of Jesus Sounds."[1]

In 1980 my wife and I were in Germany on a lecture tour with Dr. and Mrs. Bobby Joe Saucer, our great friends of Atlanta, Georgia. One of the places we visited was the Jewish concentration camp at Dachau outside Munich. What an awful encounter we experienced as we were confronted with the fact of man's inhumanity to man! Because of the oppression of African Americans we were all of a sudden caught up in the oppression of other people. Yet we were cognizant of the fact that only Jewish people can really feel the pangs of Auschwitz, Dachau, Treblinka, Buchenwald, etc. In 1987 this truth became existential for me and my wife, Pat. While visiting Gambia and Senegal in West Africa, we had occasion to visit Goree Island which is outside Dakar, Senegal. This was the processing point for millions of Africans as they embarked upon their new life as slaves. It was an awesome experience to go to the "door of no return." As we peered through the door at the mighty expanse of the Atlantic Ocean, we could feel the dread, the fear, and the confusion of our foreparents as they embarked upon their journey to experience four hundred years of destruction. What an enlightenment!

It is a truth that slavery has been with us for multiple millennia. Lerone Bennett declares:

> Slavery was old when Moses was young. In Plato's Athens and Caesar's Rome men, white, black, and brown, were bought and sold. Slavery existed in the Middle Ages, in Christian Europe and in Africa. Slavery was so prevalent in ancient times that Plato said, "every person has slaves among his ancestors."[2]

But as we peruse world history we discover that ancient slavery was based on war rather than race and economics. Later religious wars were fought between Moslems and Christians and the religious factor emerged. Those who were captured were forced to convert or die. Though evil within itself, their rationale was religious. They wanted to spread the teachings of the Koran as it had been revealed to the Prophet Mohammed. Based upon this fact many say that the modern Jew is not a Jew in the ethnic sense. They were originally called Khazars. Pressured by both Moslems and Christians, rather than converting to either, they adopted Judaism. This idea can be found in a book written by Arthur Koestler entitled The Thirteenth Tribe.[3] In biblical times one became a slave either as a prisoner of war, or by voluntary servitude for a period of time until a debt could be paid. Such was the situation in Paul's letter to Philemon. Apparently Onesimus owes a debt that he has reneged on paying. Rather than pay his debt, he becomes a runaway slave. While being on the run he comes in contact with the Apostle Paul who encourages him to return and says to Philemon to receive him as a brother and if he owed anything to charge it to his account.[4] This shows clearly that this was not about race but about a debt that Onesimus owed to Philemon.

The American brand of slavery stands alone as the most humiliating and debasing manifestation in history. It was begun for economic reasons but later received scientific and theological justification. In other words, since God had decreed that Africans are inferior, then it was all right to enslave a people that God had rejected. Therefore, in America, slavery is the definitive factor in clarifying the African American situation.

When we read the Book of Daniel, we see clearly the steps in the making of a slave. This book deals with four basic Jewish characters: Daniel, Shadrach, Meshach, and Abednego. This book is a classic in understanding the evolution of a slave.

1. Geographical dislocation -Daniel 1:3 - Like the Hebrew, Africans were uprooted from their native land. This is devastating because no matter how long you stay in Babylon, the true Hebrew longs for Zion. So if you want to enslave me, change my nativity.

2. Change the language - Daniel 1:4 - The Hebrews were to be taught a new language, that is, the Chaldean tongue. They were not forbidden to speak Hebrew; the strategy was to get them to eventually exalt the Chaldean above the Hebrew language. And if you stay long enough, you will forget your native language.

3. Training or brainwashing in a foreign culture. These new slaves had to be de-culturized - Daniel 1:5. For three years the Hebrews had to be broken in to the folkways of Babylon. In so doing, they were made to feel that they and their culture were inferior. This is necessary, if one is to be a slave. If a person does not feel inferior, no matter the physical impediments, that a person is not a slave, incarcerated maybe, but not a slave.

4. Changing one's name - Daniel 1:6-7. In Alex Haley's <u>Roots</u>, Kunta Kinte, as part of the breaking in process, fights against the notion of having his name changed to Toby. The Hebrews had their names changed as a symbol of their hopelessness. To change one's name is to change one's identity . In the midst of the African American oppression it is understandable why Malcolm Little became Malcolm X.

5. Make a distinction between house slaves and field slaves - Daniel 2:48-49. This was the most critical period in the oppression of the four Hebrews. To be a favorite in the oppressor's court is dangerous. For it is ultimately designed for the purpose of dividing the oppressed community.

6. Change one's religion - Daniel 3:1-25. Of course it didn't work in this instance. But the apex of challenges is to face the possibility of making the transition from the God of the oppressed to the god of the oppressor. If the oppressor can give you a new theology he can control your sociology.

7. The threat of persecution - Daniel 3:11 - The oppressed are invariably kept in line through the fear of pain and death.

Once these steps have been taken, you have a bonafide slave, who will demonstrate all of the idiosyncrasies of serfdom.

Slavery has taken its toll upon African American people. Its impact is ubiquitous. And any attempt to deny this fact categorizes one as a psycho-historical amnesiac. Dr. Na'Im Akbar says:

> Slavery is the modern genesis experience for Africans in the western world. Contained in this genesis is much about the continued social, economic, political and cultural reality of African Americans. There is contained in this tragic drama the nucleus of a mind wrought with the agonies of oppression of the most inhuman form, and simultaneously the image of man's greatest triumph over conditions of the flesh.[5]

The mind altering experience of slavery haunts us like the ghost of Banquo in Shakespeare's Macbeth. My present has been shaped by my vicious past. Both African Americans and Caucasians recoil at the suggestion that slavery still informs and influences the social situation of African Americans. The Caucasian gets upset because he doesn't want to be reminded of his sin against humanity. And the African American finds it too painful to remember. But remember we must. In 1985 my wife and I led a tour group to the Holy Land. Once we landed in Israel, one of the most magnetic sites was the Yad Vashem, which is a museum or memorial built in honor of the six million Jews who died in German concentration camps. As a people, we, too, need a memorial built in honor of the forty million plus who died in the middle passage and on Southern plantations. The Jews remember and are vigilant. We try to forget, only to go from one socio-economic-political defeat to another. Again Na'Im Akbar says:

> The chattel slavery of Africans in America for almost 300 years serves as one of the saddest commentaries of man's inhumanity to man. The tales of this period of our history are so morbid that they will arouse vehement hostilities at the very thought of what occurred. The level of cruelty was incomparable to anything recorded in modern history, including the Nazi atrocities at Auschwitz which were fleeting and direct, destroying bodies but leaving the collective mind intact.[6]

However, the danger of cynically focusing on the past is that it instigates paralysis of achievement. One becomes so obsessed by what was that he or she cannot claim what can be. Akbar goes on to say:

> There is a certain hesitation about dwelling on events of the past. On the one hand, it creates an atmosphere of determinism which removes the volitional possibilities of people to alter their condition. It tends to excuse the perpetuation of past events which could be altered simply by initiative. It preoccupies people unnecessarily and purposelessly with old hurts, tending old wounds. It is an emotional tirade that ultimately provides no constructive solutions for the

> present. But, those who deny the lessons of the past are doomed to repeat it. Those who fail to recognize that the past is a shaper of the present, and the hand of yesterday continues to write on the slate of today, leave themselves vulnerable by not realizing the impact of influences which do serve to shape their lives.[7]

Racism and the Oppressor

Probably the greatest legacy of slavery in America is racism. Racism is alive and well in America. It is more than prejudice. For we all are prejudiced. That is to say, we make discriminatory choices in life. I have a right not to want to live next door to the person who dumps his garbage in the street. But if this choice is based on ethnicity rather than public health, then I am a racist. However, for the sake of clarification, racism needs to be defined as prejudice plus power. It is that socio-psychological ideology that shapes the behavior of the oppressor and the oppressed.

Racism gives the oppressor a false sense of superiority. Because of their parental training, and their participation in racist structures, whites in general have a superior disposition towards African Americans and other oppressed groups. Nobody is born a racist. Yet millions are the inheritors of this evil ideology.

But again racism makes a liar out of the oppressor. We think of the Founding Fathers who drafted the Constitution and the Declaration of Independence who penned profound words that had no meaning for the oppressed. When they wrote "all men are created equal" they did not have African Americans in mind, because we were not considered to be human beings. Lerone Bennett, the African American historian said:

> America is what it is today largely because of the oppression of blacks and reds. The oppression of blacks and reds made the Constitution a lie and the Declaration of Independence a hollow mockery. More than that, oppression made Washington, Jefferson,

> Lincoln, Wilson, and both Roosevelts trimmers and hypocrites.[8]

Because of this lie, oppressed people are never at home in America. They find themselves perpetually confused. Even when the oppressed describe America as their country, they sound unconvincing or crazy.

Racism has made the oppressor into a thief. His very existence derives from his fraudulent rapacity. The land that he possesses was stolen from the Native Americans in the name of Manifest Destiny; and her economy was built upon the backs of African Americans who labored for 246 years without a paycheck. Even today because of America's greed, she makes up 5% of the world's population and controls about 40% of the world's goods. This is evil personified! Yet, we console ourselves with the self-proclaimed notion that we are a blessed nation who has the go ahead from God to oppress other people as long as we salute Him fifty-two times a year in this thing we call the church.

Because of racism's power, the oppressor is free to be an historical revisionist. He or she can rewrite the rules and change the facts to protect the guilty. A classic example is William Styron's book entitled <u>The Confessions of Nat Turner</u>. Everything that the oppressed community knew about Nat Turner was revised by Styron's book. Again Bennett says:

> The real Nat Turner was a virile, commanding, courageous figure. Styron rejects history by rejecting this image of Nat Turner. In fact, he wages literary war on this image, substituting an impotent, cowardly, irresolute, creature of his own imagination for the real black man who killed or ordered killed real white people for real historical reasons. The man Styron substitutes for Nat Turner is not only the antithesis of Nat Turner; he is the antithesis of blackness.[9]

Beyond this, racism empowers the oppressor to define an oppressed people. Historically the oppressor has categorized African Americans as lazy, shiftless, stupid, intellectually bankrupt, and biologically inferior. The purpose for this denigration is to give himself or herself a psycho-cultural rationale for oppression. By constantly repeating these stereotypes, it becomes a maxim by which oppressors relate to the oppressed. A dog is a dog because we anthropoids have so named him. Therefore, he acts like a dog because we have defined what a dog is. Likewise, the power of racism to define African Americans is a power that has been used almost forever to cast us in a mold of inferiority. Therefore, the only way this can be changed is for the oppressed to define themselves and say "to hell with what the oppressor says", or for the oppressor to renounce his heritage of institutionalized racism.

> The point that emerges most clearly from all this is that the problem of oppression in America or, to be more precise, the problem of race, is a total problem which permeates every institution and social practice. It is, as someone has said, like a drum: strike it anywhere and it reverberates everywhere.[10]

Therefore, since racism is embroidered into the socio-economic psyche of America, there will be no liberation of the oppressed or the oppressor until this malady is faced and erased.

Racism and the Oppressed

It is a truth that African Americans suffer from a serious inferiority complex that derives from our physical and psychological enslavement. Because of the verbal repetition of our alleged infeariority by the oppressor, the oppressed have subconsciously accepted his sick premise and its devastating conclusion. In public the oppressed community recoils at the suggestion of our inferiority. However, in private we tend to resort to the routine nomenclature of the oppressor. This can be demonstrated by the comfortableness of African Americans in the context of frivolity, who call themselves niggers.

This can also be shown by the attitude that African Americans have towards their leaders. Because we have bought into the notion that white is right, the oppressed community invariably responds to its leaders with skepticism and outright rejection. In many instances the ultimate social compliment to be paid an African American leader is legitimization by the oppressor. Therefore, African Americans must reject oppressor appointed leadership. Acceptance of such leadership causes African Americans to get caught up in the choose your leader syndrome, in which we can have but one leader. So, we always have to choose between:

1. Martin R. Delany and Frederick Douglass
2. Booker T. Washington and W.E.B. Dubois
3. W.E.B. Dubois and Marcus Garvey
4. Malcolm X and Martin Luther King, Jr.
5. Jesse Jackson and Louis Farrakhan

Until we can see good in all of our leaders, and things to be rejected in all of them, we will continue to have our leaders chosen for us. This is the trick that J. Edgar Hoover tried to pull on the African American community with his perverse desire to discredit Dr. Martin Luther King, Jr. and to exalt the late Roy Wilkins as the oppressor's chosen leader. This in no way illegitimatizes the contributions of Roy Wilkins; it is simply a statement in regard to a racist majority community that continually tries to appoint and anoint black leadership.

> As a people, African Americans must begin to recognize the disposition which has been conditioned in us to reject natural, effective leadership. If we understand that we have been programmed through our history to reject our natural heads, we may begin to become more conscious of recognizing true leaders.[11]

Therefore, any evaluation of our leaders must not be done through the white media, but within the moral parameters of the oppressed community. One of the great travesties of our history has been the appointment of the "Stop Gap Negro" who is anointed to control the oppressed community, to serve as a racial buffer, and as a tool whereby the racist oppressor can mitigate his guilt. Such a person was Booker T. Washington, the legendary founder and president of Tuskegee Institute in Alabama. Yet, we must be fair in our assessment, because any discussion of Booker T. Washington must be done contextually. In context he was torn between racist white power and the devastation of post-Reconstruction Black America. However, the fact that he was used by the oppressor must not be de-emphasized. Let me go on record by saying that no appointed African American leader in this country's history has wielded as much delegated power as Dr. Washington.

> The control he had over Federal appointments for blacks and over foundation grants to black institutions greatly curtailed most opposition. The Tuskegee Institute News Bureau flooded newspapers with releases supporting Washington's views. He and his supporters secretly subsidized, or bought control of, several influential black newspapers and magazines, in which they promoted Washington's viewpoint without the public being aware that these periodicals were controlled by him.[12]

In spite of Dr. Washington's eminence, such a man or woman is a serious handicap to the community of the oppressed, because he or she causes the oppressor to labor under the erroneous notion that all is well in the camp. Such an individual is an impediment to the radical repentance that is necessary to liberate both the oppressor and the oppressed. This malignancy continues to haunt us today, for the oppressor has the money and the power to make it stick, unless we refuse to participate in our own destruction.

Probably the most malevolent derivative of racism has been the self hatred that is so ostensible in the African American community. Black on black crime is a by-product of white on black crime. Because of the violence done to him, he cannot in many instances take his revenge out on the oppressor so he takes it out on his own community. In reality he hates the oppressor, but he knows that an African American usually gets the death penalty for killing the oppressor and very little prison time for killing one of his own. Thus, the message is clear; whites are superior to blacks. While I am not an expert in the history of jurisprudence in America, I would wager that there have been few whites who have received capital punishment for killing an African American. Several years ago while I served as Visiting Professor at Southern Baptist Theological Seminary in Louisville, Kentucky, a conference was held on campus that was sponsored by the Home Mission Board of the Southern Baptist Convention. At this conference was a black man who was going throughout the country praising Southern Baptists for saving his soul while he was in prison for killing two black men. While he put down the Black church and exalted the white church, he was reminded, before the session ended, by the great theologian, Dr. George Kelsey, that if he had killed two white men he would not have lived long enough to have his soul saved. He got his soul saved, because in America, black life is not valuable. Such soteriology breeds justifiable atheism. No wonder we kill ourselves!

Beyond this, the American media, both literary and cinematic, underscore and exude the inferiority of the African American and the Native American. Both television and the movie theaters have been instruments in the name of entertainment that have been used to perpetuate myths of the oppressor, such movie concepts as: the good guys wear the white hats and the evil guys wear black hats; Jack Benny and Rochester; Amos and Andy; the westerns where cowboys kill off the Indians; "Tarzan the Ape Man;" "Rocky;" "Rambo;" "The Jeffersons;" "Good Times," etc. All these serve the pernicious philosophy of the oppressor.

The message of many comedies is that oppression is funny, and the oppressed is someone to be made fun of. One notes that African American movie stars receive very little serious dramatic offers. Although I am a personal fan of Bill Cosby both as a man and an artist, I wonder if he would do as well in America in a serious drama. Even though "The Cosby Show" has substance and authenticity, I believe that the only medium open at this time for African Americans is comedy. Comedy is not to be frowned upon, except when it is used to perpetuate racial stereotypes. Another myth that has been thrust upon us by the movie theater is the figure of Tarzan the Ape Man. The message of Tarzan is that a white man, no matter how ignorant, is to be in control of his environment. Here is a white man with a "mini-skirt" and a dagger, swinging through trees, with Cheetah his fabled chimpanzee, who can holler, and everything in the jungle moves. He can single-handedly whip all the black savages, all the alligators, tigers and lions. I remember sitting in the theater as a boy cheering for Tarzan as he whipped thousands of my ancestors all by himself. No wonder I must pray.

The power of racism again comes through in such movies as Rambo and Rocky. The message of these two box office hits is that truth is what the oppressor says it is. A child that views Rambo would get the notion that here is one white man who could do what the United States armed forces could not do, and that is win the war in Vietnam. Several years ago a poll was conducted asking little white boys who was the heavyweight champion of the world. The boys responded by saying, "Rocky is the champ." The truth of the matter is that the last white American to be heavyweight champion was Rocky Marciano who retired in 1956. So the power of the oppressor is able to accomplish on the movie screen what no white fighter has been able to do in over thirty years.

Finally the media strikes at the heart of the African American community every time it portrays a black male as unintelligent. This comes out in the television series of the 1970's and '80's called "The Jeffersons," starring Sherman Hemsley and Isabel Sanford. George Jefferson is a millionaire, but he is ignorant. He often has his wife to take sides with others against him because of his moronic behavior. He is loud and uncouth. Nobody respects him, including his maid. So everything he has accomplished seems to be a fluke or pure luck. It is a truism in America that the oppressor will allow the African American male to have a little of everything but some brains. The message, then, is clear: a brainless man cannot think; a man who cannot think cannot lead; a man who cannot lead has to be led; and if one has to be led, he can be led to lose his wealth. For years the myth of the brainless African American male has kept him out of decision-making positions.

Since 1947, African Americans have basically controlled (performance wise) football, basketball, track and field, boxing, and baseball. But in spite of black domination, we still operate at the participatory level rather than the ownership level. So sports in America are just the microcosm of the macrocosm, a fact simply revealing that at all levels of American society African Americans work for white people.

Sports in America can be a medium of liberation economically, if we would wake up and smell the coffee. Yet in recent years the myth of the unintelligent or the instinctive African American athlete has been perpetuated by such men as Al Campanis who was an official in the Dodgers' organization. He said on ABC's "Nightline" that "blacks are not intelligent enough to be managers." A few weeks later Jimmy "the Greek" Snyder suggested that because of some selective cross breeding in slavery the African American athlete is bigger and stronger than white athletes. Both of these men simply reaffirmed what whites have been taught about blacks from day one. Thus these two men became the scapegoats for this racist society. However, as long as we allow the Caucasian definition of what is good and great to stand, we will be defined continually as inferior to whites. For example, Josh Gibson, the great African American baseball player probably the greatest hitter who ever lived, was called the "black Babe Ruth". In the clerical realm, a black preacher receives the ultimate compliment when he is called the "black Billy Graham." Both of these statements are racist and insulting. Therefore, we must strive to come up with a new way of thinking about ourselves and the oppressor.

Individualism

This is the fallacy that all is well if I make it. This is suicide for any oppressed people. Unless we develop a corporate ethnic agenda we will not be victorious. We must remember that, individually, African Americans have always done well. Even in slavery the house slave, though still a slave, had it made in comparison to the field slave. He had certain privileges that other slaves did not have, but he was still a slave. The mentality which says "I have mine, you get yours" must be abandoned, because a drop of water does not an ocean make. Several years ago I compared notes of oppression with a Jewish Rabbi in Louisville, Kentucky. He noted three of the major differences in Jewish and African American oppression. One is the fact that Jews, because of their numbers, did not have the luxury of individualism. He said, "In our community both Cohen and Leibowitz have to make it in order for Jews to survive." Secondly, he noted that African Americans were the only oppressed group that used the oppressor as their model for liberation. Thirdly, he noted that our love for the enemy thwarts us in our struggle for liberation. Jews do not love Hitler and are suspicious of Germans. However, in reality, it is not that African Americans love whites; the truth is that they hate themselves.

The "hole in the fence" concept of success, while a reality for some individuals, is only a frustrating mirage for the masses. The American myth is that anybody can make it in this country. But the one who perpetuates this doctrine holds the keys to success in his hands. The system is so designed to let a few through the hole in the fence in order to make them propaganda tools for white oppression. Thus, the oppressor readily throws up in the face of the frustrated masses that Oprah Winfrey, Michael Jackson and Bill Cosby have made it; so can you. However, when the masses start running toward the hole in the fence which leads to success, they discover that the hole in the fence has been mended, and there is great despair on the outside looking in. Now we have a problem. The question is, "What is going to be our attitude toward those who got through the fence?" That depends on the attitude of the brother or sister who made it over. If their attitude becomes that of the oppressor, then they simply replicate the oppressor and therefore become the enemy of the oppressed. But if they are on the other side of the fence sharing expertise, money, presence, and other resources for liberation, then they are the blessed of the earth. In other words, if we are going to build a great people, we must adopt a collective approach in overcoming oppression. Therefore, we do not have the luxury of playing the game of "one-upmanship." As someone has said, "We will either hang together or we will simply hang."

War

General William Tecumseh Sherman, the Civil War general said, "War is hell." To this, African American people can say, "amen" because no scourge is greater than war, in the strategic liquidation of an oppressed people. African Americans have fought in most of America's wars since the Revolutionary War. It is ironic that the first to die for America's independence from Great Britain was an African by the name of Crispus Attucks, on March 5, 1770. In spite of the heroics of Attucks and others such as: Peter Salem, Cuff Hayes, Lemuel Haynes, and Caesar Dickerson, America's quest for freedom did not include freedom for all her subjects. An estimated 5,000 blacks fought with the colonial forces of the American Revolution.[13] Yet it is interesting that early in colonial America every man, white or black, freedman or slave, was called upon to help defend the country against Indian uprisings, European transgressors, and other threats to peace.[14] But because of the fear of slave rebellions, the colonies soon adopted a policy of excluding blacks from military service.[15]

Lerone Bennett, Jr. said:

> Blacks fought in the land and water battles of the War of 1812. Two battalions of black soldiers were with Andrew Jackson when he defeated the British at the Battle of New Orleans.[16]

It was at New Orleans that Jackson issued an eloquent oration of the exploits of his black soldiers on December 18, 1814.

> To the men of color! Soldiers! From the shores of Mobile I collected you to arms; I invited you to share

> in the perils and to divide the glory of your white countrymen. I expected much from you, for I was not uninformed of those qualities which must render you so formidable to an invading foe. I knew that you could endure hunger and thirst and all the hardships of war. I knew that you loved the land of your nativity, and that like ourselves you had to defend all that is most dear to you. But you surpass my hopes. I have found in you, united to these qualities that ennoble enthusiasm which impels to great deeds.[17]

It is hard to find a more eloquent piece of nonsense to peruse. In a time of war, America is everybody's country. But in peacetime, it is the white man's country.

During the Civil War, African Americans carried their share of the load. Again Bennett says:

> Black soldiers participated in 410 military engagements and 39 major battles, including Port Hudson, Fort Wagner, Olustee, Petersburg Mine Assault, Chaffin' Farm, Nashville, Overton Hill, Honey Hill, Yazoo City, Poison Springs, Tupelo, Bermuda Hundred, Dutch Gap, Hatcher's Run, Fort Fisher, the Fall of Richmond, Deep Bottom and Appomattox. Sixteen black soldiers received Congressional Medals of Honor for gallantry in action.[18]

Although African Americans were kept out of the war by the Lincoln administration early on, they still proved to be of incalculable importance. It was during this War that Harriet Tubman proved to be the Union Army's greatest genius of espionage.

African Americans also served in the following wars: Spanish American War; World War I; World War II; the Korean Conflict; the Vietnamese War; the Invasion of Grenada; the Invasion of Panama in 1989; and the Persian Gulf War. It is a matter of record that thousands of Black men and women have given their lives in order that rich White men could keep their monies. The Vietnamese War really hit hard on me as a teenager growing up in Ocala, Florida. I remember vividly the existential pain that I felt when eight of my schoolmates from Howard High School lost their lives in Vietnam. What was so poignant was that most of them never had the chance to exercise their right to vote in this great nation. It is ironic that one of the most prophetic statements about the War did not come from the lips of Billy Graham or the leaders of many other ecclesiastical bodies, but from the gifted musical genius Stevie Wonder in his hit song "Frontline." It reads as follows:

> I am a veteran of the War. Up and Joined the Army back in 1964. At 16, got to be a man at any cost. I volunteered for Vietnam where I got my legs shot off. I recall a movie which said who's more a man than a man with a reason worth dying for. They had me standing on the Frontline, but I stand at the back of the line when it comes to getting ahead. They gave me a uniform and a tiny salty pill. Stuck this urge in my cap for the wrong kind of thrill. They put a gun in my hand and said shoot till he's dead. It's hard to kill when pain of your friend echoes through your head. Brought up in church no man should take another life. But then put in a jungle where life has no price. They had me standing on the Frontline, but I stand at the back of the line when it comes to getting ahead. My niece is a hooker, my nephew's a junky too. They say I have no right to tell them how they should do. They laugh and say quit bragging 'bout the war you should never been in. My mind is so brainwashed I'd probably go back and do it again. They had me standing on the Frontline, but I stand at the back of the line when it comes to getting ahead.[19]

Beyond a doubt this song profoundly, prophetically, and poignantly captures our collective frustration as defenders of this racist nation. The depth of our brainwashing was demonstrated when Dr. Martin Luther King, Jr. opposed the War in Vietnam. Not only was he castigated by President Lyndon Baines Johnson as an ungrateful nigger, but he was also vilified by some of the leading Civil Rights leaders for mixing Civil Rights with global politics. History has already proved Dr. King to be right. Vietnam was a colossal error, from which the African American community has not recovered.

Why do we fight for a nation that oppresses us? (1) Sometimes African Americans have fought out of ignorance of this country's ideology in going to War. The code word "communism" was enough to send thousands to their deaths in Korea and Vietnam. In no way do I defend communism anymore than I would defend capitalism, for both are repugnant to the Kingdom of God. But most of the blacks who fought in Vietnam were not familiar with Karl Marx's <u>Das Kapital</u> or the <u>Communist Manifesto</u>. They fought against only that which made the oppressor uncomfortable. (2) Some fight because they believe this is their country. This belief is twofold in that some feel that the blood they have spilled and the labor they have given entitle them to a share of the title deed of this nation. On the other hand, there is a group in every oppressed situation who feel a certain kinship with the oppressor. They feel that whatever the master has belongs to them as well. (3) Others fight because they fear governmental reprisals such as prison sentences. (4) Others fight out of loyalty. They are afraid that refusing to fight would make matters worse for African American people. (5) Still others fight out of a subconscious belief that if we fight gallantly, the oppressor will accept us. It was pathetic the way America used Joe Louis during World War II. Joe Louis was probably the greatest heavyweight champion in history and the hero of millions of disenfranchised blacks. But to hear Joe Louis standing before American troops saying, "We will win because God is on our side," was nothing but racist propaganda. The question, then, should be what God is on our side? And in what sense can it be proved that this God loves African Americans?

Traditionally the poor and the disenfranchised go to war in order to defend the interests and ideologies of the oppressor. We know not why we fight, except that the oppressor sends us forth as "lambs among wolves." Fighting the oppressor's wars makes the oppressed guilty of complicity in the evil of oppression. We must decide if we are Americans pure and simple, or whether we are a nation within a nation. If we are Americans, we ought to shut up and fight. But if we are a nation of thirty million, we ought to have a strong voice in deciding who is the enemy and what battles we will fight. We cannot continue to lose thousands of our people for a nation that is persistently retrogressive in its attitude towards African Americans.

Skin Color

This skin that the African American carries is a tremendous socio-psychological burden in America. The great African American novelist Ralph Ellison said in the Prologue to Invisible Man:

> I am an invisible man. No, I am not a spook like those who haunted Edgar Allen Poe; nor am I one of your Hollywood ectoplasms. I am a man of substance, of flesh, and bone, fiber and liquids - and I might even be said to possess a mind. I am invisible, understand, simply because people refuse to see me.[20]

People can see this skin and draw immediate conclusions about my intelligence and my worth as a created being. There is something about the melanin in my skin that causes my Intelligence Quotient to diminish in the company of my white superiors. My own I.Q., last tested in the late 1960's, was 160. However, a white student of an I.Q. of 85 is my superior.

Because of our black skin, we were kept out of everything that was white. The great baseball player Josh Gibson was not kept out of the major leagues because he was not good enough, but because he was black. Those who saw him play declared him the greatest hitter ever. Not only in sports, blacks experienced color discrimination in public facilities, schools, neighborhoods, and churches.

This fallacy of ethnic inferiority based on skin color is the primary ingredient of apartheid in South Africa, where 5 million whites have rule over 23 million blacks.

Nobody has a monopoly on suffering, but to suffer because of the color of one's skin is the apex of inhumanity. In 1989, my wife and I, along with a travel delegation of fifteen, visited the Italian cities of Rome, Florence, and Venice. I remember vividly the conversation I had with a Jewish doctor from Montreal, Canada. As we compared notes on oppression I said to him that Jews can hide by changing their names from "Cohen" to "Cantrell" or from "Greenberg" to "Green". And if he is not caught buying Kosher food or worshipping in a synagogue, he is home free, because his skin color will allow him to blend into the larger society. However, because of the skins of African Americans we are not allowed the same survival luxury. This fact was demonstrated very poignantly by John Howard Griffin in his book entitled Black Like Me who found out first hand what it means to be black in America. In this book Griffin points out how he would paint his face black and try to enter white establishments and would be faced with venom and death. He would go out and wash the black from his face, and he would be accepted because of his white face, and, of course, all of this was not known or made public until the experiment was completed. To have a black skin in America and other parts of the world is still disadvantageous. The late Dr. Paul Scherer told a story that originated toward the close of World War II. The graduating class in a high school was assigned as the subject for a composition, "What just punishment should be meted out to Adolph Hitler?" An African American girl won the prize by developing the thesis that he should be put into a black skin and set down in the midst of a white neighborhood.[21] This insanity is further illustrated by Taylor Branch in his Pulitzer Prize winning book entitled Parting the Waters. He records the true story of a black man who applied for admission to the University of Mississippi in the late 1950's only to be arrested and committed to the state mental institution on the grounds that only an insane Negro would seek admission to Ole Miss.[22]

All of this would engender hilarity if the consequences were not so devastating. In response to the white man's preoccupation with our skin color we have reacted in several negative ways. (1) For many years blacks tried to bleach their skin in order to be accepted. (2) The straightening comb effectuated a revolution in the black community because we had been taught that whites have "good hair" and African Americans have "bad hair." This is why African American women started getting their hair straightened. But this was not reserved for women, for male entertainers of ebony hue soon got in on the act. They began to get a stylistic hairdo called a "process". In the early years the majority of African American entertainers had a "process" such as: Sammy Davis Jr., Little Willie John, Little Richard, Sam Cooke, etc. I remember my own confusion when the late Sam Cooke abandoned his "process" for an "Afro" hairstyle. In my own brainwashed mind I thought the white look was superior. (3) The oppressor's hatred of my skin inadvertently led to my self hatred. This is why we kill each other so rapidly. The black skin in our collective psyche is repugnant, and to be able to get rid of it would be liberating in itself. But we are stuck with it! (4) Probably the most debilitating result is the game of colorism that has been practiced for years in our own community, where the closer one approximated white skin the more opportunities he or she had. This in turn caused light skinned African Americans to feel the pangs of rejection that were meted out by those of a darker hue. For many years this nonsense was also played out in the African American churches in this country. In almost every community African Americans were divided not only along economic and academic lines, but also by color. To be accepted in many churches one had to be almost white. In regard to the African American church, its practice of colorism is a manifestation of its pathetic plight as a derivative of racism based on color. Though this practice is no longer as apparent as in the past, it still is a sore spot in the collective consciences of African American people. To be judged because of incompetence based on equal opportunity is just. But to judge one based on skin color is asinine.

Integration

In the last twenty-five years nothing has been more confusing to African Americans than the issue of integration or desegregation. It needs to be stated unequivocally that we are not an integrated society. Integration was a desire for equity and justice based on the following: (1) the promises found in the U.S. Constitution (2) land (3) money (4) identity and (5) opportunity. To say the least, we have been short changed, because if our goal was simply to achieve moderate toleration and physical proximity, then we are collectively imbecilic. I am the first to admit that the African American community did not fully understand the ramifications of desegregation. We naively believed that if we could just sit next to white people, there would be a great social transformation. Needless to say, this has not yet become a reality. Neither is there a pregnant cloud on the horizon ready to shower us with hope. In the African American community, there is widespread hopelessness, while the oppressor wants to know, "What is it that you want?" The answer to the question was so aptly put by a black brother who said, "Write a list of everything you want and then sign my name." What do we want? We want to be able to control: our destiny, our economics, the education of our children, and all the institutions of our community.

However, because of our historical brainwashing, the masses of African Americans believed that being with white people was the ultimate in socialization. The late Dr. Benjamin E. Mays caused a slight furor when he served on the Board of Education in Atlanta, Georgia. He suggested that African American boys and girls did not have to sit next to whites in order to learn. He was right, and his words are still valid.

Those of us who grew up between 1865 - 1968 must admit that whites had the best facilities, and even though they were in control, there was still a modicum of institutional stability that we no longer have. Ladies and gentlemen, boys and girls, we have been tricked. Desegregation means that it is legal to make whites richer. In the process the infrastructure of the African American community has been dismantled: the family is in disarray; we no longer have discipline in the home or the school (to be discussed in later chapters), the reason being that white parents were not going to allow black teachers to discipline their children, so black parents said, "If you can't discipline whites you are not going to discipline my children either." Black businesses, by and large, have been abdicated; we also lost control of the education of our people. In the early years, black principals were demoted to assistant principals in charge of discipline; and successful football coaches were demoted to teaching physical education. So desegregation, as it presently stands, is a reaffirmation of white power and superiority.

Am I then arguing for resegregation? The question is not about resegregation but about 30 million people controlling their destiny. Our position is that the oppressor has no right to tell me where I can go, or where I should live. What we fought for at a profound level were God-given rights. God gave a loaf of bread to be shared by all the people of this stolen nation. But instead of sharing the loaf, the oppressor took the loaf and ran off with it. In order to keep the loaf all to himself, he erected the dehumanizing institution of slavery. He worked the oppressed for 246 years without a paycheck and has the nerve to ask me what I want. Furthermore, he fought a War in order to keep the loaf. We thought that when the War was over, we would have our share of the loaf. During Reconstruction 1867 - 1877 we had our share of the loaf to a degree; but then when the smoke cleared, he ended up with the whole loaf all to himself once again. He then erected a fence to keep me away from the loaf (legal segregation). When we tried to go through the gate, he made it legal to keep the loaf all to himself (Supreme Court Decisions). He then tried to confuse the issue by saying that we wanted to be with him. The issue was not about social intercourse, but social justice. The whole life and martyrdom of Dr. Martin Luther King, Jr. and the Civil Rights movement were about getting our share of the loaf. As of this writing, the crumbs continue to fall, but our rightful share of the loaf remains as elusive as the rediscovery of the Ark of the Covenant.

The Criminal Justice System

It is a truth that the criminal justice system works best for those in power. Therefore, those not in power are invariably shafted. No scenario is more frightening to me than to see a black lawyer and client, facing a white judge and jury. This is clearly stated in African American folklore. Sister Goose wanted justice from Br'er Fox but she only got fox justice, because everybody in the courthouse was a fox. Again, the Goose was in the tree, and Br'er fox told the Goose to come on down and mingle with the rest of the animals, because the animals had passed a law that no animal must be hostile towards another animal. But just when the Goose was about taken in by this suggestion, a dog started barking in the woods. As the fox started to trot off, the Goose said, "You ain't afraid of that dog is you? Didn't all the animals pass a law not to bother each other anymore?" "Yes," replied the fox as he trotted away quickly, "the animals passed the law; but some of the animals round here ain't got much respect for the law."[23] These tales are accurate in describing the African American dilemma.

This can be seen by the general hostility that exists between law enforcement officers and the African American community. Beyond this, the disproportionate number of African American men in jail and prison is eloquent testimony that either there is an unusual pathology of dysfunction that exists in the African American community, or our problem is a derivative of a racist judiciary.

The denial of justice can also be seen in the evil act of lynching. Ralph Ginzburg in his book <u>100 Years of Lynchings</u> gives a chilling chronicle of known lynchings of African American people in America between the mid-nineteenth century to the 1960's. Lerone Bennett records such a nauseating account:

> The Mary Turner lynching of 1918 was unquestionably one of the most barbaric acts ever committed in a civilized country. Though pregnant, the black woman was lynched in Valdosta, Georgia. She was

> hanged on a tree, doused with motor oil and burned. As she dangled from the rope, a man stepped forward with a pocket knife and ripped open her abdomen in a crude caesarean operation. "Out tumbled the prematurely born child," wrote Walter White. "Two feeble cries it gave - and received for the answer the heel of a stalwart man, as life was ground out of the tiny form."[24]

Although I have not witnessed this uncivilized behavior personally, my maternal grandmother told me that my maternal grandfather was killed by his white employer in the early years of the twentieth century. He killed my grandfather for the simple reason that my grandfather mildly protested the fact that his employer had cussed my grandmother for praising God too loudly. This dastardly act occurred in the State of Alabama. This murderer did not spend one minute in jail. He was totally cleared of all charges. After this experience, our family moved from Alabama to Defuniak Springs, Florida in 1910. In 1917 my mother's brother, who was in his early teens, got in a fight with a white boy, and because he got the best of the white boy, my uncle had to be slipped out of town in order to avoid being lynched. Because of conditions in the South at that time, my uncle never saw his mother alive again. There were forty-three years between the time my uncle ran away and the time of my grandmother's death in 1960. If there is any salvific merit in the whole affair, it was the fact that my mother finally had a reunion with her long lost brother in 1974, fifty-seven years after he was driven away from his family by the threat of death. This reunion was maintained until my uncle's death in 1985. The law in both instances offered no basic civil rights for our family. Other white on black murders have gone unsolved on through the years. One of the classic works on the subject of injustice was the book written by Bruce Wright entitled <u>Black Robes, White Justice</u>. The author points out the fact that the Judiciary is inextricably tied to racism:

> <u>The New York Times</u> on June 28, 1985, reported that a judge in Kentucky awarded workers' compensation

> to a white man based on the latter's fear of working with black people. The 39 year old beneficiary of this largesse was said by a psychiatrist to suffer from paranoid schizophrenia.[25]

All this gives credence to the fact that it is hard for a goose to receive justice in a court of foxes.

Another issue that needs to be raised in the history of American jurisprudence is the number of whites who have been executed in this country for killing an African American. The answer is commentary.

African American Apologists for Racism

I guess the quintessence of oppression is when an African American male or female who is thoroughly Eurocentrized academically, becomes an apologist for the establishment. I must add that not even a Klansman is more adept at arguing racism's cause. If the oppressor really wants to feel good about his or her racism, brainwash an African American and pay him or her well and he will find him or her to be of inestimable value. Such men of ebony hue as Dr. Walter Williams and Dr. Thomas Sowell, while they are competent Eurocentrically trained scholars, add very little to the building of the African American community. Without a doubt, they have many insights that ought to be shared in the community of the oppressed, and not with the oppressor-controlled media. To see a Benjamin Hooks or a Jesse Jackson debating the consequences of racism on a white forum with a black apologist is ludicrous.

Many times this group is composed of the Black bourgeois which suffers from the illusion that they are somehow superior to the oppressed masses. This crowd is into the same things as the oppressor such as: status, class, materialism, conservatism, and an "America, right or wrong attitude." If this group were given the opportunity it would be just as oppressive as the oppressor. Paulo Freire in his book Pedagogy of the Oppressed said:

> It is a rare peasant who once promoted to overseer, does not become more of a tyrant towards his comrades than the owner himself.[26]

It is indeed a sad commentary on the history of African Americans in this country that much of our undoing comes from us. The greatest fear is when the apologist becomes a polemicist. As Pogo said, "I have met the enemy and he is us." This must be changed if we are going to survive the twenty-first century.

References - Chapter One

[1] Lerone Bennett, Before the Mayflower, (Chicago, Il: Johnson Publishing Co., 1982), 29-30.
[2] Ibid., 31.
[3] Arthur Koestler, The Thirteenth Tribe, Random House, New York, 1967.
[4] Philemon.
[5] Na'Im Akbar, Chains and Images of Psychological Slavery, New Mind Productions, Jersey City, New Jersey, 1984, 1.
[6] Ibid.
[7] Ibid.
[8] Lerone Bennett, The Challenge of Blackness, Johnson Publishing Co.; Chicago, 1972, 145.
[9] Ibid., 150-151.
[10] Ibid., 146-147.
[11] Akbar, 19.
[12] Edgar A. Toppin, A Biographical History of Blacks in America Since 1528, David McKay Company, Inc., New York, 440.
[13] Martin Binkin, Mark J. Eitelberg, Alvin J. Schexnider, and Marvin M. Smith, Blacks and The Military, The Brookings Institution, Washington, D.C. 13.
[14] Ibid., 11.
[15] Ibid., 12.
[16] Bennett, Mayflower, 192-193.
[17] Ibid., 452.
[18] Ibid., 206.
[19] Stevie Wonder, "Frontline."
[20] Ralph Ellison, Invisible Man, 192-193.
[21] Georgia A. Buttrick, ed., Interpreters Bible Commentary Vol. 3, 1023, 1954.
[22] Taylor Branch, Parting the Waters: America in the Kings Years 1954-63, Simon and Schuster, New York, 233.
[23] Langston Hughes and Arna Bontemps (eds), Book of Negro Folklore (New York: Dodd, Mead, 1958), 13.
[24] Lerone Bennett, Before the Mayflower, 352.
[25] Bruce Wright, Black Robes, White Justice, Carol Publishing Company, New York, New York, 1987, 214.
[26] Paulo Freire, Pedagogy of the Oppressed. New York: Continuum Publishing Corporation, 1985.

Chapter Two

The Impact of Religion in the African American Community

Negative Impact

Any authentic search for freedom must begin with the question of religion. The impact of religion on the community can be demonstrated by the fact that overwhelmingly most African Americans in a nominal sense are theistic and Christian. This in no way minimizes the other religious expressions to be found in the community such as the Muslim faith and other media of spirituality. However, in this chapter our primary focus will be on Christianity. We have chosen to do so because of its impact, numerical strength, and the fact that the author is an adherent of the Christian faith. Religion can be both friend and foe of an oppressed community. In the case of African American Christians vis-a-vis the white community it has been socially, spiritually, and psychologically unhealthy. In other words, it has often been an opiate given to anesthetize our revolutionary propensity.

When our African forebears first came to these shores, and particularly after slavery was legalized, the problem faced by the white church, which incidentally endorsed slavery, was what to do about the souls of the slaves. The earliest response was that nothing should be done, because the slaves had no souls. Therefore, soteriology was not a theological consideration. Later on, due to the work of evangelization sponsored by the Society for the Propagation of the Gospel in Foreign Parts, early in the eighteenth century, the church reached another level of theological insanity. It concluded that Blacks did have souls, but they were inferior, so they must be fed a steady diet of Bible passages that would reinforce their inferiority, and encourage their docility and subservience. For almost three hundred years, the latter conclusion has been the social, political and theological underpinning for racism in America. I am of the opinion that racism is still very alive in America because the White church is primarily racist. The Supreme Court, while it can regulate public behavior, cannot change attitudes. It is the role of the church to lead the way in the transformation of attitudes. Racism is not the burden of the African American community; it is the burden of the white ecclesiastical community. It is a truth, that for economic reasons, Branch Rickey did more for the dignity of African Americans than the sum total of White American evangelists in this century. On this issue the White American church continues to be an abysmal failure.

If we are to be mentally free, we must, as a people, take a long, serious, and collective look at American Christianity. We must admit that the African American church is either the result or the reaction against racist Christianity. To ignore this historical reality is to live in a world of perpetual fantasy. Pierre Berton in his provocative book entitled the Comfortable Pew said:

> Indeed, the history of the race struggle in the United States has been, to a considerable extent, the history of the Protestant rapport with the status quo. From the beginning, it was the church that put its blessing on slavery and sanctioned a caste system that continues to this day. It is a negation of that Christian equality before God which the church preaches.[1]

It behooves the African American theological-kerygmatic community to explain the Carpenter's Gospel in light of the biblical-existential situation. Too many lives have been ruined because of the false anthropology of White American Christianity. This in turn has led to an unthinking enthusiasm which becomes a substitute for socio-economic action. Let me digress to say that African Americans ought to treasure our emotive expression in worship, but unless the cognitive (mind); the affective (feelings); and the conative (decision) are all joined, at best one has a mutilated worship experience. One of the great criticisms of the African American church is that it has an ongoing romance with ignorance. It confuses muscularity with spirituality; perspiration with inspiration; and sociosexual frustration with biblical praise. Therefore, historically we have not had an adequate pneumatology.

Because of racist White American Christianity, the African American church has followed the path of denominationalism. We must view denominationalism as a milestone in our pilgrimage towards the Christ, but it must never be a millstone. Many things could be accomplished for the African American community and the community at large if we were not impeded by our denominational affiliations. The late Malcolm X warned us of this albatross, but we did not have the oppressor's permission to listen. Baptists, Methodists, Catholics, Pentecostals, etc., are all labels that keep us divided and defeated socially, economically, and politically. This does not mean that I am impervious to Christian Doctrine, ecclesiology, or church order, but at the level of sociology, we have already been categorized. We must find ways to maintain church order and at the same time participate with the broader community of brothers and sisters in the liberation of our people. Therefore, we must voluntarily accept segregated religion as a blessing in disguise, because it gives the oppressed an opportunity to strategize for freedom. The late Dr. George Buttrick, former pastor of Madison Avenue Presbyterian Church of New York City, said that if he had to live his life over again he would not invite any blacks to join his church, because he had come to the conclusion that the White church had nothing to offer blacks but stolen funds. This scathing denunciation by one of the great giants of Protestantism and one of Christian history's greatest pulpiteers is commentary. Many take solace in the fact that many white churches have some black members, but this is not progress; this is retrogression. We had our Christian beginnings in this country in the white church in the seventeenth century, but we were a powerless people in a powerful institution. We therefore remain a powerless people. The presence of African Americans in a white church does nothing to change institutional and structural racism. The only benefits which derive from this forced and hypocritical relationship is that Whites feel that they no longer have a race problem, and Blacks feel that they have arrived in paradise. Let me say unequivocally that I am in favor of integrated worship, but not on the terms of the White church. I am in favor of Whites joining the African American church provided it is not an ebony replica of the White church, which is perverse. Whites could be liberated in the right kind of an African American church. An African American church with Whites such as: John Brown, Rev. James Reeb, Viola Liuzzo, Clarence Jordan, Carlyle Marney, and other authentic Whites would be a medium through which America could be liberated from the great bondage of racism. Many Blacks join White churches under the pretense of wanting to be under a trained minister who is able to teach the Bible, and a desire to get away from immorality in the African American pulpit. Let me say that there are unlearned and learned clergy among Blacks and Whites. For example, my church, the Mount Olive Baptist Church, offers an expansive Socio-Christian Education Ministry. Yet, many of the same people who will not attend my teaching ministry will attend a White church. Several years ago my able colleague in ministry at Mount Olive, Rev. Wayne Lomax, spoke to one of our parishioners about attending our Wednesday night Bible study. She responded by saying that she lived so far out west in the county that she could not make it. But then six months later she gleefully reported that she was attending a Bible study in Pompano Beach which cost her one hundred dollars per course. The irony of her behavior rests on the fact that she had to pass our church on her way six miles north. My Bible study was without cost, except the physical effort to get there; yet she was willing to pay two hundred dollars for two courses at a White church. Incidentally, my formal education was equal to that of any of the teachers in the White church. On the other issue of immorality, the moral failures of Jim Bakker, Jimmy Swaggart, Oral Roberts, etc., prove beyond a shadow of a doubt that sexual and financial sins know no color. So the issue is not immorality, but an inferiority complex based on almost four centuries of relentless oppression. The power of the White face when projected off the screen of the African American mind is awesome! The Grand Inquisitor, in Dostoyevsky's The Brothers Karamazov, declared that the ruler of human kind is "he who holds their conscience and their bread in his hands."[2] Therefore, we must face the fact that White American Christianity is impotent in the liberation of our people. Again, we do not reject Whites who are also willing victims of racist religion, because to make a blanket rejection based on pigmentation is to close the door on a John Brown or Clarence Jordan. The issue is not pigmentation, but identification.

Yet, the evil of White American Christianity is a poignant reminder of the need to clarify what we mean by the term "Christian." The early Malcolm X said, "Christianity is the white man's religion. The Holy Bible in the white man's hands and his interpretations of it have been the greatest single ideological weapon for enslaving millions of non-white human beings."[3] Again he said:

> Black people were supposed to be a part of the Christian Church, yet we lived in a bitter world of dejection... being rejected by the White Christian Church. In large numbers we became victims of drunkenness, drug addiction, reefer smoking, in a false and futile attempt to escape the reality and horror of the shameful condition that the slavemaster's Christian religion had placed us in.[4]

Was Malcolm X simply a religious malcontent who had ingrained anti-Christian feelings? The answer is an emphatic, No! His father was a Baptist minister who was killed by White racists. With all due respect to the religion of Islam, Malcolm X providentially could have been an authentic Christian prophet-theologian if it had not been for the violent racism he and his family encountered.

Carter G. Woodson in his book <u>The Miseducation of the Negro</u>, said of African Americans:

> His religion is merely a loan from whites who have enslaved and segregated the Negroes; and the organization, though largely an independent Negro Institution, is dominated by the thought of the oppressors of the race.[5]

This is a fact often overlooked by African American religionists. The African American expression of Christianity gives one the feeling of being not only a second class citizen, but also a second class Christian. Until this fact is confronted by the African American theological-kerygmatic community, our churches will continue to fail our people at a psycho-spiritual level. The theological-kerygmatic community must work unceasingly to heal the damaged minds of our community. As we are being more enlightened in our community, we must come to the conclusion that a religion that is only a replication of the Oppressor's faith is to be totally rejected, unless we are collectively masochistic.

Conservative Christianity's Missionary Agenda

Beyond the theological sanctioning of slavery as being the will of God, one of the most dastardly deeds promoted by American Christianity has been the engineered divisiveness between African Americans and our other brothers and sisters of the Diaspora. This has been wrought through missionaries who have purposely gone to Africa, Latin America, and the Caribbean Islands and have told our brothers and sisters there that they are different from African Americans. Many of them have been trained to believe that what we suffered in this country is simply an illusion. In other words, African Americans are the causative factor in their own predicament. In contrast to the hard working Africans of the Islands, we are shiftless and lazy. It is interesting to see the number of Africans from the Caribbean who come to America and completely separate themselves from their brothers and sisters in America: Many do not attend Black churches; they do not associate with their brothers and sisters; godparents for their children are often White; and in the case of death, a White mortuary is engaged. I remember my experience at Southern Baptist Theological Seminary in Louisville, Kentucky with the almost paranoid aversion of students from Africa towards African Americans. It was always a cold relationship at best. When I tried to engage several in conversation about the greatness of Africa and its contributions to the world, and our need to learn more about the Motherland, they replied, "The only thing one needs to know is Jesus." These two gentlemen had been thoroughly brainwashed by a Christological concept that undergirds self hatred and cultural ignorance. This kind of stupidity goeth not out but by a complete rejection of a Christology that teaches me to accept my alleged inferiority.

Conservative Christianity's Social Agenda

It is absolute folly for African Americans to be caught between the Oppressor's argument as to who is conservative or liberal. Both camps leave us disenfranchised. At the time of this writing the Southern Baptist Convention is engaged in a rerun of the Modernist-Fundamentalist controversy of the 1920's. I heard a very discomforting discussion on the part of a Black pastor who is a member of this organization. He was taking the side of the conservatives on the issue of biblical inerrancy and infallibility. This man, when further engaged, was totally oblivious to biblical interpretation as it comes to bear upon sociology. When I asked him about a biblical hermeneutic for supporting or destroying slavery, he became irritated because it was not hermeneutics that ended slavery in America; it was the United States Supreme Court. But if one holds tenaciously to biblical infallibility, then the question must be raised whether Blacks should return to involuntary servitude. An infallible Bible would give such a clarion call. Are African Americans correct in rejecting those passages that seem to condone slavery? If not, what hermeneutic must be employed to get to the heart of the matter? As the heat was rising and light was being dispelled, the dialogue was soon drowned in a sea of heated confusion on his part. This is not a major issue for African Americans. Only when we have been confused by White American Christianity does the issue become a burning matter. African American Christians have traditionally believed what the Bible teaches about itself:

> *All scripture is given by inspiration of God, and is profitable for doctrine, for reproof, for correction, for instruction in righteousness: that the man of God may be perfect, thoroughly furnished unto all good works.*[6]

While conservative Christianity debates biblical infallibility, the social situation of African Americans remains the same. Some televangelists rape the public of millions of dollars and say absolutely nothing about the oppression of the masses, except receiving Jesus Christ as one's personal Savior. This vertical Salvation completely ignores human responsibility. Apartheid in South Africa has received much visual support from some White American evangelists who have gone there and have come back to report the number of converts won in an integrated audience. In several weeks of preaching and touring South Africa, Jerry Falwell came back to America as an authentic expert on the social realities of South Africa. Although Bishop Desmond Tutu, Nobel Peace Prize winner, has lived the horrors of this damnable racist ideology all of his life, Falwell learned more in his short stay than Tutu had learned in a lifetime. He was therefore qualified to declare Bishop Tutu a phony.

Beginning with Ronald Reagan in 1980, the Religious Right once again gave impetus to selective morality with such issues as abortion and homosexuality. These issues are not ignored by the African American church. However, we feel that at the core of what is wrong socially in the African American community is a direct result of a racist society. Once again Salley and Behm address this situation:

> Another recent indication of White Christian rejection of Blacks and Black concerns is the selection of moral issues in America which are not high on the Black agenda. Groups such as the Moral Majority seek to make America moral by prohibiting abortions, gay rights and so on. But they say little or nothing about the pregnant issue of White racism which has oppressed and continues to oppress millions of Blacks and people of color within America and throughout the world.[7]

White flight to suburbia is another indication of the insincerity of Conservative White American Christianity. Many White congregations have left the inner city in order to get away from urban chaos and blight. Some claim to have left for more elbow room but the issue is not space; it is race. Conservative White American Christians do not feel comfortable with African Americans. Once this is admitted, the door is open for salvation. The irony is that the same Christians who have fled our urban areas with their sophistication and resources will then turn around and fund a program for the problems of the inner city which are the result of their abdication. This is high class hypocrisy. Gibson Winter gives insight into this matter in his book, The Suburban Captivity of the Churches:

> Negro migration which increased rapidly during World War I and after 1920..... uniformly accelerated the withdrawal of white Protestantism. The retreat from the Negro occurred in a two phase movement: higher status congregations withdrew with the first threat of Negro invasion; middle and lower- middle class congregations moved more slowly; consequently, the secondary withdrawal of Protestantism came about through attrition.[8]

This needs to be confronted and repented of if the church is to have an authentic witness. However, it needs to be stated that a few White churches have remained in the inner city and are struggling to bear witness because they also have been abandoned by White flight.

Again with the election of Ronald Reagan in 1980, we saw once again the public resurgence of cultural religion. Much of White American Christianity is cultural religion: where the flag is hoisted above the cross; God is a God of western civilization; and the Biblical Christ has been domesticated into the American Christ. Therefore, the church cannot take sides on any issue until she discovers where Jesus stands. Christians are good citizens, but by the very nature of our commitment to Christ, we cannot exalt nationalism above the Kingdom of God. Whenever governmental policies deviate from the Kingdom of God we must be loyal to Christ and His Kingdom, even to the point of death.

Another phenomenon that arose in the 1970's was the advent of Christian television. Television traditionally has been a medium of entertainment, and the church has fallen prey to the seductive wiles of Christianity Hollywood style. This in turn has led to celebrity Christianity. Since much of what we see on television is fantasy, much of what we see on Christian television is also fantasy. In a thirty minute broadcast the religious host or hostess must try to heal all sickness, restore all broken relationships, and dispel the mystery of existence. Incidentally, it's going to take God a little longer. No wonder so many people have latched on to the Health-Wealth gospel. It is not only heretical, but it is Hollywood pure and simple.

With the rise of celebrity Christianity, we acted as if God should be grateful that some confused movie star or entertainer embraces the faith. It is painful to watch many celebrities dogmatizing and preaching to millions across the Planet when they ought to be a student in a New Member Training Class or an accredited theological seminary. Praises be to God for the celebrity, who takes the Biblical Christ seriously, but far too many that I have heard do not have the faintest notion of what the Kingdom of God is all about. It is an understatement to say that a number of African American celebrities are caught up in this movement which paralyzes them in terms of their commitment to the African American community. Watching Christian television has often been painful for me, because of the use of African American entertainers and athletes as propaganda tools to assist in the continual oppression of their people. This can be demonstrated by the number of Black evangelicals who went to North Carolina to campaign for Senator Jesse Helms. This is just like having Jews campaigning for a Nazi candidate. Such mental sickness deserves immediate psychiatric attention.

Relevant Theological Issues For the African American Church

Does God love African American people?

This question needs to be dealt with forthrightly, if we are to be authentic in our appropriation of the Christian faith. There are many, including William Jones in his book, Is God A White Racist?, who basically declare that there is nothing multievidential to prove that God does love African American people. As one travels across the world, African people are conspicuously oppressed everywhere. On the continent of Africa the oppression is due to bad economic policies, colonialism, and malevolent dictators. However, we cannot ignore the perpetual worldwide rape of our people in Africa, America, and across the world. To the naked eye it appears that God, if He loves us, loves us less than White people. This is a tremendous burden to bear as a theistic people. If God is partial to White power, then we need to have a collective abdication. If our era of greatness as Africans has passed, then where do we go from here? Another reality is that unless there is a massive shift in pigmentation vis-a-vis the African American and the White community, we cannot expect any shift of power in the decades ahead. We will not see a predominantly Black House of Representatives, Senate Chamber, or U.S. Supreme Court. The economic and military power will remain in the hands of the oppressor, unless God intervenes. In light of these stark realities, we must face the fact that we may be confused about what freedom and liberation mean. One of the basic tenets of liberation theology is that God is always on the side of the oppressed. Therefore, God is always opposed to the oppressor, even when in His permissive will He allows him or her to take advantage of the disinherited. Since the two categories are the oppressor and the oppressed, how will we be able to identify the liberated?

Therefore, the historical Jesus is the model for defining our liberation. The social liberation we seek, such as power and possessions, is the antithesis of the Kingdom of God. Jesus as our model, then, was liberated in the sense that Caesar had nothing that He wanted.

Therein lies the secret of His freedom and the mystery of His crucifixion. Jesus was not crucified because He was oppressed, but because He was free. Freedom is hazardous to one's health. As Jacques Ellul says, "What we really want is security such as power and possessions which is nothing but slavery."[9] To be free of security is to be truly liberated. A man or a woman who defines himself or herself in terms of political power, possessions, or military might is a slave. Because the oppressor nor the oppressed takes the Biblical Christ seriously, we are both confused about the true meaning of freedom. So unless the oppressed views their liberation through the eyes of Jesus, their quest for freedom becomes a deeper enslavement.

Therefore, socially maybe we only doubt God's love when we are in pursuit of Caesar's throne.

What does it Mean to be Born Again?

Although this subject will be discussed in Chapter Four, a word needs to be said here. Several years ago I was privy to a forum in which one of the world's leading theologians from Latin America was lecturing. He said that we need new metaphors to capture the essence of the faith in the face of earthshaking lexicographical changes. Among these changes he said, "We need a new metaphor for being saved." My reply to him was, "What is wrong with the original one? For nothing is more threatening to human autonomy than Jesus' call in the Johannine Gospel, Chapter 3, for a declaration of non-existence." The theologian readily agreed that the reason "the new birth" life-experience is not taken seriously is that it is too personally and socially threatening.

However, American Christianity has managed to tame it and make it a completely subjective experience, rather than an experience which guides one in all areas of life, for all of life. The model for one's life, then, is the Biblical Christ. What is so devastating about American Christianity's appropriation of this tenet of the faith, is that once the individual gets saved, there may not be any social evidence of it, other than church attendance. The great abolitionist and former slave, Frederick Douglass, had this to say in describing his change from one slavemaster, a Mr. Covey, to a Mr. Freedland:

> Among the many advantages gained in my change from Covey's to Freeland's, startling as the statement may be, was the fact that the latter gentleman made no profession of religion. I assert most unhesitatingly that the religion of the South, as I have observed it, and proved it, is a mere covering for the most horrid crimes; the justifier of the most appalling barbarity; a sanctifier of the most hateful frauds; and secure shelter, under which the darkest, foulest, grossest, and most infernal abominations fester and flourish. Were I to be reduced to the condition of a slave again, next to that calamity, I should regard the fact of being the slave of a religious slaveholder, the greatest that could befall me. For of all slaveholders with whom I have ever met, religious slaveholders are the worst. I have found them almost invariably, the vilest, meanest and basest of their class.[10]

It is a fact that in America the old metaphor has not been tried and found wanting, but rather it has been left waiting to be tried. Since the metaphor has been cheapened to fit the socio-economic agenda of this country, the term has no objective relevance. Since the election of Jimmy Carter to the Presidency of the United States in 1976, and the emergence of the White religious right as a political entity to be reckoned with, it has been politically feasible to be "born again." Such names as: Ronald Reagan; George Bush; Jesse Helms; and former Panamanian dictator, Manuel Noriega, all claim some form of the new birth experience. Reagan, a man who had one of the most corrupt administrations in American history, was favored by the religious right. It can be said, that not only politics but religion makes strange bedfellows. Someone had the audacity to question Manuel Noriega's conversion experience in 1991. Whether one views it as legitimate or not, on paper, at least, it is as genuine as President Reagan's. Noriega was using his alleged conversion to get out of prison, and Reagan used his to get into the White House. What does the Christian mean when he or she says that he or she is saved?

I heard a very pious lady say to a young man who was considered a street thug, "Are you saved, young man?" He replied, "Are you?" She then said, "Yes I am." He then said, "What does it mean?" She said in response, "It means that I will go to heaven when I die." The young man brought the diatribe to a close by asking, "What in the hell do you do in the interval while you are waiting to go to heaven?" Out of the mouths of thugs, truth is often articulated.

Somehow or other, the radicality of the "born again" metaphor has gotten lost not only in politics, but in modern day mass evangelism as well. What does it mean to be born again when President Bush gives the signal to go to war against Iraq, and at the same time invites Billy Graham to the White House for prayer and consultation? What could Billy Graham say in light of the radicality of the "New Birth" metaphor? Thousands attend the crusades of not only Billy Graham, but other televangelists as well. Thousands are reported to have had a "born again" experience. Yet there is no necessary demonstration of that objectively. Anthony Campolo said:

> During the civil rights era of the 1950's I became very aware that it was possible to achieve a high level of personal righteousness while participating in the maintenance of a sociopolitical system that had demonic characteristics. During that time I witnessed revivalistic movements sweep through various communities in the Deep South. In each case the lives of a host of individuals were significantly changed. However, regardless of their achievement of personal righteousness through religious conversions, these people continued to be part of a Jim Crow system that perpetuated racial segregation and discrimination.

> While those whites who were converted might be motivated to treat blacks with compassion, they nevertheless did little, if anything to challenge the social system that relegated their black brothers and sisters to second-class citizenship and diminished their humanity. Such persons might feel pangs of guilt if they hurt black people individually in face-to-face encounters, but they seemed to feel no guilt from their collective support for a political system that attacked the dignity of blacks. Social Justice did not necessarily follow the creation of individual righteousness through personal conversions. As far as the oppressed were concerned, the demonic system continued to exercise its evil in spite of the exorcism of evil from the individuals who created and supported the devastating system of racial segregation.[11]

I concur, that from the perspective of the African American community, nothing is more dangerous than a White person who talks about God. The danger will continue unless we can bring this revolutionary metaphor to bear upon horizontal liberation as well as vertical liberation. The heritage of White American Christianity is that once personal salvation has been established, you are still free to be a racist. Again, Campolo said:

> Christianity is an invitation to do battle with the principalities and powers and rulers of this age in the struggle to realize a new social order built upon justice and love. What Jesus seeks is far more dramatic than simply to make humanity into a herd of nice people who conform, more or less, to ecclesiastical requisites. He would have each person aspire to a heroic place in the history of the world's salvation. Christianity at its best does not attract people with cheap grace promised to those who give minimal intellectual assent to certain theological propositions and offer a semblance of obedience to religiously pre-

> scribed behavioral expectations. Instead, true Christianity is a challenge to offer up one's life to live out a heroic calling of eternal significance.[12]

Finally, the Nat Turner rebellion of 1831, wreaks havoc with American Christianity's view of soteriology. Turner, the mystic-preacher, was convinced that God had led him to rise up against the institution of slavery. Turner, along with 60 to 70 other slaves, killed 60 Whites, including his master in the State of Virginia. Eventually Turner, along with about 20 of his followers, was executed, and other innocent slaves were killed. Was Nat Turner saved or lost? Or was his master saved or lost? The answer will reveal that we are liberationists, racists, or universalists.

What is the Soul?

This is not a query into the mystery of Hellenistic metaphysics. It is an existential question. The answer is a matter of life and death. It is a matter of oppression or liberation. There are two basic views of Soul in the Biblical Canon: the Hebrew and the Greek view.

In the Old Testament one does not have a soul; he or she is a soul. Genesis 2:7 says:

> *And the Lord God formed man of the dust of the ground and breathed into his nostrils the breath of life; and man became a living soul.*[13]

The term for soul in the Hebrew language is the word <u>nephesh</u>, which means self or a person. So a paraphrase of verse 7 would read thusly, "God breathed into humankind's nostrils the breath of life, or the human spirit, and they became living human beings." In the Old Testament human spirit, when it is connected with flesh, equals soul. Another passage that is instructive is Ezekiel 18:4,20 which says:

> *Behold all souls are mine; as the soul of the father, so also the soul of the son is mine: the soul that sins, it shall die.*[14]

Contrary to the Greek view which taught the immortality of the soul, the Hebrew view taught that the soul dies. The soul dies because I am soul. In Greek philosophy, soul was a nebulous essence inside me, caged like a squirrel and the ultimate goal of humankind was to have his or her soul set free from the prison called the human body.

In the New Testament a passage such as First Thessalonians 5:23 is often used as a scripture to support the tripartite view of the soul, which says that one is body, soul and spirit.[15] Even though the New Testament was written basically in Koine Greek, the Apostle Paul was not rejecting Hebrew psychology. He was writing to a Greco-Roman audience who would have been familiar with the Greek understanding of the soul. Therefore, his appeal was to his audience. Yet, Paul's exalted emphasis upon the human body meant that he was more in line with Moses than Plato. He says:

> *What? Know you not that your body is the temple of the Holy Ghost which is in you, which you have of God, and you are not your own? For you are bought with a price: therefore, glorify God in your body, and in your spirit, which are God's.*[16]

Therefore, we conclude that although Paul was conversant in both Hebrew and Greek culture on the issue of the soul, he never forsook his Hebrew roots. Even though he used the tripartite model in his epistles, he was basically saying body plus spirit = soul (psyche).

A proper understanding of soul is liberating. The Greek view which denigrates the human body, and the Hebrew view which sees it as a gift from God are in conflict. This can be seen when we study the Greek concept of the immortality of the soul, which basically taught that the soul lives on after death forever, as it is joined to the Universal Soul. Ezekiel 18:4, 20, says "the soul that sins, it shall die." The soul dies because I do not have a soul; I am a soul or a person, and all humankind will ultimately die.

The present discussion is not about being on a philosophical kick. It is about oppression and freedom. This analysis is therefore important because a misunderstanding of this leads to oppression. In short, our slavemasters bought into the Greek view of the soul when they enslaved our foreparents. The soul, after the oppressor eventually concluded that we had a soul (though inferior), became the focal point for brainwashing people of African descent. We were not to be concerned about our social situation, because the body was not important. The body's only significance was that it housed the soul. Only the soul mattered. This philosophy given to us by our religious oppressors, caused us to endure 246 years without a paycheck, because going to heaven after death was our chief goal. No wonder American Christianity has very little social significance except as a maintainer of the status quo. No wonder Billy Graham is such a religio-cultural phenomenon; his preaching does not connect earth and sky. When you are busy saving souls for heaven, society goes to hell. One wonders if this view of the soul is one of commitment or convenience, because with the rise of Jimmy Carter and Ronald Reagan to the presidency, the oppressor started imitating the African American church with its involvement in sociopolitical issues. It would have been great to have had the white church on the cutting edge of the Civil Rights movement. Instead it lost a gallant opportunity to be an authentic witness. The question was asked during the Civil Rights era, "Where is the white church?" The answer came back, "They are busy saving souls, who once saved, have no earthly significance whatsoever." What a powerful statement it would have made to America if Billy Graham had joined forces with Dr. Martin Luther King, Jr. The church missed its finest hour. Instead, white clergymen led the verbal assault on Dr. King, which led to his writing his famous "Letter From The Birmingham Jail." They would rather deal with the alleged sexual escapades of Dr. King. But even if Dr. King had sex twenty-three hours a day, he was still right about America. David was guilty of murder and adultery, (2 Samuel 11-12), yet, his ultimate significance was not destroyed , because Jesus gladly wore the title Son of David (Matthew 9:27; 15:22, etc.). Like David, the center of Dr. King's life was on target. The radius, diameter, and circumference were flawed, like in all humanoids. No posthumous revelation about Dr. King will ever destroy him, because his center was correct. Therefore, he will outlast J. Edgar Hoover, like the anvil survives the hammer. But in all fairness, there were many African American clergypersons who opposed Dr. King on the grounds that he needed to stay in the pulpit and save souls. This ignorance can be understood only in light of the teachings that they had received from the oppressor in regard to the Greek view of the soul. This view has been a curse to African Americans for over three centuries, and there is no cure but a complete rejection of this nonsense.

Will We Get It Together?

Frankly, there must be an admission that there is a radical difference between the African American Church and the White Church.

Dr. William A. Jones said, "When compared with the White Church in America, sharp differences are readily observable:"[17]

Black Church	White Church
Church of the Oppressed	Church of the Oppressors
Theology of Survival	Theology of Success
Theology of Immanence	Theology of Transcendence
Prophetic	Priestly
Free Pulpit	Restricted Pulpit

The question is often asked, "Can whites and African Americans worship together?" It is a fact that Amos and Amaziah are poles apart in their appropriation of the faith (Amos 7). Therefore, they cannot worship together. "Can two walk together, except they be agreed?"[18] As a follower of the Carpenter from Nazareth, I will never reject white people; my beef is not with white people, but with the White Institutional church.

With the presidency of Ronald Reagan we saw a resurgence of overt racism in this country. With all the decisions by the United States Supreme Court, attitudes, by and large, have remained constant, though at times they fluctuate between overt and covert. I blame the White Institutional church for this problem. Its failure to preach a gospel of liberation which embraces the imminent as well as the eschatological makes it guilty of complicity in the oppression of our people and others. While laws can regulate public behavior, they cannot transform attitudes. Racism is a moral problem, both individually and institutionally. In this, the White Institutional church has failed miserably. Therefore, it has no right to pontificate or preach to African Americans. We must reject any planting of churches in the African American community. We have too many churches now that have been influenced by the "saving my soul" philosophy. We don't need more churches; we need businesses, banks, and factories. We must wean ourselves from a perverse ecclesiastical dependency on the White Institutional church. The community of the oppressed does not need the oppressor to say, "Here is God," but rather, "Here is your money." In no way do I seek to over romanticize the African American church, for it is also flawed. However, an institution that has stood in the vanguard of a movement to keep an oppressed people sane and theistic is superior to that of the oppressor. Therefore, I offer the following steps as a plan of action.

Step One - Repentance

One of the most dreaded words in the Bible is the word <u>repent</u>. In Greek it is the word <u>metanoia</u> which literally means to change one's mind, attitude, lifestyle, behavior, focus, and direction. Such a definition is threatening because it aggravates human arrogance, pride, and autonomy. No wonder John the Baptizer (Matthew 3:2), and Jesus (Mark 1:14-15) were killed. Both of them preached repentance. Listen to John the Baptizer:

> *In those days came John the Baptist, preaching in the wilderness of Judea, and saying, repent ye: for the Kingdom of heaven is at hand.*[19]

Jesus also had the theme of repentance as the prelude of his Kingdom:

> *Now after that John was put in prison, Jesus came into Galilee, preaching the gospel of the Kingdom of God, and saying, the time is fulfilled, and the Kingdom of God is at hand: repent ye, and believe the gospel.*[20]

In both of these gospel accounts the verbal form of repentance is a second person plural present active imperative. Therefore, autonomous humankind has an imperative to deal with. Unless one changes his or her behavior, he or she will not, and cannot be part of the Kingdom of God.

The chief task of the White Institutional church is to repent of its history, heritage, and heresy. She must confess that she has crucified the Biblical Christ and has created the American Christ. She must also purge herself of her history of worshipping at the altar of racism, materialism, and militarism. There will be no move towards overcoming racial hostilities in this country until the White Institutional church repents of its negligence in proclaiming the Biblical Christ.

Unless the White Institutional church leads Whites to the point of hating the ugliness of her racist manifest destiny, there is no hope for White America, in spite of bulging institutional religion. There will also continue to be African Americans who are members of White churches. Why any African American would join a White church that proclaims the American Christ is beyond my power to comprehend. The fact that there are African Americans in White churches must be seen as token progress. The White pastor must not be naive enough to see this as the ultimate goal, for such a worship experience is dangerous for the collective psychological health of its ebony worshippers. Most African Americans who worship in White churches are escapists and are not really a part of the African American community.

While a student at the University of Florida in the late 1960's, I gained a new insight into this problem of racism and repentance. My area of concentration was philosophy, and I had taken a test on existentialism. The professor bragged one day that I consistently made the highest score in the class. After class had ended, a White student who was on the verge of flunking out said to me, "I know you are a better student, but my parents taught me to believe in the inherent mental inferiority of Blacks. Therefore, I cannot accept your intellectual superiority, even though I know you are a better student; unless I call my parents a liar." He then said, "Mack, it is hard to call your parents liars even when you know that they are." I conclude then, that somebody must have the courage to call his or her parents liars. If this is not done, this country will die from an overdose of racism.

On May 17, 1991, I saw a White woman who was a member of the Ku Klux Klan come to grips with her racism and renounce her racist heritage. This was the Salley Jessy Raphael show. Tears welled in my eyes as I said out loud, "This is what the White Church ought to be doing." Then I was saddened by the thought that maybe the White church cannot effectuate such a change, until she ceases to be the White church. Maybe from a white perspective, shows such as "The Salley Jessy Raphael Show," "The Oprah Winfrey Show," "The Phil Donahue Show," and "The Geraldo Rivera Show" will be the forums for bringing about authentic change. Sometimes God baptizes alien movements for his salvific purposes.

In the award winning movie Dances With Wolves, starring Kevin Costner, I was profoundly shaken by its message. A lieutenant played by Costner went out West to take command of a fort in the remote West. This fort was on Indian land. Upon his arrival he found that everyone was dead. He then went on to establish his command, raised his flag and waited for other troops to arrive. In the interval he made contact with the Indians. While he was getting to know them, he learned their language and customs. Then they gave him the name "Dances with Wolves". After years had passed, other troops arrived, and they accused him of treason because of his alliance with the Indians. They accused him of abandoning his post while he had lived among the Indians. He was severely beaten, publicly ridiculed, and while being transported to prison, he was rescued by his Indian friends. The Indians then become the target of the soldiers' attack. The lieutenant then joined forces with the Indians as they wiped out the troops.

The message of the movie to me was that unless Whites with their arrogance become one with the oppressed, even to the point of risking their lives as they take sides against their oppressive heritage, nothing will change!

Step Two - Reparations

In a nutshell the term means to restore, redress, make restitution, for wrong done to the victim. The term is always pejorative in the oppressor's community. However, it is at the very center of repentance and justice. Restitution is the objectification of repentance. But before we can deal with the question of reparations, we must deal with what is wrong in America.

Any attempt to deal with what's wrong in America must begin with the oppression of Native Americans. This is a continuing evil that makes this country corrupt at its very core. The period beginning with the colonial days to the massacre at Wounded Knee in South Dakota in 1890, was one violent nightmare as Indians were slaughtered, tricked, and driven off their land, and placed on reservations. These reservations are violent reminders of what happens when a godless manifest destiny, inspired by greed, receives the silent and verbal endorsement of the church. No wonder the German-Swiss theologian, Karl Barth, believed that Western culture, especially the United States, might pose a greater threat to the church than communism.[21] Because of the church's negligence in the past, I tremble in the face of Western Christianity's invasion of Europe, now that communism is collapsing. Can a racist church that has failed to liberate Native Americans, African Americans, women, and all oppressed groups, liberate Europe?

I was again disturbed on July 4, 1991, when President George Bush rededicated Mount Rushmore in the Black Hills of South Dakota. This land is sacred Indian land. However, the message was loud and clear: Indians have no rights which rich white men have to obey. This monument depicts the faces of four presidents who were enemies of Native Americans and African Americans: George Washington, Thomas Jefferson, Abraham Lincoln, and Theodore Roosevelt. So in light of America's sordid history against Native Americans, how much do we owe them and do we plan to pay them? Would two trillion dollars be adequate for a down payment? Is God a God of Justice? Or is He simply the spiritualized sycophant of Western culture? Can the Kingdom of God be built on the graves of Sitting Bull, Geronimo, and Cochise? If God blesses violent thievery, then we need to canonize Jesse James, Billy the Kid, Ma Barker, John Dillinger, and Al Capone. These questions are not addressed to the President of the United States but to the President's pastor.

Not only is America's soul contaminated by the Red problem , but its psyche is messed up by its history of oppression of African Americans from 1619 to the present. In 1991, such code words as affirmative action and quotas were being used to confuse the American public in Orwellian fashion. If not affirmative action, then how much do you owe my people for 246 years without a paycheck? How much do you owe for the irreparable damage done to the African American family structure? How much do you owe for the thousands of our people who were lynched by white mobs? How much do you owe for cutting off our legs and inviting us to run against you? And when we fail, you further defeat us psychologically by calling me inferior. How much do you owe for every African American who had lands stolen (cheap prices) after World Wars I and II? What do you owe us for teaching us to feel inferior and to hate ourselves? What do you owe us for robbing us of our history and teaching us that Africa has made no contribution to the world? What do you owe for all the African American men and women who have fought in every war that you have put on, in order that rich white men might be free to continue oppressing us? I know what White unbelievers will say, but what about White Christians?

On May 4, 1969, James Forman, walked down the aisle of Riverside Church, in New York City, and demanded the modest sum of $500,000,000.00. Boy was he kind! Many people, including some

African Americans, criticized Forman not for asking for reparations, but for interrupting its worship service. The point was and continues to be that the Oppressor does not worship the God that "sets the captives free." Dr. Ernest Campbell, then pastor of Riverside Church, became a point of light, to borrow President Bush's phrase. He said:

> The Christian Church has taught that restitution is an essential part of penitence. You don't simply say, "I'm sorry" to a man you have robbed. You return what you stole or your apology takes on a hollow ring.[22]

Campbell proved that God has a witness even in the White church.

Several years ago a White political leader asked me, "If given reparations, what would you do with the monies?" I replied, "It is the Oppressor's job to pay his debt, not to be the financial planner for the oppressed." Yet, the question needs to be raised, not in order to let the Oppressor off the hook, because it is none of his or her business. However, because of our enslaved and oppressed psyches, it would be better to train our people in nation building before we would start passing out checks. A people who have been miseducated for 372 years would turn around and give the monies right back to the Oppressor.

The Hebrews at the Exodus plundered the Egyptians as a form of reparation for 430 years of slavery.

> *And the children of Israel did according to the word of Moses; and they borrowed of the Egyptians Jewels of silver, Jewels of Gold, and raiment: and the Lord gave the people favour in the sight of the Egyptians, so that they lent unto them such things as they required. And they spoiled the Egyptians.*[23]

Reparation is costly! It literally ruined the economy of Egypt. But what was that compared to four hundred and thirty years of oppression.

What would it cost America? I, too, am tired of affirmative action. Pay your debts! Gayraud S. Wilmore said:

> Great Britain, France, the Netherlands, and the United States received reparations from Japan after the hostilities of 1864; Spain from Peru in 1869; the United States from China in 1900. West Germany assumed the liability of 2 billion dollars for victims of the Nazi persecution. In 1953 the Federal Republic of Germany undertook the payment of 820 million dollars (to resettle 500,000 Jews), to indemnify individuals inside and outside of Hitler's Germany for their persecution.[24]

Another story of interest is the story of Zaccheus, the tax collector. He was an executive officer with the Jewish Internal Revenue Service. The story is told in Luke's gospel.

> *And Jesus entered and passed through Jericho. And behold there was a man named Zaccheus, which was the chief among the publicans, and he was rich. And he sought to see Jesus who he was; and he could not for the press, because he was little of stature. And he ran and climbed up into a sycamore tree to see him: for he was to pass that way, and when Jesus came to the place he looked up, and saw him, and said unto him, Zaccheus, make haste, and come down: for today I must abide at your house. And he made haste, and came down, and received him joyfully. And when they saw it, they all murmured, saying, that he was gone home to be guest with a man that is a sinner. And Zaccheus stood, and said unto the Lord; Behold, Lord, the half of my goods I give to the poor; and if I have taken anything from any man by false accusation, I restore him fourfold. And Jesus said unto him, this day is salvation come to this house...*[25]

This Scripture is a story about Zaccheus the Oppressor. He was literally ripping off his own people as he worked for the Roman government. He was a traitor and an Uncle Tom to his people. Then he met Jesus in a radically transforming way. Jesus' presence was enough to mess up his bank account. Suppose he had a million dollars. He told Jesus up front that he would give $500,000 off the top to the poor. That left a balance of $500,000. Just suppose he owed someone $250,000 multiplied times four = $1,000,000. And he had only $500,000 left. So reparations would have left him $500,000 in debt. The Biblical Christ is dangerous.

Does America owe Native Americans? Yes! What does America owe them? Maybe a thousand dollars for every acre in the country. But who am I to speak for Native Americans?

Well, then, how much does America owe African Americans? Would a trillion dollars be fair? A better way of dealing with this question is to ask what Whites would want if they had worked for 246 years without compensation. So both Native Americans and African Americans want the same thing Whites would want if they were the oppressed. But my advice to both groups is that we must not be foolish enough to wait until Uncle Sam pays off! Without divine intervention, the situation will remain the same.

Step Three - Forgiveness

The question has often been asked of me by White acquaintances, "Do you hate White people for what they have done to people of African descent?" I respond by saying, "No, I do not hate Whites because I have been empowered by the Resurrected and Living Christ to appropriate love and creative goodwill towards all humankind." Therefore, I must love creatively and redemptively, but not foolishly. Because of the Nature of divine love that was concretized in the Cross of Jesus of Nazareth, forgiveness can never be the casual dismissal of wrongs done by simply letting bygones be bygones.

Calvary is a statement that sin and oppression are serious and God just couldn't let human alienation slide. It had to be dealt with. The cost was the life of the Son of God. Unless sin is dealt with creatively, it will come back to haunt you time and time again. We saw this in 1991 as we faced another presidential election in 1992. A quarter of a century ago, Whites were forced to make certain public behavioral adjustments. Since they never repented, they simply tolerated the pronouncements of the Warren Court. Now that the Supreme Court is overwhelmingly conservative, many of the racist attitudes are being displayed once again. In 1991, there was an attitude in this country which said, "Niggers, get back in your places." So there has been no repentance, because there have been no reparations, and therefore there cannot be any authentic reconciliation. The only relationship that is open between African Americans and Whites en masse is a slave-master relationship. Individuals from the oppressed community may slip through to success, but they still have their "places" in the collective psyche of America.

The problem in both communities centers around a misunderstanding of Jesus' ethic of love and forgiveness. In Luke 23:34, Jesus said while dying on the Cross, "Father, forgive them: for they know not what they do." Many Whites and African Americans interpret this to mean that Jesus was giving a blanket amnesty to Herod, Caiaphas, and Pilate. To do such a thing would be immoral. Jesus was appropriating forgiveness, but actualization comes with repentance and reparations. Just suppose that I invited a starving person to my house for dinner. The table is spread with a most delectable cuisine. Then the call comes out from the kitchen, "Dinner is served," but nobody moves. The starving one sits there stubbornly and refuses to eat and dies of hunger. In this case food was appropriated, but the actualization required the starving one to eat. So, in a nutshell, Jesus set the table for Herod, Caiaphas, and Pilate, but there is no canonical evidence that they ate the meal. So I conclude by saying, "I have love appropriated for all humankind, but it can only be actualized on the other end."

Step Four - Reconciliation

Because of the White church's failure to repent, it does not have the power to lead White America to forsake its arrogance and historical amnesia. The issue will also be confused by African Americans, who will say that Whites don't owe us anything. But such a person must not be taken seriously, for he or she is a serious impediment to the liberation of this racist nation. Such a person is in a catatonic state of insanity. Therefore, I conclude that things will continue as they are, unless the White church, like Zaccheus, is transformed by the Biblical Christ. I predict that racial hostility will increase in this country, and that there will be no authentic reconciliation between Whites and African Americans.

References - Chapter Two

[1] Pierre Berton, The Comfortable Pew, J.B. Lippincott Company, Philadelphia, PA, 1965, 29.
[2] Fyodor Dostoyevsky, The Brothers Karamazov, translated by Constance Garnett (New York: New American Library, 1957), 238.
[3] Malcolm X, Autobiography (New York: Grove Press, 1965), 24-42.
[4] C. Eric Lincoln, The Black Muslims In America (Boston: Beacon Press, 1961), 69-70.
[5] Carter G. Woodson, The Miseducation of the Negro, Hakim's Publications, Philadelphia, PA, 1933, 57-58.
[6] 2 Timothy 3:16.
[7] Columbus Salley and Ronald Behm, What Color Is Your God? Black Consciousness and the Christian Faith, Intervarsity Press, Downers Grove, Illinois, 46.
[8] Gibson Winter, The Suburban Captivity of the Churches, (New York: MacMillan, 1962), 50.
[9] Jacques Ellul, The Subversion of Christianity, Eerdmans Publishing Co., Grand Rapids Michigan, 166-168.
[10] William L. Andrews ed. My Bondage And My Freedom by Frederick Douglass, University of Illinois Press, Chicago, 158.
[11] Anthony Campolo, We Have Met The Enemy and They Are Partly Right, Word Books Publisher, Waco, Texas, 45.
[12] Ibid., 81-82.
[13] Genesis 2:7.
[14] Ezekiel 18:4, 20.
[15] I Thessalonians 5:23.
[16] I Corinthians 6:19-20.
[17] Harold A. Carter; Wyatt T. Walker; William A. Jones; Blacks Look At The Bicentennial, The Progressive National Baptist Publishing House, Elgin, Illinois, 125.
[18] Amos 3:2
[19] Matthew 3:1 -2.
[20] Mark 1:14-15.
[21] Clyde E. Fant, Jr., and William M. Pinson, Jr., Twenty Centuries of Great Preaching, Volume X, Word Books, Waco, Texas, 98.
[22] Gayraud S. Wilmore, and James Cone, Black Theology A Documentary History, 1966-1979, Orbis Books, New York, 97.
[23] Exodus 12:35-36.
[24] Wilmore and Cone, 97.
[25] Luke 19:1-9.

Chapter Three
The African American Family

The Problem

It is an understatement to say that much of the African American family and community are on the verge of extinction. Statistically, visually, and experientially, it is a woeful drama that is being lived out daily upon the stage of every hamlet, village, and metropolis in America. Sociologically, all the statistics would have African Americans dead, embalmed, and ready for viewing.

Let us look at some of the available data: African Americans make up 13 percent of America's population, but 50 percent of all those arrested for murder are African Americans, as are 41 percent of the victims; the leading cause of death for African American men between the ages of 16 and 34 is murder. The homicide rate of African American men is six times higher than that for White men; African American men make up 6 percent of the population, but make up 50 percent of the male prison population; 35 percent of African American men in urban populations are drug or alcohol abusers; 46 percent of African American males ages 16-62 are unemployed; 32 percent earn less than the poverty level; 30 percent of all African American families live below the poverty level; the African American infant mortality rate is 50 percent higher than that of Whites; African American out-of-wedlock births in the past twenty-five years have risen from 15 to 57 percent; 89 percent of all births by African American teenagers are illegitimate; 43 percent of African American families are headed by women who are abandoned by men; and of African American families earning less than $4,000 a year, 80 percent are headed by women. These depressing statistics reveal that our situation requires immediate attention.

The Proposal

Anybody who says that he or she has the absolute answer for our situation is megalomaniacal. Our situation will not be solved by an ebony messiah, but by the collective gifts of our people. The question that is being asked is, what is wrong with the African American family? What are some of the reasons why it is in such disarray? Some of the reasons are as follows:

1. Slavery - At the root of our problem is the historical fact of slavery and its continuing legacy of self hatred, divisiveness, and hostility at the male/female level.

2. The collective assault of racism - Personal racism is not a major concern for African Americans. The major concern is institutional racism where African Americans are guaranteed to have a second class orientation.

3. The pseudo premise of integration - This is the philosophy that what the White man has is better. (A fuller discussion is in Chapter One.) This is damaging to the self esteem of our people.

4. The permissiveness of the 1960's - This was brought on by the disillusionment with American domestic and foreign policy.

5. The drug culture - Drugs became a medium of escape for oppressor and the oppressed. They also became an economic medium for much of our community.

6. The War in Vietman - This war led to an attitude of cynicism and despair in regard to those in positions of authority.

7. The disappearance of the structures of discipline such as: the community, the church, and the school.

8. Parental delinquency - This leads to juvenile deliquency. Parents in many instances gave up on trying to guide their children, and instead became partners in permissiveness.

9. A sexual ethic of exploitation - This leads to "babies having babies."

So, as a part of the situation, and hopefully the solution, I offer the following judgments from my experience and the Judeo-Christian ethic as it concretizes in my community.

Why the Family?

It is very important that we answer this question because without an answer we will live in perpetual aimlessness and confusion. I often look at people who have had children and I say, "Why did this couple choose to curse these children? Why get married? Why have children?" All of these questions need to be answered. Therefore, we need a philosophy for victory. For me the Judeo-Christian faith as it was transmitted through Abraham the Chaldean-Hebrew; Moses the African; and Jesus the Jewish Carpenter provides the basis for my path to victory. Others in the community will have another philosophy. It is not our purpose in this book to take issue with other socio-religious philosophies, for the whole community must be summoned to action in the salvation of our people by building and rebuilding the family.

In the Book of Genesis it appears that Elohim in Chapter Two underscores purposeful creation. First of all Chapter 2:7 says:

> *And the Lord God formed man of the dust of the ground, and breathed into his nostrils the breath of life; and man became a living soul.*[1]

In this passage it appears that God's purpose in creating Adam was because of divine prerogative. God took the initiative. Therefore, love was at the center of God's movement towards structuring the family. It appears on the surface to be a very boring prospect until we get to Chapter 2:15-17 which says:

> *And the Lord God took the man, and put him into the Garden of Eden to dress it and to keep it. And the Lord God commanded the man, saying, of every tree of the garden you mayest freely eat: But of the tree of the knowledge of good and evil, you shall not eat of it: for in the day that you eat thereof you shall surely die.*[2]

This passage teaches that man and woman are more than a physique; he and she have been called to be partners under God in the continual enhancement of His creation. Next God (Elohim) warns them of their finitude. Man is not God. He will never be God. Therefore, this is their ultimate frustration. They can take a rifle and kill a lion or an elephant, but they can't terminate God. God created man and woman to be disciplined. So therefore, they are given the choice between autonomy (self rule) and theonomy (rule by God). The choice one makes is between paradise and predicament.

In verses 18-24 there is also the theme of companionship, not only with God, but between Man and Woman:

> *And the Lord God said, it is not good that the man should be alone; I will make an help meet for him. And out of the ground the Lord God formed every fowl of the air; and brought them unto Adam to see what he would call them: and whatsoever Adam called every living creature, that was the name thereof. And Adam gave names to all cattle, and to the fowl of the air, and to every beast of the field; but there was not found an help meet for him. And the Lord God caused a deep sleep to fall upon Adam, and he slept: and he took one of his ribs, and closed up the flesh instead thereof. And the rib, which the Lord God had taken from man, made he a woman, and brought her unto the man. And Adam said, this is now bone of my*

bones, and flesh of my flesh: She shall be called Woman, because she was taken out of Man. Therefore, shall a man leave his father and his mother, and shall cleave unto his wife: and they shall be one flesh.[3]

These verses teach the following:

1. The family is divinely formulated. (vs.18)
2. As important as man was as a partner with God, his aloneness appears to be an impediment to his continual creativity. (vss. 18-20)
3. The family is to be built upon a divine-human partnership. (vss. 21-22)
4. The family is strong when we are in agreement with God. (vs. 23)
5. There was no superior/inferior relationship: it was complementary. (vs. 23)
6. Nothing human must break the bond between the husband and his wife. (vs. 24)

As we continue to peruse the Bible we also see the theme of the individual family having universal significance. This can be seen in the introduction of Abraham upon the stage of biblical drama:

Now the Lord had said unto Abram, get out of your country, and from your kindred, and from your father's house, unto a land that I will show you: and I will make of you a great nation, and I will bless you, and make your name great: and you shall be a blessing. And I will bless them that bless you, and curse him that curses you: and in you shall all families of the earth be blessed.[4]

Through Abraham and his extended family we can see the cosmic significance of the family. Therefore, God did not ordain the family just for the purpose of enjoying legalized sex. The family under God can and must accomplish great things for God, themselves, and others.

The Bible teaches us that God has a purpose for the family in salvation history. When the parents are not alienated from God, children can be blessed. It is ironic that Adam and Eve did not have children until they became alienated from God (Genesis 3-4). Prior to their alienation (Genesis 2) they were on speaking terms with God. But then they tried to have family without God and brought upon themselves and theirs, alienation both vertically and horizontally. Because of this alienation, they lost the ideal environment for the rearing of children (Genesis 3-4). Yet in the midst of alienation (Genesis 4:1-15; Hebrews 11:4) there is a witness for God consciousness in the family.

What is the purpose of having children? I made a mistake; for income tax purposes; someone to perpetuate the family tree; someone to love since I was never loved by my parents. All of these reasons are foolish and selfish. Biblically speaking, the purpose for having children is for the recycling of souls (human beings), who will fulfill the purposes of God within and without the family. The sage tells us in Proverbs 22:6, "Train up a child in the way he should go: and when he is old, he will not depart from it."

Making Marriages Work

What is marriage? It is a commitment between God, a man, and a woman to live their lives according to the principles of God's word, and to train their children to do the same. Whenever the family attempts to live without God, the marriage is in trouble. One can have a socially successful life without God, but one cannot have a God-centered marriage without God. Some of the enemies of marriage which lead to dissolution by separation or divorce are as follows:

1. Marrying for selfish reasons - such as sex, physical beauty, money, or power.
2. The "Burger King philosophy" which says,"Have it your way."
3. Religious differences- such as a Baptist marrying a Jehovah's Witness.

4. Money - the lack of, or bad financial decisions.
5. Who is the boss? - This is a persistent problem in an age of feminine assertion and aggressiveness.
6. Sex - the lack of; too much of; or infidelity.
7. Lack of communication - Every marriage has a chance as long as we continue to keep open the lines of communication.
8. Taking each other for granted - This is "when the newness wears off your crystal chandelier" syndrome.
9. Failure to handle the invasive tendencies of the extended family and friends - This has to do with the expectations of family members, the possessiveness of in-laws, the wife and "the girls" syndrome, and the husband and his "being with the boys" syndrome.
10. Failure to magnetize the little things. Good marriages are much deeper than fur coats, Rolls Royces, diamonds, mansions, and vacations on the French Riviera. Marriages are built on the little things such as: thank you; I love you; excuse me; let's talk about this; forgive me; happy birthday, dear; happy anniversary, love; let's pray about this.
11. A lack of patience - It is said that the wife of the Greek philosopher Socrates was exceedingly mean and ill-tempered. When the philosopher was asked why he continued to live with her, he replied, "She teaches me patience." In an age of feminism and "I don't need" or "I don't want a man" attitude, marriages are falling apart because of an unwillingness to work it out.

If we are going to save the African American community, we must make the building of the family our number one priority. Therefore, we must strive collectively to have strong marriages. If we can fly and sail around the world in war time to defend the interests of others, then we must be just as vigilant in saving our own people. Let's have a war against the extinction of our people.

I am convinced as a pastor for almost a quarter of a century that in dealing with the issue of marriage, the church starts in the wrong place. Many churches have some form of pre-marital counseling. But it is routine and perfunctory at best. If we are serious, then we must begin with our children between the ages of 3-5 until they finish high school and/ or college. This training sponsored by the church, in coalition with the home, will be geared towards teaching young girls and boys what it means to be married. This boy or that girl may never get married, but they will have an understanding of the commitment that marriage requires. To perform a ceremony for a couple who has not received any basic spiritual training on the true meaning of marriage is immoral. Marriage is the cornerstone of any civilization. And when it is no longer strong, any culture will ultimately collapse. If we are looking for perfect marriages, they do not exist, because there aren't any perfect people. But I am still a fan of the institution.

What we need in our community are models to be studied and used as resource persons. While we are not anti-intellectual, it is no time for textbook theories and analyses. It is time to talk to the people who have made marriage work. In every community, church, fraternity, and sorority there are hundreds of people who have been married for 25,30,40,50,60, and some 70 years. These are resource persons that are being neglected in our communities. I have many in my own parish who can give testimony to how they are making it over. All of them will tell you that, "It has not been easy." Maybe therein lies part of the solution to the problem. Marriage has to be worked at constantly, progressively, and prayerfully. My mother and father stayed married for forty- five years, from 1928-1973, the latter being the year of my father's death. My in-laws, as of this writing, have been married for forty-eight years, from 1943 to the present. Also my wife's aunt and uncle have been married from 1945-present. These relationships are not testimonies to perfection, but to a bulldog determination which says, "I won't let go."

Overcoming Male/Female Hostility

We need to review our history in order to determine why African American men and women are adversaries rather than allies. I am convinced that both react with hostility towards each other because both are ignorant of their history. From the outset, slavery destroyed the bond between our men and women. Richard Williams said:

> Slaves were treated like animals and bred like cattle. To the slaveowner and White America, the black female was just a cow, the black male just a bull, and the black child just a calf. White America treated blacks as though they were insensitive to pain, fear, and loneliness.[5]

Because America has forced the African American male and female into such a self defeating confrontation, it is foolish for us as a people to continue this path of destruction. Even today the White male power structure uses the African American female against the African American male. This perfidious power structure does not love the female (except sexually) any more than he likes the African American male, but it is to his advantage to exalt African American women above African American men. This breeds a venomous friction in the African American community. The African American males become jealous of their sisters, and the sisters often develop an attitude which says, "You are no longer in my league. I do not need a man. And if I do decide to get one, he will probably be white." The imagined apex of this tension is when an African American female college president instills this notion in the minds of her all black, female student population. Then you know beyond a doubt that we are in serious trouble.

Living in a racistic society has forced many African American men into a mode of self-destructive behavior. The African American woman then reacts to his reaction rather than dealing with the action that produced the reaction.

In the table below, we can catch a glimpse of the images of conflict that exist between African American men and women. While these do not represent all male/female relationships, it is a clear indicator of what is generally true on a broad scale.

The Image of the Male	**The Image of the Female**
1. No self-esteem	1. Possessive
2. Violent	2. More educated than the male
3. Unemployed	3. Feelings of superiority over African American men
4. Lazy	4. A constant nag
5. Uneducated	5. Lack of encouragement for her man
6. Physical rather than intellectual	6. Economically superior to the African American man
7. Practitioner of vices such as drugs, alcohol, and gambling	7. Matriarchal - holding the family together
8. Womanizer	8. The moral leader of the family
9. Deserter of his family	
10. Incarcerated	
11. Anti-religious	

If we are going to overcome this battle between the sexes, the following suggestions are offered:

1. Parents must teach their boys and girls the virtues of love and respect.
2. Parents must become educated in the psychological effects of oppression on the African American family in order to break the cycle of hostility.
3. Parents must teach their boys and girls what it means to be an African American in a racistic society.
4. Parents must teach their boys and girls the responsibilities of marriage and parenthood.
5. Parents must teach their boys/young men how to love an African American girl/woman.

6. Parents must teach their girls/young women how to love an African American boy/man. Pre-marital sex and irresponsible baby making are to be rejected.
7. Parents must teach their children how to use the evil impact of oppression to forge a mindset for unity rather than divisiveness.
8. Any relationship will view the female as queen and the male as king of his castle. Both must treat each other with dignity and respect.
9. Since both are victims of oppression, they must become comrades in liberation.
10. Parents should begin this training when their children are between the ages of 3-5 years old.

The Question of Roles

Early on, the question of roles to be played must be settled before any legal commitments are made. Therefore, it will be necessary to come to grips with the fact that the roles each will play will vary according to strengths, weaknesses, and mutual consent. What will be the norm in one family may not be in another. But all must work towards nation building. The Bible can aid us in overcoming this problem.

Characteristics of The Biblical Husband/Father

1. He must have a personal walk with God (Deuteronomy 6:1-5).
2. He must teach the faith to his children (Deuteronomy 6:7).
3. He must be the spiritual leader of his family (Ephesians 5:22-24).
4. He loves his family (Ephesians 5:25).
5. He provides for the needs of his family. And if he fails, he is worse than an infidel (I Timothy 5:8). A man is not measured by how many babies he can produce, but by how many he can support.

6. He is faithful to his wife (Hebrews 13:4).
7. He instructs and disciplines his children (Proverbs 22:6; Ephesians 6:4).
8. His ultimate goal is to leave his family in God's Will (First Kings 2:1-4).

Characteristics of The Biblical Wife\Mother
(Proverbs 31:10-31)

1. She is a woman of character.(vs. 10)
2. She is preeminently valuable. Things do not take precedence over her family.
3. She is respected by her husband. (vs. 11)
4. She is a paragon of perpetual pleasure for her husband. (vs. 12)
5. She is not diminished by domesticity. (vss. 13-15)
6. She is industrious. She is not confined to being a housewife although she is comfortable in that role. But she transcends domesticity. (vss. 16-19;24)
7. She has a social conscience. (vs. 20)
8. She has her family under control, thereby mitigating their anxiety. (vss. 21-22)
9. She is not unequally yoked.(vs. 23)
10. She is strong. (vs. 25)
11. She has dignity. (vs. 25)
12. She has no fear of the future.(vs 25)
13. She has widsom. (vs. 26)
14. She instructs her children gently.(vs. 25)
15. She is the domestic engineer. (vs 27)
16. She does not waste time. (vs. 27)
17. She is loved, respected, and praised by her husband and children. (vss. 28-29)
18. She fears the Lord. (vs. 30)
19. She is praised beyond her immediate family.(vs. 31)

The above biblical references reveal the following contemporary insights:

1. Working parents can operate without major conflicts, but it is difficult.
2. Financial need is not the only motivation for a career outside the home.
3. Though difficult, there can be a balance between career and household; it depends upon the couple involved.
4. Working parents can have well-adjusted children.
5. A husband and wife must be supportive of each other rather than competitive.
6. Much can be accomplished in marriages where there is complementarity rather than subordination of one spouse to the other.
7. If one chooses to be a housewife, she is not to be frowned upon. She must be praised.

The Children are our Hope

Beyond a doubt, we must start a children's movement in order to secure our future. Some time ago, I read a very disturbing picture of children in general in America.

> Across America, children are failing to flourish. Rich kids, middle-class kids, poor kids, all deal with risk and neglect on a scale unimagined in previous generations. Twenty percent of all children are growing up in poverty, a 21 percent increase since 1970. Twelve million children lack basic health insurance. Fifteen million children have been abandoned by their fathers. The rate of suicide among adolescents has tripled over the last 20 years. Scholastic Aptitude Test scores among college- bound youngsters have fallen 70 points since 1963. Twenty-seven percent of teenagers drop out of school (compared with 6 percent in Japan and 8 percent in Germany).[6]

If this is the case for children all over America, it is worse for African Americans. Therefore, it is important for us to go to the Motherland for our example.

> The African child receives more body contact than his Western counterpart. Most children are breast-fed and for longer periods of time than in other societies. Before and after a child learns to walk, he spends a great deal of time being held by his mother on her lap or being carried on her back or the back of an older sibling. Usually the child sleeps with his mother during infancy until a new baby arrives. The African child learns early in his childhood to embrace relatives and friends in greeting them or thanking them for a special favor. Thus, the child grows up in a social network characterized by physical closeness, acceptance, and care. He expects to receive affection and comfort and learns to give it when it is needed by others. By the time an African child is six years old, he begins to take responsibility for providing care for a younger sibling. He carries the child on his back, cradles the child on his lap, and learns to respond with body contact and caring behavior to fit the various needs of the child. The African modes of child rearing give rise to the development of humane attitudes and the care syndrome. Unlike western child rearing, African socialization emhasizes the closeness of man to man. Physical and psychological closeness are encouraged by body contact between people.[7]

Therefore, the social salvation of our people demands that we look unashamedly to our roots in West Africa, for Eurocentricity has proved to be poison for the African American family.

A classic example of the rearing of an African child is the biblical story of Jochebed (Exodus 2:1-10)and Moses. This is no diminution of Amram's influence in the rearing of Moses, but circumstances threw Jochebed on the center stage of salvation history. The story unfolds in the Book of Exodus 2:1-10.

> *And there went out a man of the house of Levi, and took to wife a daughter of Levi. And the woman con-*

> *ceived, and bare a son: and when she saw him that he was a goodly child, she hid him three months. And when she could no longer hide him, she took for him an ark of bulrushes, and daubed it with slime and with pitch, and put the child therein; and she laid it in the flags by the river's brink. And his sister stood afar off, to witness what would be done to him. And the daughter of Pharaoh came down to wash herself at the river; and her maidens walked along by the river's side; and when she saw the ark among the flags, she sent her maid to fetch it. And when she had opened it, she saw the child: and behold the baby wept, and she had compassion on him, and said, this is one of the Hebrews' children. Then said his sister to Pharaoh's daughter, shall I go and call to you a nurse of the Hebrew women, that she may nurse the child for you? And Pharaoh's daughter said to her, go. And the maid went and called the child's mother. And Pharaoh's daughter said unto her, take this child away, and nurse it for me, and I will give you your wages. And the woman took the child and nursed it. And the child grew, and she brought him unto Pharaoh's daughter, and he became her son. And she called his name Moses: and she said, because I drew him out of the water.*[8]

This passage reveals the overwhelming influence of even a single parent in the life of a child, provided that parent is imbued with a sense of liberation. Even in the midst of an oppressive situation she (Jochebed) made the difference in the life of Moses, in spite of insurmountable odds. Because of the faith-cultural training that Moses received from his mother, he was able to handle the various phases of life: from peril to the palace; from the palace to the pastures of Midian; and to the position of God-ordained liberator. Dr. Janice Hale-Benson said:

> Even though Moses grew up in the house of Pharaoh and became his son, there was a difference between

> Moses and the other sons of Pharaoh. Pharaoh's sons grew up to become oppressors, but Moses grew up to become a liberator. The difference between Moses and Pharaoh's sons was the difference made by Moses' Nurse, who was his mother. Moses' mother not only nursed him with the milk of her breast, but she also imbued her child with a clear understanding of who he was, who the enemy was, and what he must do. She provided Moses with an identity, a god, and a heritage, so that when his moment in history arrived and he saw an Egyptian overseer striking a Hebrew slave, he did not experience an identity crisis. He immediately knew whose side he was on and what had to be done. Without Jochebed, there would have been no Moses.[9]

Parental guidance in the structures of faith and culture are indispensable in nation building. Therefore, it is crucial that we begin our journey towards liberation, not by looking for Moses, but with the father and mother of Moses (Exodus 6:20). Theocentric and ethnocentric parents are jewels in the crown of freedom. If we are going to have great children, we must teach our children what parentage is all about. The reason marriages fail in our society is that the church and the family become involved only a few months before the wedding ceremony. The couple will spend all of its energies and money on the wedding and hardly any time on the marriage. But if we are going to have strong families, we must begin our teaching in the formative years of infancy.

Respect For Our Elders

Any nation that does not respect the elderly is doomed. One of the great problems that we have faced since the 1960's is a diminution of respect for our parents and our elders. The Decalogue says:

> *Honour your father and your mother: that your days may be long upon the land which the Lord your God gives you.*[10]

The Apostle Paul said:

> *Children obey your parents in the Lord: for this is right. Honour your father and mother; which is the first commandment with promise; that it may be well with you, and you may live long on the earth. And you fathers, provoke not your children to wrath: but bring them up in the nurture and admonition of the Lord.*[11]

Again he says:

> *Children obey your parents in all things: for this is well pleasing unto the Lord. Fathers, provoke not your children to anger, lest they be discouraged.*[12]

He further declares:

> *Rebuke not an elder but intreat him as a father; and the younger men as brothers; the elder women as mothers; the younger as sisters, with all purity. But if any widow have children or nephews, let them learn first to show piety at home, and to requite their parents; for that is good and acceptable before God.*[13]

In all of these Pauline passages we see clearly the call for mutual respect between parents and children. To obey one's parents is a divine mandate. Prior to the 1970's this was a glaring strength in the African American community. My parents taught my brother Frank, my late sister Geraldine, and me to respect not only the nuclear family but adults in general. Every adult in the community was a potential disciplinarian. This was dramatized by my Sunday School teachers Ollie Kincaid and Nellie Williams reporting to my mother about my disturbing rascalities in the class. What made the difference was that my mother did not question the veracity of either of them. This has been lost within the last 20-25 years.

Andrew Billingsley said:

> If the position of mother and child was the closest, and that of brother and sister the most fraternal, that between a person and his grandparents was the most revered in all of West African society. In Ashanti, for example, the grandparents on both sides are the most honored of all one's kinfolk. Their position and status were of the greatest importance for the whole social system, in part because they stood between ordinary citizens and their ancestors. If the ancestors got their status because they stood between man and God, the grandparents got theirs because they stood only a little lower on the ladder of infinity. Among the Yoruba, it was the duty and privilege of grandparents to name newborn children. Among the Ashanti, grandmothers, both maternal and paternal, exercised great influence and responsibility in the care and protection of children. It is from the grandparents of both sexes that children learn family history, folklore, proverbs, and other traditional lore. The grandparents are felt to be the living links with the past.[14]

A return to the veneration (not worship) of our elders is a gallant step towards nation building in the African American community.

Twelve Commandments for Children

1. You must develop an authentic relationship with God.
2. You must worship regularly.
3. You must love and respect yourself.
4. You must respect your elders and those in authority.
5. You must be a servant to all humankind irrespective of skin color. But you must be especially involved in the African American community.

6. You must get an education. This will include learning about yourself as well as other people.
7. You must become a student of the Bible. For the Christian, it is God's written, revealed, and authoritative word.
8. You must abstain from all non-marital sex.
9. You must practice honesty.
10. You must work diligently to be a good steward of your body. "It is the temple of the Holy Spirit." Therefore, you must avoid drugs, alcohol,cigarettes, and harmful foods.
11. You must be a good steward of possessions. Therefore, you must have a good work ethic. You must learn how to make, share, and invest money.
12. You must be a good citizen, but not at the expense of violating your relationship with God.

Teaching Wholesome Values to Our Children

In order for this to be done, babies must stop having babies, and parents must get off the "finger popping" kick. You can't be a child and a parent at the same time. Parenthood is not for children. It is about a mature man and a mature woman coming together to share a life that will honor God and to transmit the structures of faith-culture to their children.

I am convinced from a Christian perspective that no men or women should have children in the African American community unless they are able to teach the basic content of the Judeo-Christian faith and are able to instruct their children in African and African American history and culture. Therefore, our whole concept of church must change from being an arena for sociopolitical masturbation where we get a good feeling, but no life is produced, to that of being an equipper of families to move from chaos to community. This will be a challenge in the African American church because feeling usually takes precedence over fact. The church, if it is to be relevant in the years ahead, must train boys and girls how to be men and women. It must also teach men and women how to be husbands and wives. A Christocentric family grounded in faith-culture will produce children who will do the same.

What the African American community is lacking now, on a broad level, is a failure to communicate and transmit wholesome values to our children. This is impossible to do when parents have a problem in this area. When parents are willing to spend $40,000.00 for a car rather than a house, that's a value problem. But parents who have been grounded in faith-culture must take the offensive in teaching wholesome values to our children. A sample directive is as follows:

1. Teach our children that we live in a God-centered universe rather than a human-centered universe.
2. Teach them strategies for overcoming the exigencies of racism.
3. Teach them the value of honest work.
4. Teach them about ultimate concerns:
    a. the meaning of life
    b. the importance of the stewardship and the sharing of possessions
    c. the value of good health
    d. respect for elders
    e. respect for the environment
    f. the reality of death as the termination of physical life
    g. the afterlife
    h. the purpose and the danger of power
5. The accoutrements of ghetto success are to be negated such as:
    a. expensive cars
    b. gold chains
    c. gold teeth
    d. ghetto music boxes
    e. expensive sneakers
    f. video games
    g. weird clothes
    h. weird haircuts

One of the evils of capitalism is that through advertisements, oppressed people are lured into investing in transient things, rather than things that are liberating. Anthony Campolo says:

> The questionable nature of capitalistic practices arises not only in reference to the ways in which land and natural resources in Third World nations are exploited, but also with regard to what capitalism does to the poor. For instance, serious concern is being expressed over such products as video games. While the inventing and constructing of video games has produced multi-billion dollar profits, there is doubt as to whether they serve any real need. Nevertheless, millions of teenagers are lured into spending a great deal of money as they play these games. Time that should be spent in study is consumed in video game arcades. There are some sociological studies showing correlation between video games and declining school grades among the poor youth in urban areas.[15]

Reestablishing the Nuclear and the Extended Family

The basis for structuring the nuclear family will be healthy marriages informed by faith-culture. We must no longer trivialize such an important lifelong commitment. Several years ago I was visited by a boy of seventeen and a girl of sixteen who wanted to get married. The conversation went as follows:

Pastor: "Are you serious?"
Couple: "Yes, we are."
Pastor: "Are you saved?"
Couple: "No."
Pastor: "Why do you want to get married?"
Couple: "We love each other."
Pastor: "Have you finished high school?"
Couple: "No sir, we quit."
Pastor: "Do you have jobs?"

Couple: "No sir."
Pastor: "What do your parents think?"
Couple: "They don't know about it."
Pastor: "Don't you think that you need parental consent?"
Boy: "My mama is a wino, and I haven't seen my old man in five years. So, I really don't have anyone to ask."
Girl: "My dad is dead, but my mom would kill me if she knew what I was doing."
Pastor: "And you still want to go through with this?"
Couple: "Yes sir."
Pastor: "Are you ready for a lifetime of sexual fidelity to each other?"
Boy: "Pastor, I can't promise that because I don't see anything wrong with having me a woman on the side, as long as I satisfy my main squeeze (woman)."
Girl: (laughing)
Pastor: (to young lady)"Why are you laughing? I understand where this boy is coming from, but your laughter baffles me. What's funny?"
Pastor: (Dismisses them both, and calls the mother of the girl who intercepts their marriage plans.)

Such trivialization of marriage must stop if we are going to build great families where men are kings; wives are queens; boys are princes; and girls are princesses. Therefore, the lustful experimentation of marriage in the form of pre-marital cohabitation must be abolished. It is time to get serious or become extinct. Western culture will not be the model for the restructuring of the family, because it is the cause of my continuing oppression. Therefore, we must look into our own experiences, culture, and the traditions of West Africa for our victory! Again Billingsley says:

> Marriage in Africa was rarely an informal matter between two consenting partners and their relatives. Ceremony and exchange of property were important aspects of an elaborate process which consisted of two basic types: those marriages based on the initiation of the two consenting partners and those based on the initiative of their parents and kin. In both cases the partners and their parents had to give their consent.[16]

The nuclear family is the foundation for a strong society, but it is not the only expression of sound family life.

The nuclear family is prelude to the extended family. While the nuclear family includes husband, wife, and children, the extended family includes grandparents, aunts, uncles, and cousins. Both the nuclear and the extended family offer opportunities to strategize for liberation. However, the extended family offers an enormous incentive for self-determination. This became alive for me and my wife Pat, when we visited the West African countries of Senegal and Gambia. First of all I suffered cultural shock when I saw the legacy of French (Senegal) and British (Gambia) colonialism. But beyond this, we were mesmerized by the power of the extended family. Everybody was connected to the family compound, and all shared to make it strong. I remember our African guide telling us not to feel sorry for the beggars, because all were part of an extended family, and some of them made as much as $35,000 per year in American money. The beggar would then bring all his monies into the compound's general fund. This is a way of life that must be adopted by African Americans. Since 1979 our church has supported a Haitian mission. One is inspired when he sees this concept of African communalism come into focus. Twenty Haitians will live in a three bedroom house or less until they can do better. They think corporately rather than individually.

This attitude needs to be adopted by African Americans in our quest for freedom. Instead of the individual or the nuclear family going it alone, it is time to engage the extended family against the citadel of oppression. The economic implications of this will be discussed in Chapter Six.

Strengthening the Single Person

First of all we need to look upon singleness as a gift from God. Not all people will get married. Beyond the frustration of answering questions by inquisitive family members and friends, life as a single can border on exasperation. Again, not all will be married. And not all will be single, but both can be productive in the building of the African American community.

> The single life in the city has been romanticized by the mass media as a swinging, carefree kind of existence revolving around luxury apartments, fancy sports cars, bright discotheques, exciting singles bars, and weekend excursions. For many urban singles, however, this way turns out to be more fantasy than fact. For them, life in the city can become a drab, cheerless struggle for survival.[17]

The categories of singleness as it embraces male/female are as follows:

1. single and celibate, without children
2. single and celibate with children, by adoption
3. single as a result of divorce, without children
4. single as a result of divorce, with children
5. single as a result of separation, or desertion, without children
6. single as a result of separation, or desertion, with children
7. single as a result of the death of a spouse, without children
8. single as a result of the death of a spouse, with children
9. single without children, but sexually active
10. single with children, and sexually active
11. single, but not willing to settle for a less than suitable mate
12. single with children and never married

13. single because of spouse being in prison or a mental institution
14. single with children, for the sake of governmental assistance

Regardless of the categories, the African American church must be prophetic, compassionate, understanding, open, encouraging, and reaffirming, as we proclaim a gospel that affirms marriage and singleness. The church, through its ministry to singles, can go a long way toward liberating the single person from societal gossip and innuendos. It can also liberate a marriage-oriented culture from presumption. Then both married and single can become co-partners in liberation, as we remember that Jesus of Nazareth lived a life of celibate singleness.

Re-establishing the Concept of Neighborliness

Since the 1960's the African American community has lost its sense of being neighborly. Who is my neighbor? My neighbor, someone has said, is the one who fills my space when I do not want to have it empty. In the 1950's, when I was growing into adolescence, a sense of community existed on "Tucker Hill." Tucker Hill was one of several sections where African Americans lived in Ocala, Florida. This concept of community was demonstrated in the following ways:

1. The sharing of foods.
2. The sharing and the lending of small amounts of money.
3. Payment of debts owed.
4. Possession of keys to each other's houses.
5. Each neighbor was a medium of security in other neighbors' absence.
6. One could leave his or her house unlocked and the neighbors would take care of the domicile.
7. Neighbors visited each other but not ad nauseum.
8. The neighbors were surrogate parents to each other's children.

9. The common courtesies of greeting each other by saying, "How are you today?" Shaking hands or embracing was the expected norm for neighbors.
10. In time of sickness or death neighbors could be counted on to keep their vigils, and to do whatever was necessary to minister to the family in distress.

To talk of neighborliness today is almost to sound mythical. To say to our children that there was a time in many of our Southern towns that African Americans could leave their houses unlocked, is to be accused of lying or painting an imaginary picture of Utopia. Yet we must be honest in saying that this concept of neighborliness was more adaptable to the South rather than the North. Because of industrialization and urbanization, the North, early on, became an asphalt jungle not conducive to neighborliness.

As we view the landscape today, neighborliness is extinct even in small Southern towns. What has brought about this drastic change? The following are suggested reasons for the breakdown:

1. The War in Vietnam - The war did not damage the soul of America; it revealed the soul of America. Too many African Americans died in this imperialistic war. In turn the violence witnessed, perpetrated, and endured has created a cold, callous, and calculating African American. It has produced an attitude of cynical despair. It reduced many African Americans to resort to the law of the jungle where "only the fittest survive." So there goes the neighborhood.
2. The permissiveness of the 1960's - When immorality takes precedence over morality then any society is in serious trouble.
3. The breakdown of the nuclear and the extended family - No neighborhood can remain strong and safe if the family unit is destroyed.
4. The loss of discipline in the home, church, and school - These three are the basic foundations of any community, and when these operate without any sense

of moral correctness, it is over for the neighborhood and society in general.

5. The emergence of the drug culture, which is a derivative of the War in Vietnam – Our neighborhoods have almost been destroyed by drugs. There is an attitude of trepidation, which keeps our communities on alert. The oppressor brings the drugs into the country, into our neighborhoods, and into our veins. Even rich white men come into our communities and buy their drugs and ride back to the serenity of suburbia.
6. Drug related crimes such as burglaries and vandalism – No one feels safe in the African American community.
7. Meism - This is the attitude which says, "Look out for number one. As long as I make it everything is cool." This attitude was proliferated during the Reagan years in the White House. It was inadvertently adopted by many African Americans who feel they are doing all right. Such an attitude destroys the community and keeps us from the task of nation building.

Family Time Together

Too much time outside the home disrupts domestic equilibrium. If families are to be strong, we must come to grips with the fact that anything that cannot be shared by the whole family must take a back seat, such as sororities and fraternities. This is no denunciation of these organizations, but family must be prioritized next to God. Families must spend time together. Everyone needs his or her individual space, but too much space leads to family problems. There ought be a time for husbands and wives to share together. And there need to be regular times when the entire nuclear family can be together. There is often difficulty in doing this, but we must make the time.

The Church in the House

One of the most pregnant phrases in all the Bible is "the church in your house." (Romans 16:5; First Corinthians 16:19; Colossians 4:15) A fundamental error in the African American religious community is the separation between religion in the home and religion in the corporate worship experience. Ofttimes there is no connection between church and the home other than eleven o'clock on Sunday morning. Religion ought not be a way to kill an hour on Sunday; it should be a way of life. In spite of the fact that the church has been at the center of the African American community from its inception, there is often no visible evidence of the appropriation of the faith in the home.

For example, very few churchgoers ever read the Bible, and few have a family time together for study, prayer, and reflection. This fact is intensified when biblically illiterate people sit before the preacher on Sunday morning. No wonder worship is such a tedious affair for many churchgoers.

The purpose of the church in our community is to save the lost and to disciple (train) the saved. Beyond this, the church must equip parents to teach the Faith and their culture to their children, who in turn will do the same. The church fails because it cannot do in one hour on Sunday what the home has failed to do in 167 hours. It is the church's responsibility to equip the home, so that the community will in turn be strenghtened. If we don't we will end up as pious failures.

Again the corporate worship experience must include the nuclear and the extended family. Since I speak from a Christian perspective, the family in worship will come to gain knowledge about the Biblical Jesus of Nazareth, who is the model for our liberation.

The African American male must take his place in the corporate worship experience. He must overcome his hostility toward the African American preacher, who is often looked upon as his competition. I still believe the African American husband/male should be the moral leader of his home. This is no time for tyrannical and chauvinistic games. It is time for liberation. Nothing is more exhilarating to me than to see the nuclear family in worship reading, praying, singing, studying, reflecting, repenting, and preparing to go out and liberate others.

Family worship must be a time when the seeds of liberation are sown. By this I mean being set free from that which enslaves the oppressor both imminently and eschatologically. Family worship must not be a time where we dispense opium. We must stop seeking religious fixes for our sociopolitical-sexual frustrations. We need a cure. The cure is the Carpenter from Nazareth. When we take Him seriously and move from praise to practice, a revolution has been set in motion that the oppressor cannot stop.

References – Chapter Three

[1] Genesis 2:7.
[2] Genesis 2:15-17.
[3] Genesis 2:18-24.
[4] Genesis 12:1-3.
[5] Richard Williams, They Stole It But You Must Return It, Hema Publishing Co., Rochester, New York, 1990, 11.
[6] Sylvia Ann Hewlett, Fort Lauderdale Sun Sentinel, July 14, 1992, "A Wilting Generation," Fort Lauderdale Sun Sentinel, July 14, 1992.
[7] Akpan Ebsen, "The Care Syndrome: A Resource for Counseling in Africa," Journal of Negro Education 42:205-211.
[8] Exodus 2:1-10.
[9] Janice E. Hale-Benson, Black Children: Their Roots, Culture, and Learning Styles, Johns Hopkins University Press, Baltimore, Maryland, 1986, 45-46.
[10] Exodus 20:12.
[11] Ephesians 6:1-4.
[12] Colossians 3:20-21.
[13] I Timothy 5:1-4.
[14] Andrew Billingsley, Black Families in White America, Simon and Schuster, New York, 1968, 47.
[15] Anthony Campolo, We Have Met the Enemy, and They Are Partly Right, Word Books Publisher, Waco, Texas, 1985, 163.
[16] Billingsley, 41.
[17] Anne Davis and Lucien Coleman, Review and Expositor, "The Single Person in Contemporary Society", Review and Expositor Vol. 74, No. 1, 1977, 34.

Chapter Four

Toward a Theology For Ministry To The African American Community

Theology is indispensable in shaping the faith-culture process. Theologian J. Deotis Roberts speaks forthrightly:

> It is just not true that activism is sufficient in itself. The black church needs a theology both for its self-understanding and for its sense of mission. We need to know not merely that we should act; we need to know why we should act. Theology and ministry are inseparable.[1]

Along these lines, theologian Dr. C. Eric Lincoln has the following to say:

> The black church has traditionally relied upon a preached theology...Now that era may be past. The Blacks of this generation, and possibly for generations to come, are going to write their own theology in light of their circumstances and their needs. A white Jesus, whether preached, taught or implied by cultural habits, simply won't do. In a society like ours, he can't do anything for black folk! A white church that is painfully adjunctive to institutionalized racism - the consequences of which are devastating the whole society - can't do anything for black people. It can't do anything for itself.
>
> White theology suffers mortally from the sin of omission. It has sent its theologians to study in Europe

> where the problem isn't, or imported the best European theologians to bring us the light, but not for our darkness.
>
> In consequence, American theology has had few words to speak to our condition. White theology has not done anything for black people except ignore them.[2]

Therefore, we must minister to the African American family through the medium of our history and culture as it is informed by Jesus of Nazareth.

Clarifying the God Question

In the 1960's, America was bombarded with the "God is Dead" theology, and as usual, the church made the wrong response. We stated such pious irrelevancies as, "If God is dead, why was I not invited to the funeral?" Or, "If God is dead, who woke me up this morning?" While these statements evoked an ecstatic response from the congregation, they did not come within a million miles of the central question. The response should have been, Who is God? Some gods need to die.

In the African American community the mass devastation is a derivative of our failure to answer this question. Failure to answer this question has wreaked havoc upon thirty million African Americans. In Exodus 5:1-2, we find the basis for our discussion:

> *And afterwards, Moses and Aaron went in and told Pharaoh, thus saith the Lord God of Israel, let my people go, that they may hold a feast unto me in the wilderness. And Pharaoh said, who is the Lord that I should obey his voice to let Israel go? I know not the Lord, neither will I let Israel go.*

This passage is instructive because it forces us to differentiate between the God of Moses and the god of Pharaoh. Unequivocally, they are not the same. The God of Moses (Yahweh) is a God of freedom (vs. 1a). The God of Pharaoh is a god of oppression (vs.2). Therefore, any authentic attempt to minister to the African American family and community must take seriously this distinction between the God of the disenfranchised and the god of the oppressor. At least in this passage (vs.2), Pharaoh is very explicit in stating that he did not know the God of Moses. In stating his ignorance of Yahweh, he defined his anthropology and his sociology. His theology was the basis for his view of man and society. Apparently, he felt no compunction for his enslavement of the Hebrews because he had a theological undergirding. Therefore, Pharaoh's theology cannot suffice for an enslaved people.

The problem with American theology is that it does not take seriously the need to deal with this question. Our view of God is the very foundation of what we are, think, and do. It influences every single institution in our society: philosophical, educational, military, political, economic, and ecclesiastical. Therefore, it is liberating to oppressed and oppressor to reexamine our God concepts. James Cone says:

> The lives of a black slave and white slaveholder were radically different. It follows that their thoughts about divine things would also be different, even though they might sometimes use the same words about God. The life of the slaveholder and others of the culture was that of extending white inhumanity to excruciating limits, involving the enslavement of Africans and the annihilation of Indians. The life of the slave was the slave ship, the auction block, and the plantation regime. It involved the attempt to define himself without the ordinary historical possibilities of self-affirmation. Therefore, when the master and slave spoke of God, they could not possibly be referring to the same reality.[3]

America will never reach her true potential until the American church rectifies its god concept. If we are going to have theocentric families, only a God who is a God of love will suffice. African

Americans cannot love a God who does not love them, unless we are collectively masochistic because a God of love does not will our destruction. Many African Americans have rejected Pharaoh's god and have called themselves atheists; when in reality they have rejected a fallacious god concept. Pharaoh's god supports racism, imperialism, materialism, militarism, and every other ideology that robs us of our dignity. In other words, the god of Pharaoh is never on the side of the disinherited; he is on the side of the majority. Wherever the biggest guns and budgets are, there he will be also.

From a psycho-theological perspective, the problem among African Americans stems from the fact that we are torn between allegiance to a God who wills our destruction and the God who wills our well being. Those with an unhealthy view of God are self destructing. And those who embrace the God of Moses, experience triumph in the midst of oppression.

While not all African Americans adhere to the Christian faith, most pledge some kind of allegiance to Jesus of Nazareth. However, if those of us who proclaim the Kerygma are going to effectuate a revolution in the family and the community, we must raise the question that the two disciples of John the Baptist raised, "Art thou he that should come or do we look for another?"[4] It is critical for the preacher-theologian to give help in this Christological dilemma. The question is not whether we should choose Jesus or Mohammed or Jesus or Buddha, but who is Jesus? Are we talking about the American Christ or the Biblical Christ?

If the Biblical Jesus of Nazareth is indeed the answer for our community, then we must pledge our allegiance to Him. But who is He? Let us be honest in saying that we have Americanized Jesus. He is no more than a transcendent synonym for Uncle Sam, and the American way of life has replaced the Kingdom of God in the consciousness of the Christian community. This is why President Ronald Reagan was almost canonized by the religious right.

This parody of the Faith must be rejected by the African American community. Therefore, the preacher-theologian must lead the way in setting the Biblical Christ free from His cultural incarceration. This is going to be a challenge because many African Americans have already bought into the American Christ. And in an age of upward mobility, the African American executive who drives a Mercedes Benz and who makes $100,000.00 per year will find it difficult not to buy into the American Christ as over against the Biblical Christ. But therein lies the future of the African American family and community.

I once gave a lecture at one of our leading universities in the Northeast where I challenged the white theologians to tell me why they accepted Jesus Christ. My question to them was, what is it about the Jesus of the Gospels that appeals to you? To my great surprise, most had never thought about it. But then a breakthrough came when one theologian said, "I guess we whites, considering our history, can only deal with Jesus after His Resurrection," to which I replied, "This is the quintessential Christological heresy. It is heretical because it separates the Jesus of Humiliation from the Jesus of Exaltation. This is like betting that Hank Aaron will hit 755 home runs ten years after he accomplished the feat." This is the same heresy that Kierkegaard attacked in his native Denmark. The whole manifestation of Manifest Destiny and triumphalism comes from this heresy.

Therefore, if we would minister to the family and community we must make clear who Jesus is. This is what the community had to do during slavery. We had to go through a process of theological transposition. The oppressive Christ was rejected, and the Christ of freedom was embraced. Consequently, the task remains the same in every generation for the preacher, theologian, and community. But as we become more attuned to the American myth of power and success it is going to be an enormous task to preach the Biblical Christ in the community. This is already being demonstrated in the number of young, middle class brothers and sisters who are identifying with the health-wealth heresy, which is nothing but a modern day version of Gnosticism. But my view is that we do not have to go from oppression to heresy, for there is a better way.

In my dialogue with the theologians at the great University in the Northeast, the Socratic tables were turned on me and the same question was put to me: "Why do you accept Jesus in spite of all the oppression experienced by your community?" I replied, "As an oppressed person, I accept Jesus because we are colleagues in oppression." The late preacher-theologian Dr. George Buttrick, who was my mentor and friend at Southern Baptist Seminary in Louisville, once asked me why my community never abdicated Jesus en masse, to which I replied, "We were bleeding and He was bleeding. We were oppressed and He was oppressed, and He convinced us to stay with Him until He could get out of the hole He was in."

The task for the church in the community is to present an unpopular Christ to an oppressed people as the way of salvation. We must proclaim a Christ of humiliation and exaltation. And neither must be abandoned unless heresy ensues. In preaching Jesus, we must make it clear that He is not the Western Christ, nor is He the Christ of African Americans only. He is the Universal, or the Cosmic Christ. However, at the level of particularity, He identifies with all who are oppressed irrespective of pigmentation.

We must proclaim unequivocally that God (Yahweh) was incarnated in one called Jesus of Nazareth. The Logos became flesh in one who would be considered a failure.[5] This within itself makes Jesus an outcast in America, because America loves a winner. But when Jesus was born between 7 - 4 B.C., Rome ruled the then known world including Jesus' native Palestine. In other words, Jesus' country was a subject nation. He knows what it means to be: (1) a slave, (2) a minority, (3) poor, (4) locked out, (5) homeless, and (6) persecuted. This is a major psychological breakthrough. Just think that God was humiliated and oppressed just like our community, and yet He is being victorious. Jesus in His humiliation looks like what I am. In His exaltation, He looks like what I shall become. It is not our purpose in this chapter to deal with the color of Jesus, for the White church would be the first to say that such a discussion is not important, but Jesus continues to be artistically displayed as a white man. There are reputable scholars in African and African American history such as Professor John Henrik

Clarke, professor emeritus at Hunter College in New York City, and Dr. Asa Hilliard of Georgia State University in Atlanta, Georgia, who have provided documentation that the earliest paintings of Jesus were of a dark-skinned man. While no one can prove photographically that Jesus was black, white, yellow or red, we can conclude that if it were proved that He was manifested as a Black man, Christianity in America would be dismantled in twenty-four hours. But not only would whites defect, but large numbers of blacks would leave the Christian faith because they could not allow themselves to believe that the Logos was incarnate in black skin like theirs.

Yet, it would not bother him or her if He continues to be painted white. Without a doubt, the psycho-theological confusion in the community of the oppressed is colossal. So the question is not focused ultimately on pigmentation, but identification. Not what color is Jesus, but is He the answer for the family and community?

The Image of God

It is an understatement to say that African Americans hate themselves. This is crucial because anyone who hates himself or herself cannot be rightly related to God. Columbus Salley and Ronald Behm in their earth shaking book What Color is Your God said:

> The negative forces in operation during the period of slavery, segregation, and ghettoization have had the collective effect of creating in the minds of many Black people doubt concerning their human worth and dignity. To this day, the power of white Christian society to define the ultimate worth of black people and blackness has created within many blacks a doubt about their equality with whites.[6]

Without a doubt, any theology that is going to be effective in the community must be one that embraces the Imago Dei. The creation narratives in Genesis 1:27 and Genesis 2:7 provide the basis for human dignity. Humankind is a creation ex nihilo of God. The

Image

Breathe

doctrines of creation and Judeo-Christian anthropology go hand in hand. And the Biblical affirmation is the foundation of dignity and esteem in the family and community. The Genesis account says, "God saw everything that He had made and behold, it was very good."[7] So African Americans must reject any evaluation of their personhood that does not affirm Elohim's assessment of their value. We are somebody because God says so, and this affirmation is not a human achievement, but rather a divine declaration.

But in spite of what God has declared, humankind in its alienation from God deems it necessary to oppress other human beings. In America, African Americans still suffer the psychological brutalities of slavery. And the sin of America is that she has not authentically repented of the evils against the Native Americans or the African Americans. While we are no longer physical slaves, we are still psychological slaves.

Slavery is still a psychological albatross in the family and community at large. And to deal with it is painful for whites and blacks alike. It's amazing that the Jewish Holocaust gets top media coverage, but the African American Holocaust is to be forgotten. I am reminded of a story I read about a championship bout between Joe Louis and Max Baer. Joe Louis had battered Max Baer fiercely in the first round before eventually knocking him out. When Max Baer returned to his corner after the first round, he told his trainer how hard Joe Louis was hitting him, to which the trainer replied, "Awe, Joe Louis is not hitting you." Max Baer then said, "Well, if Joe Louis is not hitting me, you better keep an eye on the referee, because somebody in this ring is beating the hell out of me."

While we still have the vestiges of slavery and oppression with us, African Americans must not lose sight of the fact that we are a great people with a great heritage. We must not ignore the psychological chains of slavery, but we must not fail to move forward to victory. For the Biblical narratives in Genesis chapters 1 and 2 lend themselves to a clear statement about the value of human worth, dignity, and glory. A Newsweek article in the January 11, 1988, issue told the story of the scientific community's findings based on

DNA molecules that our original parents, Adam and Eve, were Black, and all life derived from the continent of Africa.[8] This revelation should not be used as a means of assuming a superior attitude on the part of people of ebony hue. But it is a statement of truth that needs to be declared in the white community as well as in the African American community. For at the ground of our oppression is the ignorance of our history. No longer should African Americans tolerate a theology that is metaphysical and abstract. It must be a theology that seeks to remedy our dilemma from a Christocentric perspective. And to be like Jesus of Nazareth is to know one's history, for the historical Jesus was not ignorant of His heritage. Even though He transcended His history, He was nevertheless a part of that history.

It is liberating to all people once we learn the truth about black people. No scholar of any academic field should be taken seriously who does not know the contributions of Africa to his or her discipline. Therefore, the theological-kerygmatic community must chart a practical strategy that can move our families and communities into holistic Christian living. But it must begin with a knowledge of the God who became incarnate in Jesus and a comprehensive awareness of the contribution of Africans to every known discipline. This will go a long way towards leading African Americans out of the abyss of inferiority. Our collective feeling of inferiority is the key for interpreting the attitudes and behavioral responses in our community. Once we see that the repertoire of our people extends beyond athletics and entertainment, we are on the way to freedom. We have and can do anything for the common good. Once we get in touch with ourselves, we will be able to reverse the devastating effects of our oppression in America. Again, Na'Im Akbar says:

> We can reverse the destructive effects of slavery by looking to strengths in our past and beginning to make plans for our future. If we begin to direct our children's attention to strong images like themselves, they will grow in self respect. We must honor and exalt our own heroes, and those heroes must be people who have done the most to dignify us as a people. We

> must definitely avoid the psychologically destructive representation of God in a Caucasian form.[9]

This last statement by Akbar needs to be heeded by the white church community as well as by the African American community. Pictures of Jesus as a white man with blond hair and blue eyes are psychologically disastrous for both communities. For the white community, it leads to a sense of superiority. And for the African American community, it is the basis for an inferiority complex. Michelangelo's paintings of Deity in the Sistine Chapel, while they represent cultural bias, nevertheless precipitate an overwhelming sense of helplessness on the part of African Americans. If my oppressor has been white and God is white, then I don't stand a possible chance in God's world. Many times this feeling of inferiority is perpetuated every time we open a Sunday School publication in an African American church. To stand before African American children with all white pictures on display is a devastating psychological blow. The answer is not to hoist a Black Jesus to replace the White Jesus, but rather to take down all images that would tend to make one feel superior or inferior. However, if this is not done, then we must use black images if for no other reason than for the purpose of cancelling the white images. "God is a Spirit,"[10] but as a handler of sacred writ, I find it very difficult in my semi-intelligent state not to think of Jesus (God) as a white man. If we are going to overcome our inferiority, we must begin to take this problem seriously.

Salvation for the Community

When we survey the carnage of family and community, we are moved to cry out like the prophet Jeremiah, "Is there no balm in Gilead, is there no physician there? Why, then, is not the health of the daughter of my people recovered?"[11] It is a challenge to the theological-kerygmatic community to define and re-define what evangelical Christianity means when it uses the term "saved." We must provide a hermeneutic based upon our embracing of the Christ who identifies with the oppressed in their suffering. And at the same time, we must have an authentic interaction with the

Bible as the norm for Christian living. We will be the interpreters, for Pharaoh is not adequate as a professor of theology. Because he has a sick theology, it is fatal to the cause of African Americans to take his course on soteriology.

The danger for our people is that we will continue to buy into a "cheap grace" salvation. This is what western Christianity offers by and large. Any salvific experience that does not connect earth and sky is to be rejected by the community. If there is no fellowship between orthodoxy and orthopraxy, and cosmos and eschatos, then we must declare this kind of liberation or salvation as injurious to the psychological well being of the community. Salvation as deliverance from alienation to a holistic commitment to Jesus, Carpenter of Nazareth and Lord of History, is synonymous with the term liberation, though this is not always made clear in the writings of liberation theologians. And to be committed to the Offensive Christ, is to join Him in His humiliation. For we only gain contemporaneity with Him when we first embrace the embarrassment of who He is. We are first "turned off" by Christ before we are "turned on" by Him. I am a firm believer in the power of God in Jesus to deliver the African American family and community because the Jesus that was embraced by many of our foreparents was the Jesus who sets us free rather than enslaves us. Again, our community must reject the American Christ because He wills ethnocide. And such a Jesus must be forever banished from our consciousness.

I am convinced that much of the confusion in American theological circles over the issue of salvation stems from faulty exegesis and a misunderstanding of the relationship between Law and Grace. For example, the Apostle Paul says in Ephesians 2:8-10:

> *For by grace are you saved through faith; and that not of yourself: it is the gift of God: not of works, lest any man should boast. For we are his workmanship, created in Christ Jesus unto good works, which God has before ordained that we should walk in them.*

Simply put, Paul is saying that an authentic encounter with Jesus leads to a demonstrable life. The Apostle never suggests the "cheap grace" philosophy of letting "Jesus come into your heart." If that phrase means a commitment to Jesus that will be demonstrated in society, then it is acceptable. Paul is saying that God offers a gift that can be had only if one responds by faith. Then once we respond, we move from autonomy (self-rule) to theonomy (the rule of God). It is at this point that we begin to move from orthodoxy to orthopraxy. This distinction, except in rare instances, has been missing from American Christianity. This is why what one says is more important than what one does. This is why in our past history, one could be a Christian and slave master simultaneously. And this is why any racist in the United States or South Africa who claims to be a Christian can feel comfortable because he or she feels that profession and practice do not go hand in hand. Let us listen to James, the brother of the Lord in Chapter 2:14-18:

> *What does it profit, my brethren, though a man say he has faith, and have not works? Can faith save him? If a brother or sister be naked, and destitute of daily food, and one of you say unto them, depart in peace, be you warmed and filled: not withstanding you give them not those things that are needful to the body; what doth it profit? Even so faith, if it has not works, is dead, being alone. Yes, a man may say, you have faith, and I have works: Show me your faith without your works, and I will show you my faith by my works.*

It is amazing that even a profound scholar like Martin Luther could misinterpret what James was saying. He even rejected outright the canonicity of the epistle because he believed that James contradicted Paul's teaching on grace through faith. And if that be the case, James does contradict Paul. But if the salvific formula is "grace through faith unto good works," they complement each other. While the reading of abstract theology allows one to develop the muscles of his or her mind, it is powerless to change the existential. Therefore, only a gospel that can be concretized should be welcomed in the community.

Another scriptural passage that is often used as a test for the proponents of cheap grace is Romans 10:8-10:

> *But what saith it? The word is nigh thee even in thy mouth, and in thy heart: that is the word of faith, which we preach; that if thou shall confess with thy mouth the Lord Jesus, and shall believe in your heart that God has raised him from the dead, you shall be saved. For with the heart man believeth unto righteousness; and with the mouth confession is made unto salvation.*

Those who would support a cheap grace theology mislead at the point of verbal expression. Thus in this generation, salvation has become identified with the institutional church, emotionalism and church growth. And I am the first to admit that if salvation involves only a verbal commitment, we wonder how did Paul get killed? The answer lies in the fact that to make such a statement as "Jesus is Lord" was treason. The Romans said "Caesar is Lord." So to state publicly that "Jesus is Lord" was to be executed. Therefore, even this confession with the mouth when taken in context, is "expensive grace" rather than "cheap grace," for it did get many killed. The challenge that the African American church faces is to teach our people how to spell "relief." When we consider the historical sufferings of our people, it is going to be a tremendous challenge to lead the people away from their attraction to the American Christ, who is His enemy.

Again, Matthew 22:37-40 gives us the summation of the Judeo-Christian faith:

> Jesus said...*you shall love the Lord your God with all your heart, and with all your soul, and with all your mind. This is the first and great commandment. And the second is like unto it, you shall love your neighbor as yourself. On these two commandments hang all the Law and the Prophets.*

In this scriptural passage, Jesus gives us the essence of Salvation and the core of faith in general. This particular teaching of Jesus was later expressed in I John 4:20-21:

> *If a man say, I love God, and hates his brother, he is a liar: for he that loveth not his brother whom he has seen, how can he love God whom he has not seen? And this commandment have we from him, that he who loveth God loves his brother also.*

Any theology that does not teach and cause one to practice the love of God, of self, and humankind is a perversion and must be destroyed. When you tell a race of people for three hundred plus years that God loves them either not at all, or less than other people, the socio-psychological results are catastrophic. The three levels of love taught by Jesus are healthy and all-encompassing. Because I love God, I love myself. And because I love myself, I have the capacity to love all humankind. There is no escape because to hate any person or people is to hate God. He who is out of touch with humankind is out of touch with God. If our families are to be reached Christocentrically, then we must proclaim and practice love. We must say that it is all right to love oneself in God. Unless we do so, this self hatred in each of us will bring about our demise. Therefore, the theological-kerygmatic community must sound the alarm that to align oneself with any movement which underscores and relegates one to a position of inferiority, such a movement is to be totally rejected. Because if I accept a position of inferiority, I inadvertently accuse God of creative malfeasance. James Cone says:

> If we are created for God, then any other allegiance is a denial of freedom, and we must struggle against those who attempt to enslave us. The image of God is not merely a personal relationship with God, but is also that constituent of humanity which makes all people struggle against captivity. It is the ground of rebellion and revolution among slaves.[12]

Christian Ethics and the Family

It is a truth that unless orthodoxy can translate into orthopraxy, the end result is heresy. As has been stated, American Christianity is wrong at its center because it does not lead to commitment to Jesus of Nazareth. One can literally be a Christian in spite of one's behavior. This nonsense breeds atheism. Any serious study of the plight of African American people must begin with the family. It is an understatement to say that the family is in disarray. J. Deotis Roberts said:

> One of the most serious internal problems of Blacks is family disintegration. It would be nigh impossible to find a group of people who have been able to survive great hardship without strong familial ties. The destruction of the black family has been deliberate during our sojourn in this country. Although the black man's mere survival is a miracle of grace, it appears that the black church, as "invisible" and as a visible institution, has nurtured this suffering race and kept it alive.[13]

Therefore, we must be imbued with a sense of overcoming at a psycho-spiritual level in order to liberate ourselves through Jesus of Nazareth; for He is our liberator. Luke's Gospel is instructive at this point:

> *And he came to Nazareth where he had been brought up: and as his custom was, he went into the synagogue on the Sabbath day, and stood up for to read. And there was delivered unto him the book of the prophet Isaiah. And when he had opened the book, he found the place where it was written, the Spirit of the Lord is upon me, because he has anointed me to preach the gospel to the poor; he has sent me to heal the broken-hearted, to preach deliverance to the captives, and recovering of sight to the blind, and to set at liberty them that are bruised, to preach the acceptable year of the Lord.*[14]

Armed with the power inherent in knowing our Liberator, we must move forward in building a Christocentric people who will behave according to the principles of Christ rather than the folkways and mores of an oppressive culture.

The theological-kerygmatic community must begin a pre-school movement that will undergird the development of strong families. At an early age, a male child and a female child should be taught that marriage is a commitment and that those who get married should be responsible and mature. Too many of our homes are headed by single women. We must thank God for the contributions of our African American mothers. But a continuing matriarchy only contributes to a problem of esteem in the African American male. We must build strong black men and women in the next generation. And once we do this, divorces will decrease drastically, and we can claim the blessings of the past through the nuclear and extended family concept. I repeat, my wife and I took a delegation several years ago to the West African nations of Senegal and Gambia, and it was clear to us how powerful the extended family was in the mother continent. It was patriarchal in structure, but everyone was in support of the total family unit.

In the Yahwistic account in Genesis 2:24, Elohim gives His support to a marriage based on commitment. From this union, the world was born. Nothing short of the Biblical concept of husband-wife relationships should be tolerated by the community. Therefore, all threats to the bond of matrimony such as adultery, religious differences, money, a lack of communication, and general incompatibility must be dealt with forthrightly before one exchanges vows. The church community then must provide both precept and example in the development of strong families. In every African American congregation, there are many glaring examples of strong family life. Many disenfranchised persons in the community have not only made marriage work for many years, but, though they had very little academic preparation themselves, have educated their children. While we are not averse to the expertise of the behavioral scientists, I am convinced that the answer to our liberation is in our hands. But there needs to be a bibliocentric approach to the family. Therefore, the Pauline model for the maintenance of the Christian family in Ephesians 5:22-6:1-4 does not have to be discarded because of the fear of being called chauvinistic. The order that Paul gives for the successful family is as follows: (1) Christ, (2) the church, (3) the husband, (4) the wife, and (5) the children. As Christ nurtures and leads the church, even so must the husband be the leader of the Christian home. "Wives submitting to their husbands" does not suggest any ex cathedra wisdom, nor does it encourage a slave-master relationship. For this is obliterated through loving one's wife "as Christ loved the church." Likewise, as Christ loves and guides the church and the church nurtures the husband and the wife, even so must the husband and wife bring their children to maturity through sound Christian doctrine. "Children must obey their parents in the Lord," as Paul declares in Ephesians 6:1. He further states, "And, you fathers, provoke not your children to wrath: but bring them up in the nurture and admonition of the Lord" (Ephesians 6:4). Therefore, if our families are to be strong, we must not ignore Jesus and His teachings.

Furthermore, as we overcome, through the Biblical Christ, teenage pregnancy will be greatly reduced. As was stated earlier, eighty-nine percent of all births by African American teenagers are illegitimate. This problem will be reduced through an adherence to the teachings of the Bible through education and a healthy attitude about love and sexuality. This will also be overcome by teaching young black males as well as young ladies that sexuality is to be expressed within the bonds of matrimony. The answer to this problem as it appears even in the ecclesiastical community is not condoms but an adherence to Biblical teachings. Paul says in I Corinthians 6:18a, "flee fornication." And in I Thessalonians 4:3, Paul says, "For this is the will of God, even your sanctification, that you should abstain from fornication." While a socio-psychological analysis is important, the ultimate solution lies in the Scriptures.

Also, the issue of abortion initially must be dealt with from the standpoint of abstinence. The church and the home must coalesce in preventing pregnancies that lead to abortion. Abortion as a means of birth control is murder (Exodus 20:13). But, abortion in the case of rape, incest, or danger to the mother's life is a difficult ethical decision. Because we will be a Christocentric community, we will support pro-life from the womb to the tomb. However, the African American community must not be caught up in the hysteria of the Religious Right that advocates rights for the newborn and yet supports policies that keep most of the world in poverty. The theological-kerygmatic community must make it clear that to be a practitioner of justice is to advocate the rights of the unborn, the newborn, and all humankind.

Another crucial area of concern is greed or the unbridled lust for material things and money. Without a doubt, money is god in America. It is interesting that we put "In God We Trust" on our money but not on our church buildings. This is crucial in understanding our basic institutions. In our society, to possess money or to be rich is power. And the more one has, the more powerful he or she is. Our philosophy of education is perverse in that we have perpetuated the notion that the purpose of getting a college degree is to be able to make a lot of money. But the purpose should be that of service rather than getting rich. Jesus said in Matthew 6:24, "No man can serve two masters: for either he will hate the one and love the other; or else he will hold to the one and despise the other. You cannot serve God and mammon." To be Christian is to give absolute loyalty to Jesus Christ. Whoever chooses money over Christ forfeits salvation. Money is important as a medium of exchange, but it must not master us. However, to discuss the dangers of greed with an oppressed community is very difficult. On a practical level, an oppressed people need to develop themselves economically. Yet their philosophy must not reflect communism, socialism, or capitalism, for all of these fall short of the Christian view of the Kingdom of God. Jesus, in the parables of the "Rich Fool" in Luke 12:16-21, and the Rich man and Lazarus in Luke 16:19-31, did not condemn them for having money, but they were rejected because they didn't share. Unless God was teasing us in the Incarnation, the message is clear that God majors in people rather than in things.

Greed inevitably leads to the drug epidemic. The infrastructure of the African American family is being torn asunder by alcohol and hallucinogenic drugs. And it appears that no end is in sight. The community (African American) spends over twenty billion dollars per year for drugs. Rather than face the brutalities of reality, he or she tries an escape. Therefore, a whole generation of African Americans has lost the way. The church, then, must be the light that shines in this dungeon of darkness. We must continue to proclaim the importance of the individual and human personality in general. The church, armed in the Spirit of Christ, must sound forth the trumpet of liberation that will set the drug pusher free from his addiction to money and his hatred for African American lives. The dope users must be lifted to a level where they can feel good about themselves as they embrace our Christ. To be set free in Christ is to be paroled from the prison of greed.

Another problem that has ethical implications is unemployment. And the crisis is escalating because by the end of the twentieth century, seventy percent of African American males will be unemployed. This is going to wreak untold havoc in the family and community. We cannot afford a theology that is so abstract that it transcends the work place. Therefore, we need a transformed concept of work. We have too many unemployed African American males. And if a man cannot provide, or will not provide, for his family, his esteem will be at ground zero. Dr. Na'im Abkar says:

> One of the attitudes which have (sic) passed to us from slavery is the rather common attitude towards work. The slave was forced to work under the threat of abuse or even death, but work was not for the purpose of providing for his life's needs. Instead, he worked for the slave master. He would neither profit from his labor, nor enjoy the benefits of his labor. A good crop did not improve his life, his family, or his community. Instead, it improved the life and the community of the slave master.[15]

As a result of our oppression, African Americans, particularly in the underprivileged class, have an attitude against work, the reason being that work is always benefiting those who would oppress them, and is never beneficial to the workers. In order to avoid the possibility of work, many resort to such schemes as the lottery, Jai Alai, the numbers racket, and other tricks to get rich. This attitude also keeps many imprisoned to the welfare state. This can be and must be overcome through a healthy theology which is the ground of any authentic anthropology. This will enable us to move from consumerism to productivity. Until we begin to produce some of what we buy, we will always be a disenfranchised people. Dr. Akbar says:

> Certainly, the historical origin of the hatred of work does not completely explain the African American's orientation to work. Equally as relevant is the vast shortage of jobs and the many obstacles to receiving the same benefits from work as do other members of society.[16]

Beyond this, a real encounter with the Biblical Christ will produce a people who respect their own leaders and will in turn produce persons who will be worthy of that respect. One of the most devastating derivatives of slavery is the lack of respect for African American leadership. This does not mean that we must reject the John Browns, the Viola Liuzzos, the Rev. James Reebs, or the Clarence Jordans, but it does insist on legitimizing our leadership. What a powerful impact this will have towards building family and community. While many would not see the ethical dimensions of this problem, a careful analysis of the African American situation will reveal its glaring implications because a rejection of your own chosen, trained, and endorsed leadership reveals self hatred, and that within itself is immoral.

As of now the greatest imminent challenges facing the family and community are drugs and AIDS. But the greatest ongoing challenge will be the community's attitude toward violence to themselves and the oppressor. How one relates to any enemy is the apex of moral concerns. Jesus in the Sermon on the Mount gives a directive for solving this dilemma in Matthew 5:38-42 (TEV):

> *You have heard that it was said, an eye for an eye, and a tooth for a tooth. But now I tell you: do not take revenge on someone who wrongs you. If anyone slaps you on the right cheek, let him slap your left cheek too. And if someone takes you to court to sue you for your shirt, let him have your coat as well. And if one of the occupation troops forces you to carry his pack one mile carry it two miles.*

In the Kingdom of God the slave is master, and the master is slave. To refuse to cooperate passively with any form of oppression is Christian, but to respond with vengeance towards the oppressor is not in the spirit of the Biblical Christ. In the oppressed community, we must not waste energy in getting even with those who have wronged us, nor must we do violence to ourselves as a substitute for what we ultimately would like to do to the enemy because Jesus' principle for living the Kingdom life is not weakness but the greatest demonstration of strength. To "turn the other cheek" is not an invitation for violence but a door for repentance and reconciliation. Dr. Major J. Jones said:

> Who is the master if one does not have the inner strength to go the second mile or to turn the other cheek? Perhaps, it is the abnormal thing to hate those who hate you and to do injury to the person who injures you. To love the one who hates you is surely not to be in bondage to the other's initiative. The slave nor the master can be free as long as they hate each other or treat each other as master and slave. As long as they do, both are what they are, merely slave and master.[17]

Jesus in His Kingdom teachings never advocates any "Stepin Fetchit" response to oppression. For any acceptance of what the Jewish philosopher Martin Buber called the "I-it" relationship must be rejected. The family in Christ operates from an I-Thou relationship. This within itelf is liberating. Because I love God and myself, I am able to love others authentically.

Therefore, the African American family, as it learns to love itself through the Biblical Christ, will have the foundation for building strong communities. These Christocentric families will in turn have the moral responsibility of leading the oppressor to a true relationship with the Jesus of humiliation and exaltation. Therein lies the salvation of the oppressed and the oppressor.

References – Chapter Four

[1] J. Deotis Roberts, The Roots of a Black Future: Family and Church, Westminister Press, Philadelphia, PA, 1980, 111.
[2] C. Eric Lincoln, "Black Church", Christianity and Crisis, Vol. 30, No. 18 (1970), 226.
[3] James H. Cone, God of the Oppressed (Seabury Press, New York, 1975) 10.
[4] Matthew 11:2-3.
[5] John 1:14.
[6] Columbus Salley and Ronald Behm, What Color Is Your God? Downers Grove, Illinois: Intervarsity Press, 1981), 64.
[7] Genesis 1:31.
[8] "The Search for Adam and Eve," Newsweek, January 1988: 46-52.
[9] Akbar, 25-26.
[10] John 4:24a.
[11] Jeremiah 8:22.
[12] Cone, 145.
[13] J. Deotis Roberts, Liberation and Reconciliation: A Black Theology (Philadelphia, PA.: Westminster Press, 1971), 60.
[14] Luke 4:17-19.
[15] Akbar, 9.
[16] Akbar, 11.
[17] Major J. Jones, Christian Ethics for Black Theology (Nashville, Tennessee: Abingdon Press, 1974), 104.

Chapter Five

Education in The African American Community: The Threat of Educating The Oppressed

If you keep books away from a slave, he or she will remain a slave. If you give him or her books which only expound the contributions of the Oppressor, he or she will remain a slave. However, if the slave is allowed to learn about his or her contributions to the world, he or she will be free even in shackles. Such has been the politics of education in the United States of America. Lerone Bennett said:

> Bullets aside, there are two ways to perpetuate the oppression of a people. The first way is to refuse to educate them. And the second way is to educate them. By this we understand that education in a situation of oppression is necessarily a question either of oppression or liberation. In a situation of oppression, the oppressor always seeks to maintain and extend his domination of the oppressed by educating and refusing to educate. For the Oppressor knows that he who controls the image controls the mind, and that he who controls the mind has little or nothing at all to fear from the body.[1]

When we first arrived in this stolen nation, it became a matter of jurisprudence that the slaves were not allowed to learn to read and write. This became the law for all practical purposes throughout the South. Those who slipped and learned to read were breaking the law. If they were caught, they were severely beaten, maimed, or killed. This reaction on the part of the Oppressor was a clarion statement about the power of knowledge. During slavery, learning to read and write was the issue, not education. For one, in a sense, can be educated without knowing how to read and write. But if one is literate, he or she has the power to discern whether the education is benign or malignant. The danger of this power of discernment was symbolized or concretized in the life of Frederick Douglass who became the most eloquent spokesperson for freedom of the 19th century, after having risen like a phoenix from the ashes of slavery.

> Sophia Auld, a kindhearted White person taught Douglass his ABC's and to spell a few words, until her husband discovered it and told her it was illegal and unsafe to educate slaves. According to Hugh Auld, if Frederick was taught to read, "there would be no keeping him." Upon hearing these words, Fred became convinced that education was the key to freedom. Though conscious of the difficulty of learning without a teacher, he asserted, "I set out with high hope, and a fixed purpose, at whatever cost or trouble, to learn how to read." During the next seven years, he did favors for his white playmates in return for reading lessons. Then when he was twelve years old, he obtained a copy of The Columbia Orator. In this book he found several denunciations of slavery which made a powerful impact on him.[2]

Beyond Frederick Douglass many other slaves paid heavy prices in order to learn to read and write. However, in the midst of oppression, learning to read can be a path to liberation or further enslavement by the oppressor's Eurocentricity, which casts aspersions on anything having to do with Africa. "The mere imparting of information is not education. Above all things, the effort must result in making a man think and do for himself."[3] Nothing is more dangerous to the security of the slave master than to have a person in the field who can think. It is ironic in ancient Greece that the slave was the intellectual superior to his or her master. Therefore, he was master, while physically enduring the indignities of servitude. This is what made Martin Luther King and Malcolm X dangerous to America's racist establishment. You cannot control a thinker. You may kill the thinker, but you cannot control him or her. Therefore, the Oppressor can't make a thinker do anything but die.[4]

The Fallacy of America's Educational Philosophy

America's educational philosophy is wrong both in terms of content and purpose. Its curriculum is racist in that it teaches about the contributions of Euro-America and ignores the contributions of Africa and African Americans. Upon graduating from the University of Florida in 1970 with a degree in Philosophy, I was totally oblivious to the contributions of Africa to the world. Growing up in Ocala, Florida in the 1950's and '60's we had Negro History week each year. This event was founded by Carter G. Woodson in 1926. In a nutshell, Negro History Week, though no fault of Dr. Woodson, was a brief peek at the lives of: Booker T. Washington, George Washington Carver, Mary M. Bethune, Marian Anderson, Joe Louis, Jackie Robinson, and Jesse Owens. If America is a melting pot, its curriculum ought to reflect such diversity.

But in America traditionally, Whites have known the contributions of Whites, and African Americans have known the history of Whites. But neither has known the history of Africa. No wonder we are so violent. This insinuates that Africa has no history worth mentioning. If you would challenge the Superintendent of Schools in any city in America on the greatness of Africa in world history, the overwhelming majority would draw a blank, including the African American Superintendents. Lerone Bennett said, "Miseducation is a simple necessity of the system. The system calls for miseducation as a premise of its own existence and it creates educated men in its own image."[5]

Such truth must be confronted and internalized. If we will determine our destiny, education is critical, but it must be the right kind. Again Bennett says:

> The system could not exist if it did not multiply misinformation. And whether the system educates or refuses to educate, the aim is the same: mystification and misinformation. As a matter of fact, it sometimes happens that the oppressed with the most education are the most maimed. J. Raymond Jones was referring to this dynamic when he said that Harvard has ruined more Negroes than bad whiskey.[6]

Our oppression is underscored by this truth. Therefore, we cannot be liberated until we come to grips with this reality.

> The so-called modern education, with all its defects, however, does others so much more good than it does the Negro, because it has been worked out in conformity to the needs of those who have enslaved and oppressed weaker peoples.[7]

Anyone who has only been the beneficiary of a Eurocentric education is miseducated. If one has been introduced to Louis Pasteur and not Dr. Charles Drew, he or she is of no serious benefit to the race. Most African Americans who have finished college are not trained to help the race in a profound sense.

> We have been lynched in this country with ropes and chains, but we have also been lynched with words and symbols and quotations from Aristotle. And the abstract lynchings of the educational system reflect a deliberate will to dehumanization built into the basic structures of the educational system. It is no accident that the educational system maims our youth and saps the will of our elders. It is no accident that there is a white-out on the black man's contribution to history and culture. It is no accident that sociology and economics are heavily weighed against the poor. It is no accident; it is deliberate; it is a result of will and design. According to V.O. Key, the "educational system is a great instrument of governance, a political

> device probably more effective than police and prisons, which functions by and large as a means of aiding the dominant elements in any political order to maintain their power." The key word here is power. Education is a question of power. It is a question of the ultimate in power - the power to name, to define, and to control minds.[8]

Therefore, the person who has been trained in Pharaoh's university must decide if he or she will be a liberator or an oppressor. Many have chosen the latter, much to the chagrin of the masses.

The second fallacy is that the goal of getting an education is to make money rather than to give service. Materialism is the motivation. Lest I wax hypocritical, let me explain what I am saying. We live in a society where money is important. But when we exalt money above service to humanity, a society becomes decadent. Just like totalitarianism caused the demise of the Soviet Union, materialism will be the death of America. Everyone needs money. Nobody can go to the check out lane in a store without money and simply say, "Jesus paid it all." But when the goal of education is about making money, then, we are miseducated. One can make money and at the same time major in humanity. But ofttimes people are lost in the struggle to have more. Education in America is designed to give one justification for greed and imperialism. America's legendary frontiersmen are not castigated in American history for killing Native Americans because greed was at the heart of their adventures. No history book frowns upon George Washington or Thomas Jefferson because they were slaveholders, because at the time this was good economics. Both were educated in a system that did not provide a corrective for their violation of the human spirit.

The goal of education is to serve people, and sometimes materialism is a major product. But suppose it isn't? I always feel a sense of guilt and schizophrenia when I talk like this to an oppressed people. However, it needs to be stated over and over again. If the goal of life is to have things rather than to love God and people, then formal education is an unnecessary interlude. No one has to finish college to make money. Drug dealers make far more money than a classroom teacher. Some who are proficient can make more in a month than a teacher can make in a year. Who, then, wants to study chemistry, physics, trigonometry, and calculus unless you want to make the argument that a college degree would better aid one in counting his or her money? We need to confess that money is god in America. And this idolatry is undergirded both by the church and the school.

George Washington Carver must have seemed like a fool when he refused Henry Ford's offer to become a wealthy man by joining him at his plant in Dearborn, Michigan. Dr. Carver believed that giving service was what life was all about. Our educational system ought to put heavy emphasis on helping people regardless of compensation. Suppose someone can't pay you; will you refuse to help? People such as Mary Bethune; Martin Luther King, Jr.; Mahatma Gandhi; and Albert Schweitzer, in spite of his alleged paternalism, are to be studied, admired, corrected, and emulated.

The Strategy For Starting Black Schools and Colleges

At the end of the Civil War it became legal for African Americans to have the opportunity to become miseducated. Since it was no longer legal to stop our race from learning to read and write, the oppressor's strategy took on the role of founding schools for former slaves. These schools were founded, not for the purpose of liberation, but for further enslavement. Our bodies were freed, but our minds are still in captivity. In spite of the efforts of the Freedmen's Bureau, founded by Northern Whites, we have still been miseducated. E. Franklin Frazier said:

> The creation of the "Bureau for Freedmen, Refugees and Abandoned Lands", by an act of Congress in 1865, represented an attempt on the part of the government to systematize and assume responsibility for adjusting the freedman to his new status. One of the major functions of the Bureau was the education of the

> freedmen. The general policy of the Bureau was to erect school houses and provide the various missionary societies with funds for the salaries of teachers. There was much opposition on the part of the conservative Southern Whites to the educational efforts of the Bureau. School houses were burned and both White and Negro teachers were beaten and expelled from the communities in which they worked. As the landless and poor white farmers were won to the cause of White supremacy, they too joined the opposition to Negro education.[9]

Although many opposed the formal education of the former slaves, a Eurocentric curriculum that magnified his superiority and emphasized my inferiority was "just what the doctor ordered." Carter G. Woodson said:

> The Negro's mind has been brought under the control of his oppressor. The problem of holding the Negro down, therefore, is easily solved. When you control a man's thinking you do not have to worry about his actions. You do not have to tell him not to stand here or go yonder. He will find his proper place and will stay in it. You do not need to send him to the back door, he will cut one for his special benefit. His education makes it necessary.[10]

The sad reality of this dilemma is that most of the pseudo-intelligentsia of the African American community are not even aware of the problem. The educational system in America was designed primarily for the ruling class. When I attended the University of Florida in the late 1960's, I did not see anything or read anything that affirmed my personhood or encouraged me to change my station in life. I got the feeling that I had no business there, but since I was there I was going to be baptized in the pool of Eurocentrism. I was as good a Eurocentric student as you could find on campus. I eloquently regurgitated in parrot-like fashion all of the history of my Oppressor, which supported his seminal thesis that all Africans were inferior.

In many instances, even today, there is no intrinsic difference, curriculum wise, in attending a Black College as over against a White College. The curriculum is the same. If such is the case, then, the Black college can be a colleague in our oppression. Therefore, it could be philosophically stated that a Malcolm X was effective because he was not a victim of a Eurocentric education. Carter G. Woodson further states:

> The thought of the inferiority of the Negro is drilled into him in almost every class he enters and in almost every book he studies. If he happens to leave school after he masters the fundamentals, before he finished high school or reaches college, he will naturally escape some of this bias and may recover in time to be of service to his people.[11]

Such an education forces even the African American pulpit to quote only Eurocentric scholars constantly, without a slight reference to any work of African descent. I, too, am a victim of such academic devastation.

> Practically all of the successful Negroes in this country are of the uneducated type or of that of Negroes who have had no formal education at all. The large majority of the Negroes who have put on the finishing touches of our best colleges are all but worthless in the development of their people.[12]

Education For Certification and Liberation

It would appear from the above statement by Dr. Woodson, that he was advocating the abandonment of a formal Eurocentric education, but Woodson himself had an earned Ph.D. from Harvard University. His point was that if we are to be liberated, we must look beyond the destructiveness of an education that keeps me oppressed.

Certification

If Dr. Woodson were alive, he would agree that we are in a peculiar dilemma in this country since most African Americans reject the notion of returning to the Motherland and have given up on the hope of obtaining any territory exclusively set up for African Americans. We must, therefore, be wise enough to learn all we can about the oppressor in order to be able to provide the corrective for his perverse educational system and philosophy. This is what I call education for the purpose of certification.

We must not allow our children to drift through twelve years of public school without getting a foundation in the basics of reading, 'riting, and 'rithmetic. The parents must be vigilant. When a student has been in school twelve years and can't conjugate a verb or identify a gerund, he or she has wasted time and money.

Our students must get away from the silly act of ridiculing another African American student for speaking correct English, having good study habits, or making good grades. The "nerd" is not the student who makes the honor roll; he or she is the one who spends twelve years in school and can't read, write, or spell. Again, we must emphasize that there is no "Black Math," and while "Black English" is all right in the context of culture, in the larger community it is not good for certification. Unless we are moving to Africa or some other nation, we must be certified. One plus one equals two no matter what the pigmentation might be.

Therefore, we encourage our young people to stay in school, not waste time, be disciplined, read anything that is wholesome, and not let the trap of desegregation become a deeper trap by failing to become prepared to operate in the world of the oppressor.

Liberation

Liberation occurs when I come into the knowledge of myself. The person who knows Shakespeare and Chaucer, but not James Baldwin, Richard Wright, and Maya Angelou is not going to be any good for the race. If we do not know ourselves, we have no message, no matter how erudite and articulate we may be.

The public schools in some states are making gestures towards including African and African American contributions in the curriculum. However, at the level of certification it must be infused into the total curriculum, unless it becomes an unpopular elective. By this we mean the total contributions of Africans and African Americans upon the total thought pool of world civilization.

The home must lead the way in providing the model for the learning of one's history and culture. As I stated in Chapter 3, all future parents in the African American community must be prepared to be the transmitters of our culture. This should be one of the prerequisites before the two people bring a third into the world. The presence of two ill-informed people in a family is terrible, but the presence of three is criminal.

Beyond the home, community organizations such as churches, mosques, fraternities, sororities, and study groups such as the Association for the Study of Classical African Civilization can fill the gap. Therefore, we must lean heavily upon those scholars in our community such as Drs. John Henrik Clark, Leonard Jeffries, Asa Hilliard, et al.

When we look at this issue, the biblical character of Moses, the African, helps us to interpret our present situation. Acts 7:22 says, "and Moses was learned in all the wisdom of the Egyptians and was mighty in words and deeds." After having received the best education in the world, Moses had to wrestle with the question of what he was going to do with his education that was for the purpose of certification.

However, Moses had a heritage grounded in the Promised Land. He was imbued with a sense of liberation. In spite of his certification, he had to struggle with a far deeper issue.

> *And it came to pass in those days, when Moses was grown that he went out unto his brethren, and looked on their burdens: and he spied an Egyptian smiting an Hebrew, one of his brethren. And he looked this way and that way, and when he saw that there was no man, he slew the Egyptian and hid him in the sand.....Now when Pharaoh heard this thing, he sought to slay Moses, but Moses fled from the face of Pharaoh, and dwelt in the land of Midian: and he sat down by a well.*[13]

Like Moses, we are social schizophrenics. We are Americans, and then we are not Americans. And since Socrates, Plato, Aristotle, Descartes, Hegel, Kant, Hume, and Shakespeare can only certify me to operate in the White man's world, I need to reach into that reservoir of otherness called liberation knowledge, that aspect of my collective being that knows what sets one free.

The oppressor will not offer an education that will liberate. This is our task. I am convinced that the ecclesiastical community must lead the way in developing African American Cultural Centers or Ethnic Schools. The Jews support public education, but they are authenticated by what is taught in their cultural centers. We must do no less. In the cultural centers and private schools we must deal with the five R's rather than the three R's: reading, 'riting, 'rithmetic, race, and religion.

We must rediscover and create, once again, what Benjamin E. Mays did for Morehouse College and what Mordecai Johnson did for Howard University. Though they be dead, they must speak again to our present dilemma. Both of these educational giants created a spirit of freedom and liberation in their respective institutions, and as a result, a people caught on fire. While Dr. Mays was president of Morehouse College, a student named Martin Luther King, Jr. caught his vision of liberation. It was not the curriculum at Morehouse that inspired Martin King; it was the spirit of dignity and freedom that he found in Dr. Mays. He inspired men for twenty-seven years to believe that "Morehouse Men" were special.

I am still amazed today to hear his former students say that they used to stand on the campus and watch him walk magisterially across campus. One of his former students, Dr. Dorsey C. Miller , an alumnus and a member of my congregation, said, "He walked like a King." For twenty-seven years the men of Morehouse packed the chapel to hear and to see the embodiment of freedom. Such inspiration is greatly needed for our community, in general, and for African American men, in particular. Therefore, we must have mental development along with economic development because a person with a depraved self-esteem will end up giving his or her money to the oppressor anyway.

Dubois versus Washington

The greatest educational discussion of the late 19th century and early 20th century was the debate between W.E.B. Dubois and Booker T. Washington. Washington favored industrial education over academics. Dubois believed that the academic preparation of the "Talented Tenth" was the way to freedom. It should not have been an acrimonious debate because the oppressed must learn to discern what is for private discussion and what is for public exposure. As I said in an earlier chapter, we are constantly being negated by liberals and neoconservatives in the African American community. A public debate between Thomas Sowell and Jesse Jackson is a sideshow that only entertains the oppressor. Both must be heard. The following points hopefully bring light to this discussion.

1. Both Washington and Dubois were prisoners of their respective backgrounds. Booker T. Washington was born a slave in 1856 in the South (Virginia) and was familiar with that which he espoused. Dubois was born in Great Barrington, Massachusetts. In each case geography dictated the approach each would take. Such was the case between Martin King and Malcolm X. Martin was a Southerner. And Malcolm lived in the North. Washington was born in the South. Dubois was born in the North. In the case of

Martin and Malcolm, and Washington and Dubois, geography became the death knell for two brilliant visionaries.

2. Both were victims of racism.

3. Both believed in the power of knowledge.

4. Both reacted to racism based on what each thought was best for African Americans.

5. Both were used by the Oppressor to divide the race. This tactic is still being used today.

6. Both were wrong in the sense that they could not see beyond their respective educational programs.

7. Both were trapped by an "either/or" solution to the problem of educating the oppressed. In regard to education we need doctors, lawyers, nurses, teachers, preachers, engineers, economists, philosophers, and scientists. But we also need plumbers, electricians, farmers, carpenters, painters, tailors, and seamstresses. To choose between Washington and Dubois is to experience death. To be blessed by both spells victory.

8. Both failed in that Washington overestimated the oppressor's potential for transformation. Dubois overestimated the leadership prowess of the mythical "Talented Tenth." We are still waiting for the Oppressor to repent and accept one based on character rather than color. And we are still waiting for the "Talented Tenth" to lead the way.

9. Both cry out posthumously for African Americans to merge their respective approaches. Unless we become eclectic in our educational philosophy, we are floating

in a canoe without an oar. Education for certification and liberation is the only way out in this hostile environment.

The School As Central to Community

In African American history the church and the school have been at the forefront of stabilizing the community. Thirty-five or forty years ago the church and the school often occupied the same facilities or shared the same properties. How well do I remember Watula Baptist Church and School, Mount Canaan Baptist Church, and Calvary Baptist Church and School all in the Ocala, Florida area.

In this context, though segregated, parents, students, and teachers often attended the same church. So the student and the teacher saw each other not only at school but in church as well. The respect that one had in the groves of academe were easily transferred to the church setting. The fact that the teacher, parent, and student were in worship together made a public statement that is hard to hear in our day. It was special on Monday mornings when the teacher asked, "How many were in church or in Sunday School?" The intent was not to theologize or pontificate in regard to denominational dogma. But it was a recognition of the fact that church, home, and school must fulfill their respective roles if African Americans are going to be victorious. Beyond this, teachers were like surrogate parents. They were authorized by the church and the school to be in charge of the classroom. From 1953-1957, I attended elementary school at Belleview -Santos High School outside Ocala. There was a principal there named Matthew Everett Hart, Jr. The whole community supported his right to be the chief educator and disciplinarian. He had no baseball bat or bullhorn as he walked the corridors of the school. His mere presence cast a shadow of healthy foreboding on the part of his student body. It was at this segregated school that my love for scholarship was born. Not only was Mr. Hart a disciplinarian, but his altruism in regard to helping needy students was legendary. It was well known that he would buy a pair of trousers for a student, and if need be, he would set them on fire with his paddle.

I was also blessed with two other principals. One of them was Mr. Herbert S. Coleman of Howard Elementary School, where I was a student from 1957-1961. Besides being a disciplinarian he was also very bright. From him I gained a sense of putting a premium on the mind. He was "macho" yet scholarly. I learned from him that one does not have to be effeminate or feminine in order to be a thinker. It was at his school that I discovered my own intellectual gifts.

Orian Brock of Howard High School was my principal from 1961-1965. Having had a record as an excellent classroom teacher, Mr Brock taught me the meaning of the word <u>endurance</u> and the ability to make the best of life's situations.

In Ocala, Marion County Florida, even though segregated from the late 19th century until 1970 when our schools were phased out by desegregation, we had some of the most gifted teachers and students in the South. My school, Howard High; Booker T. Washington High School; Fessenden Academy; and Belleview-Santos High School provided a proud heritage. Not only did we produce some of the greatest athletic teams of the State of Florida, but we were also high on academics. Oh, to have that balance again!

How can I ever forget the great teachers that I had from 1953-1965. They were all African Americans:

1. Ollie Gary
2. Thelma B. Brown
3. Annie Green Fulton
4. Ruby Snow Rutledge
5. Thelma Thompson Brown
6. Lucinda K. Williams
7. Estelle L.D. Smallwood
8. Earl Speights
9. Wilma H. Stirrup Grimes

10. Alva C. Brown
11. Thelma Parker
12. Vera Coker
13. Frank George Pinkston
14. Lottie V. Donaldson
15. Helen Albert
16. Robert Stevenson
17. Ernest K. Johnson
18. Reuben E. Johnson
19. Alberta Brown
20. Bernard Barno
21. Willie Middleton
22. Willie Miles
23. Samuel C. Berry
24. Eula B. Miller
25. Shirley Shellman
26. Thelma Iles
27. Roosevelt Wilson
28. Marvia Simmons
29. Jewel James
30. Altha Berry
31. Willie Mae Cochran
32. Vernell Johnson
33. Nadine Broxton
34. Altha Flowers Anthony
35. Betty G. Jones
36. Clara Gore

These ebony giants ignited a flame in me that cannot be extinguished, even by the chilly fingers of death. For that which is authentic cannot be terminated. Thanks be to God for their immeasurable gift to me.

Education as a Medium through which Character is Strengthened

The role of the school is not to teach morality or discipline. This is the role of the home. It is the school's task to reinforce or to reemphasize what the home has taught. Yet, to make such a statement today is to make a plea for chaos. The teacher should not have to spend his or her day trying to discipline a child. This should be done at home. Yet, I confess that this is nothing but idealism, unless the home is functioning properly. The issue of education is more about the home than the school. But if the home and the church fail to shape moral values, then the school is ostensibly handcuffed.

Years ago, Judeo-Christian morality was the expected and accepted norm in our African American Schools. Teachers could not openly "shack up" without being married. Though the system was very uneven-handed in dealing with teenage pregnancy and the girl was not allowed to remain in public school, every effort was made to encourage the young lady to go on and get her diploma through the adult education program while the boy who impregnated the girl was allowed to stay in school. Teachers made every attempt to keep even the appearance of immorality out of the sight of their students. In no way do I want to paint a picture of perfection because we, too, had problems in my day. However, there was an attempt to shun the appearance of evil. Every day started with a song and a recitation of the model prayer in unison. In 1962 this was rescinded by the U.S. Supreme Court as a discriminatory practice. Were we better off when we had our daily prayer? Conservative Whites of the religious right and some African Americans would answer in the affirmative. But we must remember that our children do not wake up in the classroom. They wake up in their bedroom. Why wait until one gets in the classroom? It is far more effective to have a child who is under the influence of Godly parents, a child who will come to school prayed up, motivated, respectful, non-violent, disciplined, well read, and ready to take his or her exam in trigonometry. Were we better off when we had our regular prayer time? Some African Americans would say yes. Others would say we fared better socially once we got it removed. Most of the significant pieces of legislation of the Civil Rights movement came after 1962, when school prayer was taken out. Since we live in a pluralistic society, our schools will also reflect that pluralism. Should a student have the right to pray voluntarily in his or her own way? Sure! As a matter of fact, I never stopped praying to God after 1962 because I was never overly impressed with the routine of repeating the model prayer every morning. Prayer is more profound than that. If we restore prayer in the classroom, will personal racism disappear? If prayer is restored, will structural racism disappear? Will we be less materialistic? If so, let's restore it as soon as possible. Frankly, I am tired of religious posturing.

On the other hand, it is foolish not to include such courses as the Bible as literature and comparative religion in our curriculum.

> Religion must once more be given central place in education, lest the merely secular prove our doom.....We teach the literature of Shakespeare, why not teach also the literature of the Bible? It will pass muster, and the great masters of English-speaking literature might then be intelligently discussed. We teach the hedonistic ethic of Aristippus and John Stuart Mill. Why not teach the ethic of the Sermon on the Mount? That will also pass muster! In its sinew of thought, not to mention its mobility of content, it makes some other ethics that are taught appear like babblings from the kindergarten. The day school's present thirty hours of silence about God and Christ makes the one hour of church school seem an unreality.[14]

A cold secularism is just as dangerous as the fervent irrationalism of some fundamentalist quarters. Both add to the sickness rather than provide a cure.

Ideally, the school can be a powerful weapon in the liberation of a people. However, the public school system in America is detrimental for African Americans because the curriculum encourages the superiority of Whites and the inferiority of African Americans. How can you teach honesty when American history is a record about grand theft. Nevertheless, for the sake of certification, our children must stay in school. This is no time to play ethnic games.

Segregated Schools versus Desegregated Schools

The premise of segregation was that we were inferior, and the Oppressor was superior. Growing up in Ocala, Florida was an experience common to all African Americans in the South. Since the White Church was primarily silent on the issue of racism, we had no other option but penalized separatism. It is one thing not to want to be with me, but to penalize me because I am not is evil. For sane African Americans the issue has never been about being with Whites; the issue is getting those inalienable rights that God wills for all of us. Since the system has robbed us of these rights and has placed them in the vault of oppression, our struggle has been about opening the vault in order to get what is ours. I have never wanted to be with Whites if they prefer not to be with me. But as long as they try to control what God wants us to have, we must be a wasp in the garments of racist America, even to the point of death. Sojourner Truth, the great abolitionist, in answer to a speaker who praised the United States Constitution, said:

> Children I talk to God and God talks to me. I go out and talk to God in the fields and woods. This morning I was walking out, and I got over the fence. I saw the wheat holding up its head, looking very big. I got up and take hold of it. You believe it, there was no wheat there. I say, 'God, what is the matter with this wheat?' And he says to me, 'Sojourner, there is a little weasel in it.' Now I hear talkin' about the Constitution and the rights of man. I come up and I take hold of this Constitution. It looks mighty big, and I feel for my rights, but there ain't any there. Then I say, 'God, what ails this Constitution?' He says to me, 'Sojourner, there is a little weasel in it.'[15]

Such has been our experience in America.

One thing we must deal with almost four decades after Brown versus the Board of Education in 1954, is why did we want to integrate? (1) Was it to get what was guaranteed in the Constitution? The amazing genius of Dr. Martin Luther King, Jr. was that he saw himself in the United States Constitution, whereas Thomas Jefferson, George Washington, and John Adams thought that it referred only to them. (2) Was it to secure the rights promised by Plessy vs Ferguson in 1896? In these challenging times, as we face the 21st century, one wonders if African Americans would have been better off if Plessy vs Ferguson had been authentically realized. (3) Was integration pursued in order to be with White people? If so, we are with them, and we are paying a heavy price called ethnocide. (4) Or did we advocate integration in order to determine our destiny? If that be the case, we are failing miserably. From my perspective we have gained very little and have given up much in order to remain second class in the "Big House."

Segregated Schools

A. Positives

---

1. Our children were affirmed by most parents and teachers.

2. Our weekly assembly gave African American students an opportunity for expression and the promotion of individual skills.

3. Our schools were well disciplined, because our faculties were supported by our parents.

4. We had teachers who went the second mile, way beyond the call of duty.

5. We had neighborhood schools.

6. Once each year in many of our schools the students (Seniors) would take over the school for one school week. This instilled a sense of pride and responsibility in our students.

B. Negatives

1. Segregated schools were constant reminders of racism and second class citizenship.

2. Students were bused many miles in order to reach a segregated school. Enroute, they passed by the White schools.

3. In many smaller communities where there were no high schools, African Americans had to move away from home in order to finish high school.

4. In comparison to the White school's facilities, ours were not up to par.

5. Our books were hand-me-downs.

6. Ofttimes, our teachers practiced favoritism based on color or class. Many children, including myself, felt the pangs of rejection because of who they were. But, in our school, this was minimal.

Desegregated Schools

A. Positives

1. Physical plants are better.
2. Books are better.
3. There's equal pay for teachers.
4. A few individuals have come to grips with their racism and have changed for the better.

B. Negatives

1. There is a greater opportunity to be miseducated.

2. There is a reaffirmation of White superiority.

3. Initially, desegregated schools led to mass demotions for African American principals and teachers. Principals were demoted to assistant principals in charge of discipline (of African American students), and coaches were given physical education classes.

4. There is no discipline. Early on, corporal punishment went out because whites were not going to let an African American teacher paddle their children. So African American parents made the decision that if the whites could not be paddled, their children were not going to receive corporal punishment either.

5. Overall, the quality of education is poor. Our children are not reading, writing, spelling, counting, or expressing themselves well.

6. Many abdicated Black colleges because we believed that the White college was a superior institution.

7. There is the bane of busing which destroys the neighborhood school. Of course this is undergirded by an unjust economic system which guarantees that wherever the privileged are, there will be the best privileges also. While I am against busing, I do not oppose it as an apologist for racism because all African Americans who grew up in the South prior to the 1960's can tell about the burden of busing. I am completely turned off by the hypocrisy of Whites who mandated my being bused in the 1950's, and yet will not accept the same for their grandchildren. It is a game.

The African American Intelligentsia and the Masses

Even though W.E.B. Dubois espoused the concept of the Talented Tenth as the leaders of the African American community, there is scant evidence historically that such has been the case. Neither Dubois nor Plato, who talked about the philosopher being the king, saw his dreams become a reality. In regard to the African American intelligentsia, they have been paralyzed by an educational philosophy and curriculum that render them helpless. Woodson said:

> For the arduous task of serving a race thus handicapped, however, the Negro graduate has had little or no training at all. The people whom he has been ordered to serve have been belittled by his teachers to the extent that he can hardly find delight in undertaking what his education has led him to think is impossible. Considering his race as blank in achievement, he sets out to stimulate their imitation of others. The performance is kept up for a while; but, like any other effort at meaningless imitation, it results in failure.[16]

The African American intelligentsia, first of all, are characterized by aloofness. Because of their Eurocentric education, they ofttimes feel closed off from the masses. This can be a blessing in disguise. However, if one is not attuned to the certification-liberation perspective of African Americans, it is a tragedy. Secondly, the intelligentsia traditionally have followed a path of individualism. This is foolish for any oppressed group. To laud the achievement of one who will have no impact upon the race is an exercise in futility. Thirdly, this group has a strong impetus to imitate Whites. Again Woodson said:

> In this effort to imitate, however, even if the Negroes successfully imitate the Whites, nothing new has thereby been accomplished. You simply have a larger

> number of persons doing what others have been doing. The unusual gifts of the race have not thereby been developed, and an unwilling world, therefore, continues to wonder what the Negro is good for.[17]

Fourthly, they have often offered a critique but not a cure for the existential dilemma of the race. They are like the fabled philosopher in Thomas Carlyle's Sartor Resartus, who sat on top of a mountain with a telescope in his hand looking at the stars that studded the midnight sky. This was his way of escaping the misery in the town below. Liberation is never a movement of the elite but of the masses. William E. Gladstone, eloquent statesman and Prime Minister of Great Britain, was convinced that the elite were practically wrong on every social issue. Therefore, he said, "all the world over I will back the masses against the classes."[18]

Educational Challenges Facing The African American Community

1. The African American community must first of all recognize the danger and the dilemma of America's educational system as it impacts us. The tragedy is that most of the African American intelligentsia are oblivious to what has transpired down through the years. When we come to grips with America's philosophy of greed and racial superiority then we can understand how the educational system is used to keep us oppressed. Dr. Janice E. Hale-Benson says:

> The American educational system has not been effective in educating Black children.....The emphasis of traditional education has been upon molding and shaping Black children so that they can fit into an educational process designed for Anglo-Saxon middle class children. We know that the system is not working because of the disproportionate number of Black children who are labeled hyperactive and who are being given drugs as tranquilizers. We know that the

> system is not working because of the disproportionate number of Black children who are labeled mentally retarded and placed in special classes. We know that the system is not working because of the disproportionate number of Black children who are being expelled, suspended, and pushed out of schools. We can see that the system is not working in the high Black teenage unemployment rate and the overrepresentation of Black people in the prison population.[19]

2. The African American community must recognize that not only are we the recipients of an oppressive education, but overall it is a poor educational system. America's educational report card in 1991 was almost disastrous. Therefore, if it is bad for the Oppressor, it is doubly bad for the Oppressed. Maybe this can be the ground upon which we start moving towards creating a new educational system. Since we all agree that it is bad, let us then move towards a certification - liberation model.

3. The African American community must see to it that the educational system, which has the certification-liberation model, builds character and is geared towards helping African Americans in determining their own destiny. Anything that falls short is to be rejected.

4. The African American community must in some way overcome the frightening reality of the Oppressor teaching our children. It was bad enough just using his racist curriculum, but in segregated schools we had a few teachers who were liberationists and could imbue a few students here and there to rise up against tyranny. But when the Oppressor claims to be afraid of an African American child and does not love that child, no learning will take place. No wonder the academic status of our children is so low. Some of our children are doing well grade-wise, but far too many are failing.

5. The African American community must once again establish disciplined homes. One of the evils of desegregation is that we no

longer have a great number of disciplined homes. When parents take the side of their children against the teacher, chaos is the end result. When thuggish parents produce thuggish children, there will be no peace in the groves of academe. I remember vividly the school year 1958-1959 when I was disruptive in class, my teacher, Mrs. E.L.D. Smallwood, took me home after school. When she reported my actions to my mother, no hostility built up between the two of them. All my mother's wrath was vented towards me. Not only did she mete out corporal punishment, but she made me return to school the next day and apologize to my teacher and my classmates. This action on my part was not repeated. The real danger was after my father got home; I would be disciplined further. When he arrived he simply said, "Boy, I don't have an education but you are going to get one even if it kills you. You will not do this again." Unless this is restored, there is no future for the race.

6. Having disciplined schools will be a derivative of a disciplined home. Our challenge is to transform our concentration camps into schools. Barbed wire fences, cops, gun-carrying students, drugs, and beepers do not make for an atmosphere of learning. Our prayers are with those teachers who have to cope with our undisciplined children. My principals, Matthew Everett Hart, Jr. and Herbert S. Coleman, did not have barbed wire fences or police protection to keep anyone off campus or to keep anyone from going off campus. The mandates were given, and they were followed. When they were not, those who were guilty of malfeasance paid the price. The school is for transmitting knowledge and providing tools for the implementation of the same. When a teacher has to spend time trying to bring a student to order, very little learning is taking place. This kind of environment creates apathy on the part of the teacher and the student. And when neither cares, the whole world is in trouble. Therefore, the church and the home must work diligently to help parents and children to overcome bad attitudes, complacency, drugs, violence, suspensions, and all the other accoutrements of oppression. When you have African American children who are standing in corners, and when kindergarten students are being suspended, it is time to take action. If we don't, we are dead.

7. The church-home coalition must work together to get parents involved in their child's education. When we have parents who are too busy or who just don't care, there is nothing that the school can do. I remember the first time that my parents attended P.T.A. meeting. My mother went to the fourth grade, and my father dropped out in first grade. When my teacher reported to my father that I had made all A's while some of the other students had made A's, B's, C's, D's, and F's, my father was upset because he didn't understand why I didn't try harder to get some of the other alphabets. Even though this may cause one to laugh, this became a point for me to instruct my father. I also take pride in the fact that I taught him to sign his name and to read and write. It was a day of great joy when he no longer had to sign an X on his paycheck. But in spite of his deficiencies, he and my mother were involved.

8. If we are going to get and keep our best minds in education, our teachers then must be among the highest paid in our society. It is ludicrous to pay a football coach one million dollars to coach college athletics and pay a professor of mathematics $40,000.00 per year. Years ago in the African American community, the teaching profession had a glow about it that has been lost with desegregation. We must provide incentives to place our best minds in the classroom once again. This nation is paying high dividends for our negligence in this area. I am not insisting that money alone is the answer; but I am saying that you get what you pay for. Instead of continuing on a path where there is the proliferation of weaponry, let us secure an even greater weapon, and that weapon is a great teacher.

9. The role of education is to create thinkers, and not regurgitators. It is of no value to the race to have someone with a Ph.D. from Yale walking around expatiating loftily about the achievements of White folks. The African American community is in dire need of thinkers. Of course this is very frightening to the Oppressor. For when the Oppressed no longer think their thoughts after the Oppressor, their liberation draws near.

10. Education in the African American community must produce a people who think independently but also who act independently. We will continue to act inferior as long as we must depend upon White people to employ us. Carter G. Woodson says:

> When a Negro student works his way through college by polishing shoes, he does not think of making a special study of the science underlying the production and distribution of leather and its products that he may some day figure in this sphere. The Negro boy sent to college by a mechanic seldom dreams of learning Mechanical Engineering to build upon the foundation his father has laid, that in years to come he may figure as a contractor or a consulting engineer. The Negro girl who goes to college hardly wants to return to her mother if she is a washerwoman, but this girl should come back with sufficient knowledge of physics, chemistry, and business administration to use her mother's work as a nucleus for a modern steam laundry. A white professor of a university recently resigned his position to become rich by running a laundry for Negroes in a Southern city. A Negro college instructor would have considered such a suggestion an insult.[20]

Our education in the future must help us not to repeat the catastrophic errors of the past.

11. To counteract the conspiracy to destroy our African American boys, Jawanza Kunjufu said:

> The fourth-grade failure syndrome has been targeted as a pivotal year in the conspiracy to destroy Black boys. This transition from the primary grade to the intermediate and upper grades has many implications. The decline in male performance can be attributed to less than desired teacher competency in the primary division, few male teachers, parental apathy,

> increased peer pressure, and greater emphasis on mass media. The high performance level of Black boys in the primary division is not the result of quality teaching, but raw natural ability. The poor development of this ability is illustrated in their lack of enthusiasm to learn, low self-esteem, and poor self-discipline, and is manifested - not created - in upper grades. In conclusion, it is very difficult to be a man if you do not see positive male role models. African American boys who do not receive quality instruction, do not have a father present, nor male teachers, nor a conspiracy conscious African American minister, are left with incompetent teachers, apathetic parents, mass media, and the streets.[21]

We must get more African American men in education, especially grades 1-8.

12. One of the greatest challenges that the African American community faces is the need to support and endow our Black Colleges. If we continue to allow our colleges to be at the mercy of White philanthropy, we will not be free. When Whites are carrying our financial responsibility, then they will dominate the trustee boards of our schools, and that means control. We must overcome our aversion towards education and support the right kind of education with all of our resources. We have the monies. We lack only the commitment.

References – Chapter Five

[1] Lerone Bennett, The Challenge of Blackness, Johnson Publishing Co.; Chicago Illinois, 1972, 224.
[2] John W. Blasingame, Frederick Douglass: The Clarion Voice, Division of Publications, National Park Service, U.S. Department of the Interior, 1976, 4.
[3] Carter G. Woodson, The Miseducation of the Negro, Hakim's Publications, Philadelphia, PA, 1933, x.
[4] Richard Wright, Native Son, New York, Harper and Row, 1966, 311-312.
[5] Bennett, 224-225.
[6] Ibid.
[7] Woodson, xii.
[8] Bennett, 225.
[9] E. Franklin Frazier, The Negro in the United States, MacMillan Company, New York, 1957, 421-422.
[10] Woodson, xiii.
[11] Ibid., 2.
[12] Ibid.
[13] Exodus 2:11,12,15.
[14] George A. Buttrick, Christ and Man's Dilemma, Abingdon Press, Nashville, Tennessee, 1945, 146-147.
[15] Bennett, Before the Mayflower, 182.
[16] Woodson, 6.
[17] Ibid., 7.
[18] W.E. Gladstone, Speech delivered in Liverpool, England, June 28, 1886.
[19] Janice E. Hale-Benson, Black Children: Their Roots, Culture, and Learning Styles, John Hopkins University Press, Baltimore, 1986, 1-2.
[20] Woodson, 38-39.
[21] Jawanza Kunjufu, Countering The Conspiracy to Destroy Black Boys, African American Images, Chicago, Illinois, 1982, 15.

Chapter Six

Economics and the African American Community

The economic paralysis in the African American community is a result of the psychological devastation of slavery, and an oppressive educational system which does not encourage our liberation. So we must take our quest for freedom into our own hands. The issue now and in the twenty-first century will be "silver rights" as well as "civil rights." If we are to be successful, not only must we have money, but we must use it wisely. Dr. Martin Luther King, Jr. said:

> The economic highway to power has few entry lanes for Negroes. Nothing so vividly reveals the crushing impact of discrimination and the heritage of exclusion as the limited dimensions of Negro business in the most powerful economy in the world. America's industrial production is half of the world's total, and within it the production of Negro business is so small that it can scarcely be measured on any definable scale.[1]

Therefore, if we are to be victorious on the social scene in America, we must develop a healthy attitude about wealth.

Where We Have Been

We must come to grips with the reality that we were not brought to this country to be entrepreneurs but to make entrepreneurs. Slavery was about making the oppressor proud, powerful, and rich.

As a result, African Americans worked for almost three centuries without compensation. While this was going on, the minds of the oppressor and the oppressed were being shaped. Even unto this day the collective mindsets have not changed.

After the Civil War, many former slaves chose to remain with their former masters in order to survive. Others chose to strike out on their own as a means of economic development. But there was disappointment because of this nation's negligence in granting reparations for the former slaves. In spite of the support of the Radical Republicans such as Senator Charles Sumner from Massachusetts and Representative Thaddeus Stevens from the State of Pennsylvania, African Americans never got the proverbial "mule and forty acres." Just suppose this nation had had a "Marshall Plan" for former slaves after the Civil War, for the purpose of rebuilding or building African Americans. But instead they were set free-without education, money or land? One of the great injustices of American history is that African Americans never bombed America, but the Japanese did. Then African Americans fought with the oppressor in order to defeat them in World War II. Then in September 1945, when Japan surrendered to General Douglas MacArthur aboard the U.S.S. Missouri, America worked tirelessly to rebuild Japan and to make her into the world's leading economic power, while much of African America is in ruin and chaos. When America treats the enemy with more respect than us, a profound statement is made about both the oppressor and the oppressed. But ultimately this may have more to do with economics than race. Yet, we cannot rule out skin color as a continuing problem. Even though we are 127 years removed, the devastation of slavery upon the economic mindset of African Americans is still with us. E. Franklin Frazier said:

> Under the system of slavery the problem of the employment of Negro labor did not exist in those areas where the plantation system was being undermined. Even in such areas the Negro slaves who were not needed were sold into the lower South or the slaves might find profitable employment by "hiring their

> time." Many slaves who hired their time were often able ultimately to buy their freedom. Since the Negroes who were free before the Civil War tended to become concentrated in cities, they faced the problem of finding employment. In the Southern cities the free Negroes often enjoyed a monopoly in the mechanical trades, whereas in the Northern cities where free Negroes had to face the severe competition of immigrant labor, they were an impoverished and submerged group.[2]

Whether in slavery or out of slavery, we have not yet eaten the bread from the table of capitalism.

After slavery, African Americans moved ahead with great optimism, in spite of the fact that there was no major effort to repay the debt of involuntary servitude. Any quest for reparations would have been extinguished by the expectations of Reconstruction. In spite of the gains made during Reconstruction, the optimism of African Americans was short lived. For a period of ten years, 1867-1877, our foreparents lived with the hope that America would live up to its creed that "all men are created equal." They soon discovered that this creed referred to rich white men. After slavery, the freed slaves made a gallant effort to become landowners. After having tilled the soil of the slave master, the freed slaves early on discerned the power that derives from owning land. This is still a powerful economic tool.

Following the destruction of Reconstruction, African Americans were faced with a new form of social slavery called "Jim Crow." Because of Jim Crow laws, African Americans were forced to make their own way, though separate from the Oppressor. This was finally legalized in the Supreme Court decision of Plessy vs Ferguson in 1896. This decision, like Reconstruction, would be a living monument to the power of the Oppressor to manipulate, lie, cheat, and control the destiny of African Americans. Yet, it forced us to take care of business in the last twenty years of the 19th century. As a race, we were forced to build schools, hospitals, banks, churches, businesses (both skilled and unskilled), and communities. But in the former slaves' desire to achieve economic power they were often met with resistance from the Oppressor.

> After Emancipation, the Negro sharecropper and agricultural laborer as well as the Negro artisan were thrown into open competition with the common White man of the South. But the competition for land never became the cause for serious social conflict.[3]

The same tension can be seen today as the system is manipulated in such a way as to keep oppressed people fighting each other rather than the system. Those politicians who are masters in the art of creating race-class divisions use such terms as "racial quotas" and "affirmative action" in order to keep oppressed people confused. Thus far, the scheme has worked remarkably well. E. Franklin Frazier again says:

> When the Negro mechanic was thrown into competition with the White worker, there was often open social conflict in both the North and South. Gradually Negro mechanics were supplanted in the South where they had enjoyed a monopoly.[4]

"According to estimates, at the close of the Civil War, 100,000 of the 120,000 artisans in the South were Negroes."[5] By 1890, the skilled Negro worker had been eliminated as a competitor of the Southern whites.[6] W.E.B. Dubois attributed the plight of the Negro worker in the Northern cities to the heritage of slavery, the social disorganization following Emancipation, and race prejudice against Negroes.[7]

In spite of the heralded efforts of Booker T. Washington at Tuskegee Institute, there was still a great economic disparity between Whites and African Americans. Many previous skills that operated in the community of the emancipated were not being transmitted from one generation to the next.[8]

> It was with the view to correct this situation that Booker T. Washington inaugurated a system of industrial education for Negroes. But, as we have seen, the system of industrial education established at Tuskegee Institute and other industrial schools was concerned with handicrafts that were becoming outmoded. Moreover, industrial education for the Negro could not meet the competition of white labor.[9]

So we could say conclusively that the years between 1865-1900 were years filled with hope and despair. We had been exhilarated by the possibilities of Reconstruction, only to be devastated by the dismantling of the same. Therefore, our social situation dictated a spirit of unparalleled entrepreneurship in the African American community.

My home town of Ocala, Florida is a classic case study. In our town, the first thirty years of the twentieth century were the most productive economically for African Americans. Ocala from 1900-1940, was a town of less than 10,000 people.

> It is said, by 1914 the Negroes of Ocala and surrounding areas were the most prosperous in the South. Negroes at this time owned practically all of the business on West Broadway, from Magnolia Avenue to 16th Avenue and beyond. Negroes also owned nearly all of the businesses on Main Street South and had other businesses in the downtown area. The Metropolitan Negro Bank was located at the corner of South Magnolia and Second Street. It was one of the few colored banks in the South. It opened its doors in 1914 and went out of business in 1928. On January 1, 1925, the bank had on deposit more than $200,000.00. East of the bank was a cotton gin owned by George Giles. West of the bank was about the finest Negro hotel in Florida.[10]

Beyond these statistics, prior to 1920 most of the Negroes throughout the county (Marion) owned their own homes.[11] No wonder our community is in such chaos; we are not as progressive as we were ninety years ago. It needs to be said again that Jim Crowism forced African Americans to chart their own destiny. Our town was loaded with artisans, mechanics, farmers, grocery stores, dry goods stores, packing houses, weekly newspapers, tailor shops, seamstresses, and an investment company which provided a bank, a theater, a knitting mill, and a community center. Beyond these we had a printing establishment called the Florida Watchman, that served an entire state; electricians; plumbers; hotels; carpenters; contractors; cleaners; and other businesses. Well, what happened?

> Around the early '20's much of the Negro owned property was in the hands of whites. After World War I, many of the owners left Ocala and did not return. Some left their property in the hands of friends. This, however, often resulted in taxes not being paid and the property later being sold for taxes. Some moved to larger cities where opportunities were supposedly better. And a few were frightened away. The coming of highways engulfed a lot of the Negro property. Rather than try to reestablish, some moved to other cities. Some Negroes sold the property rather than pay the high taxes. By 1930 much of the Negro owned property in downtown Ocala had changed hands. The depression was also a factor, in that it was impossible for a lot of Negroes to pay their taxes. Out of all the struggles a few pieces of property were able to survive.[12]

These startling statistics are very depressing; however, they must also become the means of prodding us on to victory. We must restudy our history and see how we made progress, and what brought our progress to a halt. Presently we are being forced, once again, to fend for ourselves and to chart our own course. Because of institutional racism that will probably never change, we are seeing the same movie again. We must give up on integration and the desire to be with Whites. Whites en masse have never loved us; they don't love us; and will not love us. Occasionally, a White will come out as a kamikaze for our cause, but they are few. So we must take our eyes off Whites and focus on us because there is no love where there is no justice.

Where Are We?

The late Dr. Vernon Johns, predecessor to Dr. Martin Luther King at Dexter Avenue Baptist Church in Montgomery, Alabama, and one of the greatest preachers, prophets, scholars, and sages of the twentieth century once said, "The Negro is economically illiterate." He also said, "If you want a definition of perpetual motion, give the average Negro a Cadillac and tell him to park it on some land that he owns."[13] Dr. Johns' assessment of the economic situation of African Americans was definitely on target. We must become more enlightened about the power, potential, and the danger of money.

It is almost redundant to keep saying that if African Americans were a separate country we would be about the ninth largest in terms of economic power. This is a powerful statistic, but it needs to be pragmatized.

> The money that Black people earn in the U.S. (and most of our money comes from wages) stays in the Black community for about four hours. Again, it is a question of values, beliefs and knowledge. However, one should not be too critical of the Black poor and middle class when he sees the Black "well off" with after burners on escaping to live, work, shop, and play with whites. The $200 billion African American economy that Black leaders so often brag about is not an economy based upon African Americans' production of goods, or the distribution of indigenous products or services. The $200 billion Black economy is based upon Black people working for white people. Such an economy would end if White people ceased to employ African Americans. The major businesses in

> the Black community are the church, drugs, and crippling consumerism.[14]

But with an economy nearing a half trillion dollars we must rise and build or continue to flounder in the quicksand of chaos and cynicism. We must think nationalistically. That is to say, 30 million of us with almost a half trillion dollar income, do not need pity or sympathy. We need some sense about the value of money and sanity in spending it.

George Washington Carver, the great scientist, is a classic example of economic illiteracy although he will long be remembered for his scientific discoveries, humility, and the fact that he shunned greed. Nevertheless, none of the products that came as a result of his genius are controlled by African Americans. His attitude toward greed is commendable in an age of acquisitiveness. He refused to be categorically defined by possessions. This is Christ-like. But if he had been economically astute, the products that came from his discoveries could have been controlled by the African American community rather than the White community.

Integration and African American Economics

Even a blind mule can see that African America's quest for integration has been devastating to our economic liberation. Because we have labored for almost four centuries under an educational system that gives philosophical assent to our inferiority, we have constantly striven to be with and to be accepted by Whites. Our quest for Caucasian acceptance has all but killed independent entrepreneurship. In my hometown of Ocala, Florida businesses owned and operated by African Americans declined drastically after 1965. Our communities were constantly warned by the late Elijah Muhammad and Malcolm X that our quest for integration would be destructive, and economically it has been.

African Americans still live under the fallacious and degrading creed that "White is superior." After the gains of the Civil Rights movement we made a corporate effort to steer clear of any businesses owned by African Americans.

> The Negro has failed to recover from his slavish habit of berating his own and worshipping others as perfect beings. No progress has been made in this respect because the more education the Negro gets the worse off he is.[15]

There needs to be a collective confession that inside all African Americans there is a pervasive problem of self hatred. And this self hatred is the reason why we continue to suffer from economic inertia. We sought what we thought we wanted and have lost what we had. What we used to have was forced upon us by the Law of the land. We had to make it because our master who owed us reparations, did not pay his debt. Therefore, we had to swim or sink. I remember as a boy growing up in Ocala in the 1950's that all the African American preachers in our county purchased their suits, hats, shirts, shoes, etc., from Crompton's Dry Goods Store. Upon Mr. Gibbs Crompton's death in 1959, coupled with our desire to patronize White entrepreneurs, we have not had an African American clothing store since. We are therefore called "to do for ourselves, or die out as the world undergoes readjustment."[16] I am not calling for resegregation because we will die before we allow America to reduce us to common chattel again. However, we need to redefine the socioeconomic implications of integration. It was never the wishes of Dr. King and others in the Civil Rights movement for African Americans to abandon their own businesses. But almost everyone overlooked the fact that our lack of self esteem would inevitably cause such a disastrous course. Who is going to shop at our own clothing stores when there is Lord and Taylor? Who is going to shop at our own grocery stores when there is Publix? The answer is, everybody but us.

Economics and the Charismatic Leader

Historically it appears that the only persons who have been able to affect a significant portion of the African American community in terms of economic development have all been those who have taken on a god-like persona to their constituents. The mainstream, middle-class African American has not been successful to a large degree. Such persons as Father Divine, Elijah Muhammad, and Yahweh Ben Yahweh are classic examples. George "Father Divine" Baker had a tremendous following, probably in the millions. His followers were African Americans and Caucasians:

> Prosecuted by a harsh Long Island Judge in 1932, Father Divine gained national attention and thousands of followers when the judge died five days later. Converts deemed Divine omnipotent. Now moving to Harlem, he founded communal "heavens" feeding and housing thousands of Depression victims. Peach restaurants, barber shops, laundries, and other businesses sprang up, undercutting competitors by good service at unbelievably low prices..... Soon luxury hotels were being purchased in cash. He called loans sinful.[17]

Elijah Muhammad was born Elijah Poole in Sandersville, Georgia. He became the leader of the Nation of Islam, after having been instructed by Master W.D. Fard, who Elijah Muhammad believed was Allah in disguise.

> The members are taught to abstain from tobacco, pork, alcohol, gambling, dancing, card playing, drugs, cosmetics, immorality, and adultery. They are dedicated enterprising workers on their jobs and in numerous Muslim businesses, including restaurants, supermarkets, cleaning and laundry establishments, pharmacies, and apartment buildings.[18]

Another enterprising, charismatic leader is Yahweh Ben Yahweh headquartered in Miami, Florida. Yahweh Ben Yahweh, like the other two charismatic leaders, is also a native of Georgia. No other African American leader in Florida has been able to marshal masses of its people toward economic development. This leader, and his people, usually called the Yahwehs, have built housing projects, apartments, hotels, restaurants, grocery stores, supermarkets, and other establishments. At the time of this writing he has been arrested and incarcerated on charges of murder and conspiracy.

When we study the lives of these leaders, there are common threads in their movements that made them effective, at least for a period of time:

1. All of them were god-like figures. Therefore, their godness served to erase the fallacious god concept that had been taught to them by the slave master. So if one is to be liberated, the White god must be eliminated from one's thinking.

2. All except Elijah Muhammad viewed himself as a god.

3. They demanded discipline and loyalty.

4. All three were dictators.

5. All except Father Divine thought that Whites were evil.

6. All of them taught an exalted anthropology to their followers.

7. All of them changed their names and those of their followers.

8. In the cases of Elijah Muhammad and Yahweh Ben Yahweh, the slave mind was taken away. Whites

were now lowest on the totem pole instead of African Americans.

9. All three had a strong emphasis on socioeconomic development.

10. All three emphasized independence from White control and White handouts.

11. All of them suffered persecution.

12. After the deaths of Muhammad and Father Divine, their movements became splintered. Since Yahweh still lives, it is yet to be revealed what his movement will be.

These and others must be studied in order that we might discover their strengths and weaknesses, thereby coming up with a formula for victory. I believe that they were successful in a sense because:

1. They dared to tamper with White American Christianity's doctrine of God.

2. They dared to de-emphasize the importance of the oppressor, who keeps the oppressed dependent even while he (the oppressor) argues against affirmative action and quotas.

3. They controlled the education of their followers. It is doubtful if anyone who has bought in to the oppressor's educational system will ever be part of any mass movement for economic liberation. Because of their training they will always work hard to make the oppressor richer, and possibly themselves. But the race will still operate at a level of economic paralysis. Traditionally, the most successful business persons in the African American community have been those who missed out on being educated by the oppressor.

4. They appealed to the masses where the workers are to be found. The middle class is not attracted because it suffers from the malady of having a plethora of leaders and activists, who can't produce anything but some crumbs for himself or herself.

5. They have a high level of expectation for their followers.

6. However, they failed because their movements were built around personalities rather than institutions which would transmit their teachings. When they died, or were killed off by the media, their movements were affected.

Economics And The Northern Migrations

One of the great tragedies in African American history was the further disenfranchisement of African Americans through the loss of lands in the South because of migrations to the Northern cities. These migrations took place primarily after World Wars I and II. The reasons for migrations were overt racism, segregation, lynching, high property taxes, and the illusion of the North as the promised land. Until the first World War only about a tenth of African Americans in the United States were in the North, and seven-eighths of those in the North lived in cities.[19] In the South, on the other hand, up until 1920 more than three-fourths of African Americans lived on farms and plantations.[20]

Because of the migrations to the urban centers of the North, African Americans became trapped in an ongoing cycle of nationalistic negation. You cannot develop a people economically when they are landless. For many years in the South there was a stigma attached to anyone who lived in rural communities. If you were going to be "hip" you had to live in the city. Because of this idea along with my grandmother's illness, my parents sold fifty-two acres of choice land in 1957, for less than $20,000.00. Today that land would be worth several million dollars. Once again, we must capture a vision of economic development through the ownership of land.

The agony of the Northern migrations was that African Americans left overt racism in the South only to run into covert racism in the North. Here they found themselves landless, without family and friends, living in ghettoes with only a Northern accent to show for their move. For many African Americans the myth of the promised land in America centers around the fact that it is a mirage in an economic desert, produced by the aristocracy to keep the oppressed ever moving towards an oasis that exists only for the few.

Steps To A New Economy

The Bible and Wealth

Since most African Americans have been exposed to the Judeo-Christian ethic, the Bible then becomes the guide for millions in evaluating wealth and socioeconomic development.

In the Old Testament, wealth was a sign of divine favor. It was contingent upon obedience to God.

> *And you say in your heart, my power and the might of my hand has gotten me this wealth. But you shall remember the Lord your God: for it is he that gives you power to get wealth, that he may establish his covenant which he swore unto your fathers as it is this day. And it shall be, if you do at all forget the Lord your God, and walk after other gods, and serve them, and worship them, I testify against you this day that you shall surely perish.*[21]

This position is also pointed out by the Koheleth.

> *Every man also to whom God has given riches and wealth, and has given him power to eat thereof, and*

> *to take his portion, and to rejoice in his labor, this is the gift of God.*[22]

Even though wealth was a sign of divine blessing, it was not to take preeminence in one's life because it was a surplus of divine favor.

> *And God said to Solomon, because this was in your heart, and you have not asked for riches, wealth, or honour, nor the life of your enemies, neither have you asked for long life; but have asked wisdom and knowledge for yourself, that you may judge my people, over whom I have made you king. Wisdom and knowledge is granted unto you; and I will give you riches, and wealth, and honour, such as none of the kings have had that have been before you, neither shall any after be like you.*[23]

In the community of the oppressed those who worked in the "Big House" were not only to help themselves but to help their brothers and sisters.

> *For Mordecai the Jew was next unto King Ahasuerus, and great among the Jews, and accepted of the multitude of his brothers and sisters, seeking the wealth for his people, and speaking peace to all his seed.*[24]

Wealth has no power imminently or eschatologically to redeem us from sin and death.

> *They that trust in their wealth, and boast themselves in the multitude of their riches; none of them can by any means redeem his brother, nor give to God a ransom for him: For the redemption of their soul is precious, and it ceases forever: That he should still live forever, and not see corruption. For he sees that wise men die, likewise the fool and the brutish person perish, and leave their wealth to others.*[25]

Such a sobering truth did not minimize the importance of transmitting wealth to oncoming generations.

> *A good man leaves an inheritance to his children's children: and the wealth of the sinner is laid up for the Just.*[26]

However, one must always be cognizant of economic development that does not consider ethics. For there is a judgment on any wealth that was gotten illegally. "Wealth gotten by vanity shall be diminished: but he that gathers by labour shall increase."[27]

In the New Testament we are immediately confronted by the embarrassment of the biblical Christ who did not find it necessary to define himself or others in terms of wealth. Christocentrically, wealth is important, but it is not of ultimate concern. It was the Carpenter from Nazareth who said, "Take heed, and beware of covetousness: for a person's life consisteth not in the abundance of things which he/she possesses."[28] No wonder American Christianity evades the sociopolitical implications of the Incarnation of God in Jesus of Nazareth. Nevertheless, any heremeneutic that deals with sociology must begin with Christology. He who was born between animals and crucified between thieves is our embarrassing, and yet our ultimate standard. Therefore, in regard to the oppressed community we must use either the oppressor or Jesus of Nazareth as our norm for evaluating one's behavior in regard to socioeconomic development. Jesus' attitude towards wealth is disturbing to both the Oppressor and the Oppressed. The Oppressor is alienated because he or she has the wealth and is anxious about losing it. The Oppressed is at odds with Jesus because he or she wants that which enslaves the Oppressor. If we are not careful, the desire for money will cause both to crucify Him on a stick.

Jesus was not antagonistic towards money; He was cautiously affirmative. He believed that when money moved from the circumference of one's life to the center, he or she came under divine condemnation.

> *And he spoke a parable unto them, saying, the ground of a certain rich man brought forth plentifully: And he thought within himself, saying, what shall I do, because I have no room where to store my fruits? And he said, this will I do: I will pull down my barns, and build greater; and there will I store all my fruits and my goods. And I will say to my soul, you have much goods laid up for many years; take your ease, eat, drink, and be merry. But God said unto him, you fool, this night your soul shall be required of you: Then whose shall those things be, which you have provided? So is he that layeth up treasure for himself, and is not rich toward God.*[29]

Again in the story of the rich man and Lazarus Jesus condemns the individual who hoards wealth.

> *There was a certain rich man, which was clothed in purple and fine linen, and fared sumptuously every day: And there was a certain beggar named Lazarus, which was laid at his gate, full of sores, and desiring to be fed with the crumbs which fell from the rich man's table: moreover the dogs came and licked his sores. And it came to pass, that the beggar died, and was carried by the angels into Abraham's bosom: the rich man died and was also buried; and in hell he lift up his eyes, being in torments, and he sees Abraham afar off, and Lazarus in his bosom...*[30]

Any wealth that is not designed to alleviate human suffering is a curse. When African Americans talk about economic development, are we using the Rockefellers, Vanderbilts, Morgans, Fords, or Kennedys as models, or are we using Jesus as our model? The above passage of scripture not only excoriates the selfishness of the rich man, but it raises a question about what would have been the attitude of Lazarus had he been rich?

In the story of the Rich Ruler, Jesus comes down hard on the life that prizes money above the mandates of the Kingdom of God.

> *And, behold, one came and said unto him, Good Master, what good thing shall I do, that I may have eternal life? And he said unto him, why do you call me good? There is none good but one, that is God: but if you will enter into life, keep the commandments. He said unto him, which? Jesus said you shall not commit murder, you shall not commit adultery, you shall not steal, you shall not bear false witness, honour your father and mother: and you shall love your neighbor as yourself. The young man said unto him, all these have I kept from my youth up: What do I lack? Jesus said unto him, if you will be perfect, go and sell what you have and give to the poor, and you shall have treasure in heaven: and come and follow me. But when the young man heard that saying, he went away sorrowful: for he had great possessions.*[31]

Once again possessions take center stage and the Kingdom of God becomes circumferential. Jesus, in no uncertain terms, underscores the danger of wealth.

> *Then said Jesus unto his disciples, verily I say unto you, that a rich man shall hardly enter into the kingdom of heaven. And again I say unto you, it is easier for a camel to go through the eye of a needle, than for a rich man to enter into the kingdom of God. When his disciples heard it, they were exceedingly amazed, saying, who then can be saved?*[32]

Jesus in no way states that the rich cannot be saved. He says that it is difficult. And if Jesus says that it is hard, it is hard because the life that struggles to harmonize God and possessions is a miserable life.

No man can serve two masters: for either he will hate the one, and love the other; or else he will hold to the one, and despise the other. You cannot serve God and mammon.[33]

One of the most misunderstood and misquoted passages in regard to the subject of money is found in First Timothy 6:10, which says, "for the love of money is the root of all evil: which while some coveted after, they have erred from the faith, and pierced themselves through with many sorrows." Money is amoral. The love of money is the foundation or the spring from which all kinds of evils flow. The challenge of the African American Christian community, then, is to discover how to build ourselves economically without becoming prisoners of greed and avarice. The Apostle Paul gives sobering insight on this subject:

Charge them that are rich in this world that they be not highminded, nor trust in uncertain riches, but in the living God, who gives us richly all things to enjoy; That they do good, that they be rich in good works, ready to distribute, willing to communicate; laying up in store for themselves a good foundation against the time to come, that they may lay hold on eternal life.[34]

Steps To Economic Sanity

1. There can be no solid economic development in America without coming to grips with what should have happened after slavery. I repeat, if America had financed former slaves like it did Japan and Europe after World War II, we could have been economically independent. Even the affirmative action programs of the 1960's and 1970's were designed to fail in order to return to those "chilling days of yesteryears." I agree with John Jacob, the head of the National Urban League, that America needs a Marshall Plan for the rebuilding of the infrastructure of this country, particularly the African American community. While America plays genocidal games of semantics with our future, such as affirmative action and

quotas, we continue to flounder aimlessly in a sea of despair. John Jacob said:

> A Marshall Plan for America would slam the brakes on our decline by creating jobs and training opportunities while renewing and modernizing the infrastructure every society depends on. I have suggested a modest $50 billion a year, 10 year program which is really a drop in the bucket for a nation whose national government has a $1.2 trillion annual budget loaded with non-essential spending and waste. Marshall Plan funds would be targeted to priority areas developing a national telecommunications network, repairing highways and bridges, investing in early childhood programs and schools, and training the underutilized disadvantaged. A key goal would be to bring jobs, education and training opportunities to the masses of people who today have no productive role in our economy. A Marshall Plan administrator would coordinate the programs and ensure that they are efficient and cost effective, and that they do what they are supposed to do.[35]

While I support the idea of a Marshall Plan, I fear that with the political mood in this country in 1991, that conservative politicians would find ways to keep it from being effective in the African American community. Our history has taught us that what the oppressor giveth grudgingly, he taketh away enthusiastically.

2. We must realize that money is not a substitute for God; it is a medium of exchange. People are more important than possessions. When someone told Mother Teresa of Calcutta that they "could not work among the poor and the filthy of India for millions of dollars," she replied, "neither could I. I only do it for the love of Christ." That kind of wisdom is needed in this avaricious nation. Unless economic development is kept within the Christocentric parameters of service to others, our pursuit will end in a deeper enslavement.

When we want to have, for the sake of consumption, we will then replicate the oppressor.

3. We have been brainwashed for destruction and dependency, which paralyzes us with self hatred and distrust. It is a trite response on the part of many that African Americans ought to start their own businesses. This is true. However, the White community nor the African American community will do business with us because all have been trained to believe in our inferiority. Unless we can cut the umbilical cord, we shall continue to drink from the poisoned breast of the enemy.

4. We must learn the art of transmitting wealth. It is often true that the first generation creates the wealth; the second generation spends it; and the third generation goes on welfare.

5. We must develop a healthy attitude toward work. We must work diligently to instill in young boys and girls the importance of working for ourselves in order to build a strong people. There is dignity in work even when we work for the oppressor. Our collective communities must start training programs for our children which will present the negativities of working for the oppressor, and why much of poor African American communities abhors work. But we must also present positive examples of how we can triumph in spite of our racist history.

6. We must view each African American family as a business corporation or combine. This will begin to take shape when young married couples begin to chart and plan their future. Many families have more than two or three college-trained people, but they can only see themselves working for Whites. Whites go to college to work for themselves; we go to college to work for them. No wonder we are paralyzed. Until we can break the cycle, we will be perpetually disenfranchised.

7. We must also learn individually and collectively how to budget our monies and live within our means. You cannot buy a limou-

sine when you don't have cab fare. "Keeping up with the Joneses" is destructive to you and to the race.

8. We must stop the oppressor from using his game of semantics to keep us divided and dependent. Such divisive code words as "affirmative action" and "quotas" appeal only to the base character of this stolen nation. I have vowed not to discuss or debate the above any longer. I simply say, "I defer to the White church to solve this moral evil." African Americans en masse do not want handouts; we want reparations. Conservative Whites and African Americans will disagree. However, conservative African Americans also work for White people. Again, I say we want what you owe, but we know that White America does not have the moral audacity to pay its debt to us. Therefore, we will not be inactivated by the prospect of receiving our due. We will not be stupid enough to wait until pay day. Listen, my brothers and sisters. White America is not going to pay their debt for 246 years of slavery. Therefore, we must rise up and take our destiny into our own hands. We therefore propose the following:

a. Job training.
b. Tax breaks for working families.
c. Loans for needy college students. It has been suggested that students could help pay back their loans by performing governmental services.
d. Strong head start programs.
e. A minimum wage that keeps up with the high cost of living.
f. Affordable housing.
g. Health care for all Americans.
h. Strong and enforced work laws which will seek to end unemployment and vagrancy. The unemployed will be given a job at a wage where he/she can live comfortably. The vagrant will be forced to get into some type of job training in order to rescue him/her from future incarceration.

i. Let welfare become workfare except for the needy. However, we must transform the lie which says that there are more African Americans on welfare than Whites. There are far more Whites than African Americans on welfare. When Whites come out against welfare they have been miseducated into believing that welfare is a "black thing." Welfare is a "White thing." It was started by Whites, and the major beneficiaries are Whites. Welfare from an African American perspective is a deeper enslavement. The needy should continue to receive and get increases. The greedy of all races should be given job training and/or enroll in college. Again, those who refuse should be placed in vagrant centers where they must learn a trade. We must also free the term "welfare" from its stigma. The early church called it by such terms as "alms" or "gifts of love." It also declared, "that if any would not work, neither should he/she eat" (2 Thessalonians 3:10).

j. We need loans for African American businesses.

9. If our ultimate goal is to be with, to be accepted by, and to work for Whites, our goal has been perfidiously achieved. But if we want to see 30 million African Americans building themselves for the future, we need to create a Think Tank. This Think Tank will strategize for the future of our people. It will include liberals, conservatives, and separatists. For the first time in history all segments of our community will come together. This Think Tank will disclose who is for us, or who is against us. This forum will not be about performing for Whites on the Phil Donahue Show. It is about our emancipation and our liberation. This forum is not about patriotism and the love of this country. It is about the love of God and ourselves. And in that context we have the capacity to love the enemy. We need our greatest minds in business, economics, banking, finance, political science, etc., to be engaged in our liberation. A degree from Harvard is not the major criterion for inclusion. The major criterion ought to be that one must be a kamikaze for the African American cause or brace oneself for rejection by the race.

Most of those who have been trained in schools of business, finance, and economics have been trained to work for White people and have nothing to offer African American people. Most of these graduates are sent out for a lifetime of servitude to Corporate America where they will destroy themselves trying to ascend the corporate ladder that is basically receptive to the feet of White men.

10. We must become producers rather than just consumers. We are a dependent people. Therefore, we are oppressed.

11. We must become selective consumers. We must become educated as to which businesses make authentic investments in our community.

12. We must become sacrificial consumers. By this I mean that we must learn to prioritize our spending. We spend too much money on exorbitant and destructive vices such as drugs, alcohol, cigarettes, etc. Having money should cause one to leave a legacy. The Talmud said, "One should have a child; plant a tree; or write a book."

13. The African American middle class must change its attitude and begin its mission to the rest of the community that still finds America to be a nightmare rather than a dream. This group, according to E. Franklin Frazier, is characterized by conspicuous consumption and a desire to imitate Whites:

> Lacking a cultural tradition and rejecting identification with the Negro masses on the one hand, and suffering from the contempt of the white world on the other, the black bourgeoisie has developed a deep-seated inferiority complex. In order to compensate for this feeling of inferiority, the black bourgeoisie has created in its isolation what might be described as a world of make-believe in which it attempts to escape the disdain of whites and fulfill its wish for status in American life.[36]

This mental confusion still exists in the African American community. Again Frazier says:

> Since the world of make-believe cannot insulate the black bourgeoisie completely from the world of reality, the members of this class exhibit considerable confusion and conflict in their personalities. Their emotional and mental conflicts arise partly from their constant striving for status within the Negro world, as well as in the estimation of whites. Moreover, they have accepted unconditionally, the values of the white bourgeoisie world: its morals and its canons of respectability, its standards of beauty and consumption. In fact, they have tended to overemphasize their conformity to white ideals. Nevertheless, they are rejected by the white world, and this rejection has created considerable self-hatred, since it is attributed to their Negro characteristics. At the same time because of their ambivalence towards Negroes, they are extremely sensitive to slights and discriminations which Negroes suffer. Since they do not truly identify themselves with Negroes, the hollowness of the black bourgeoisie's pretended racial pride is revealed in the value which it places upon a white or light complexion. Because of their social isolation and lack of a cultural tradition, the members of the black bourgeoisie in the United States seem to be in the process of becoming nobody.[37]

If we are going to develop ourselves economically, our athletes, entertainers, and other wealthy persons must make authentic investments in our churches, colleges, and communities. I am not necessarily troubled by where individuals live as long as they don't transport their minds and their bank assets. However, this will not become a reality until the middle class overcomes its elusive obsession of being with, and being accepted by, Whites. A few athletes and entertainers are making an impact, but it needs to be focused, and it must be broad based. I am not talking about investing in order to get an honorary degree; we need major investments by those of means in our community. Although I am not contemptuous of wealthy African Americans who live in White communities, some need to stay in our community as role models for the masses.

In the biblical record Moses (Hebrews 11:24-29); Esther (4-7); Mordecai (Esther 10:3); and Nehemiah (2:1-6) socioeconomically were middle class and oppressed, yet they all made contributions to the liberation of their people. This will only be true in the African American community when the middle class (if there is a middle class) stops being a buffer between the oppressor and the rest of the oppressed community. Dr. John Henrik Clarke in a lecture given at my church in 1989 said, "We will never make it until we love what we see in the mirror."

14. We must overcome the "Driving Miss Daisy" complex. Driving Miss Daisy was an Academy Award winning movie which depicted an African American played by Morgan Freeman and a White woman played by Jessica Tandy. This movie showed the African American willing to endure insults and embarrassments in order to be the chauffeur for his employer. On a tour of Spain, Portugal, and Morocco in 1990 I was asked by several Jewish people what I thought about the movie, to which I replied, "African Americans are tired of driving Miss Daisy. We will not be free as long as we don't own the company where she buys her automobile." Ownership and control of our communities are indispensable for our liberation.

15. We must counteract the phenomena of Whites, Jews, and foreigners getting rich in our communities. In no way do we advocate violence against others who may be in our community. However, we must do what others do, and that is to support its own. I am almost tired of hearing the truth of how many times the Jewish dollar circulates in its community (10 times) while ours turns over once. It is indeed a sick race that makes others rich, but will not support its own. In every African American community other groups are "making a killing" off us. I believe when immigrants get off at Ellis Island, New York they ask, "How do you get rich in

America?" The reply comes, "Start a business, or buy a failing one in the African American community. You see they are brain-washed, and they have been trained not to support each other." My hometown of Ocala, Florida is a classic example. Businesses owned by African Americans in the past are now controlled by Asians. Until African Americans can have successful businesses in their own communities, we will continue to be oppressed. To have a successful business in the White community would require one to hire Whites almost exclusively as a front. Such a reality is appalling in "the land of the free."

16. We must emphasize the importance of caring for and sharing with our own. This needs to be reflected by the individual, the nuclear family, the extended family, and then to the larger African American community. Unless we can recapture this spirit, individuals will be successful, but as a race we will fail.

17. What can we do through our churches?

   a. Foster projects that will employ African Americans. Any such project must not violate the principles surrounding the separation of church and state.

   b. Form mini-corporations in our churches where five or more people will come together to begin business ventures. Ten people could sink $5,000 per person into a venture even if they didn't know what the venture was. These monies could be placed in a fund to draw interest until the venture was ready. Therefore, you would start with $50,000. Some ladies in my congregation did this and purchased a piece of property which has since tripled in value.

   c. Form business associations which would catalogue all of the businesses in a local congregation. In a larger sense, ministerial alliances could publish and promote such a directory for the community at large.

d. Support our own banks and credit unions. This is very difficult because of the reluctance of African Americans to put their monies in banks and credit unions that are controlled by us. We need to be deprogrammed. Our present mind is killing us!

e. Encourage selective banking in areas where there is no African American bank in operation. We need to encourage large groups of churches to do business with maybe one bank that is willing to do authentic business in our community. With this strategy, I am talking about millions of dollars that could be used collectively to build the infrastructure of our communities and to start businesses.

f. Set an example in terms of attitude and action in the community. If a new facility is being built, use African Americans as architects, carpenters, masons, plumbers, electricians, painters, carpet designers, etc. Also in terms of a day-to-day operation, use African Americans when opportunity presents itself.

g. Keep our congregations aware of the errors of the past. We must be constantly reminded that many of our most successful African American entertainers died broke, ripped off by drugs and White managers.

As philosopher Santayana said, "Unless we learn the lessons of the past, we are doomed to repeat its errors."

References – Chapter Six

[1] Martin Luther King, Jr., Where Do We Go From Here: Chaos or Community? Beacon Press, Boston, Massachusetts, 1967, 139.
[2] E. Franklin Frazier, The Negro in the United States, The MacMillan Company, 1957, 593.
[3] Rupert B. Vance, "Racial Competition for the Land," in Edgar T. Thompson (Ed.), Race Relations and the Race Problem. Durham, NC, Duke University Press, 1939, 102ff.
[4] Frazier, 595.
[5] Sterling D. Spero and Abram L. Harris, The Black Worker, New York, 1931, 159-160.
[6] Frazier, 596.
[7] W.E.B. Dubois, The Philadelphia Negro, Philadelphia, PA, 1899, 282-286.
[8] Frazier, 596.
[9] Ibid.
[10] Pinkney Wookbury (Editor), The Struggle for Survival: A Partial History of the Negroes of Marion County 1865-1976, Central Florida Community College Press, 1976, 19.
[11] Ibid.
[12] Ibid.
[13] Charles E. Boddie, God's Bad Boys, Judson Press, Valley Forge, PA, 1972, 65.
[14] Haki R. Madhubuti, Black Men: Obsolete, Single, Dangerous?, Third World Press, Chicago, 1990, 22.
[15] Carter G. Woodson, The Miseducation of the Negro, Hakim's Publications, Philadelphia, PA, 1933, 109.
[16] Ibid., 107.
[17] Edgar A. Toppin, A Biographical History of Blacks in America Since 1528, David McKay Company, New York, 1969, 280.
[18] Ibid., 374-375.
[19] E. Franklin Frazier, Black Bourgeoisie, MacMillan Publishing Co.; New York, 1957, 23.
[20] Ibid., 23.
[21] Deuteronomy 8:17-19.
[22] Ecclesiastes 5:19.
[23] 2 Chronicles 1:11-12.
[24] Esther 10:3.
[25] Psalm 49:6-10.
[26] Proverbs 13:22.
[27] Proverbs 13:11.
[28] Luke 12:15.
[29] Luke 12:16-21.
[30] Luke 16:19-23.
[31] Matthew 19:16-22.

[32] Matthew 19:23-25.
[33] Matthew 6:24.
[34] I Timothy 6:17-19.
[35] John E. Jacob, Article in the Westside Gazette, Fort Lauderdale, Florida, October 3, 1991.
[36] Frazier, Black Bourgeoisie, 27.
[37] Ibid., 28.

Chapter Seven

Politics and The African American Community: Establishment Politics and Economics

Any understanding of politics in America must begin with the realization that money is more important than people. This country is not run by the Congress, the President, the Judiciary or the people. It is controlled by a rich oligarchy, or aristocracy. Therefore, whoever plays the game of politics, and does not understand this, will continue to be confused, frustrated, and oppressed. The naivete of the African American community is that it attempts to practice the art of politics without understanding economics. If every African American voted, we would see legislation passed only to see our socioeconomic position unchanged because social power in America is based on economics. It is an awesome scenario that leaves an overwhelming majority of the American population in the dark. The few in every nation control the many, even in America.

> The distinguished prime minister of England, Benjamin Disraeli, once wrote, "the world is governed by very different personages than what is imagined by those who are not behind the scenes." Woodrow Wilson, whose principal adviser was a behind-the-scenes operator said, "There is a power somewhere so organized, so subtle, so watchful, so interlocked, so complete, so pervasive that they better not speak above their breath when they speak in condemnation of it." Historians normally recount the deeds and exploits of Kings, presidents, prime ministers, secretaries, and cabinet ministers. In truth, the real power to choose presidents and prime ministers is not in public view

> - it is behind the scenes. Such men generally prefer to operate in great secrecy, although some have a certain public face. Invariably, however, they control such enormous wealth that their collective voices can cause rulers to tremble and governments - along with their national economies - to fall.[1]

While this may sound fanciful, nevertheless it gives credence to what I have believed for some time, but was unable to articulate. While I am poles apart from Pat Robertson's theological - political views, I am nevertheless persuaded that his assessment of the American social, political, economic, and military establishment is on target. While many will disagree with his theological interpretation as it relates to eschatology, he must not be ignored. Under the imbroglio of democracy and capitalism a multitude of sins is covered. It is a fact that probably 99% of the American people of all ethnic backgrounds do not have the faintest notion as to who is running America.

> Rest assured, there is a behind-the- scenes Establishment in this nation as in every other. It has enormous power. It has controlled the economic and foreign policy objectives of the United States for the past seventy years, whether the man sitting in the White House is a Democrat or a Republican, a liberal or a conservative, a moderate or an extremist. This power is above elections, but it has been able to control the results of elections. Beyond the control of wealth, its principal goal is the establishment of a one-world government where the control of money is in the hands of one or more privately owned but government-chartered central banks.[2]

Again Robertson says:

> The visible home of the establishment is Pratt House, on the corner of Park Avenue and Sixty-eighth Street in New York City, right across the street from the So-

> viet embassy to the United Nations. This is the headquarters of the Council on Foreign Relations, and from here the Establishment reaches out to the many power centers. Here are just a few: U.S. State Department, the U.S. Treasury Department, the Federal Reserve Board, the Export-Import Bank, the Rockefeller Foundation, the Rockefeller family, the Rockefeller Brothers Fund, the Ford Foundation, the Carnegie Foundation, the Chase Manhattan Bank, First National City Bank, J.P. Morgan and Company, Harvard University, Columbia University, Yale University, the University of Chicago, The Washington Post, the New York Times, the Los Angeles Times, and scores of international corporations, investment banking houses, private foundations, and media outlets in this country, in England, and on the continent of Europe.[3]

This is a frightening reality that the majority and the minority community must come to grips with. In America everyone is powerless except the powerful few. Therefore, the American system with the Legislative, Judicial, and Executive branches is not controlled by the people, but by an aristocratic oligarchy. It needs to be said that there are no African Americans with enough money to be a part of the Establishment. All of our monies collectively would not be enough to land one African American a seat among the powers that be. While we argue over political parties, voting, electoral colleges, and presidents, the aristocracy continues to wield power in America. We all have been fed the illusion that we live in a democracy. We are ready to fight for it, propagate its fallacies, and even die in order that the invisible powers behind the scenes can continue to be exactly that.

> In government policy, the most visible expression of the Establishment is the Council on Foreign Affairs. Out of some twenty-nine hundred members, at least five hundred are from centers of influence, and the rest are influential academia, the media, business and finance, the military, or government. A few are token conservatives.[4]

From an economic perspective African Americans and the majority community need to confess collectively that politics in America is a charade for the few to control and the many to consume. Freedom, therefore, is defined as the ability to buy things we don't need. Greed dominates this country. It was founded on greed backed up by Bibles and bullets. For the Native Americans, greed undergirded by the ecclesiastical-military complex, was a mountain too high to climb. This philosophy has continued down to our day with the Establishment's policy of supporting dictatorships in Third World countries; while these countries are raped by multinational corporations in the name of democracy versus communism.

In light of this, at this time, we must get rid of the notion of power except in an ethnic sense. The more I get involved the more I recognize the powerlessness of African Americans and whites as it relates to the Establishment. Therefore, it is necessary for our collective sanity that we redefine power and freedom. When 400 White men have more money than 30 million African Americans, we need new definitions, goals, and objectives.

> How long will black ghetto children be deceived before the truth is given to them? They do not have a fair chance to succeed. They are not free to be all that they can be, regardless of what their teachers tell them. The opportunities for developing the vocabulary, the style, and the dispositions so essential for success in the social system have been denied them. The children of those who control the means of production will have easy and favored access to social success, while the children of the socially disinherited are duped into thinking that they have an equal chance to achieve the goals that symbolize success. These deprived children are told that they live in a free society in which anybody can do or be anything. They are told that they have as much of a chance as anybody of realizing the culturally prescribed dreams for achievement. In reality, however, the children of the ruling class are

> the only ones who have a good chance of actualizing their potential. It is increasingly obvious to those who work with oppressed minority groups in America that the children of these groups have the cards stacked against them.[5]

The thing that makes this statement so inflammatory is that it is true. This is not the time for lies. Those of us who call ourselves leaders must stop feeding our people false hope, because hope that is based on a lie is fantasy. Hope for our people is to be found in God and in ourselves. So when we talk about empowerment for African American people, it must be done so with a clear understanding of the politics of the Establishment. The Establishment and its goals are antithetical to the kingdom of God and to people in America and the world in general. Its goals are to control and to keep the powerless (all Americans except the Establishment) happy with the facade of power.

As African Americans we must admit that our economic situation is based on our people working for Whites. Ours is a dependent economy. It will continue to be so until we can have an individual and corporate mental revolution. However, when African Americans wake up to their potential in terms of using our resources wisely, we can go a long way towards building a greater people. We must play the hand we have been dealt.

The Politics of Race

Racism is a continuing by-product of Establishment politics. While the Establishment, because of its pinnacle of power, does not get involved in the day to day manifestation of racism, nevertheless it is strengthened because of it; while Whites and African Americans continue to fight each other, the Establishment continues to wield unchallenged control of the structural institutions of America. Racism is necessary in order to divide and conquer. Whites must realize that not only have African Americans been hurt, but they also continue to be harmed by racism.

Initially, greed was the definitive issue in our enslavement rather than racism. However, as time went along, our alleged inferiority was based on the fact that our skin color was a curse from God. Early on, after receiving theological sanction, the politics of race was set in motion and continues until this day, though a few United States Presidents, e.g. Harry Truman, John F. Kennedy, and Lyndon Johnson took the high road in a small way. Yet none of them can truly be said to have been radically liberated on the question of race.

With the election of Ronald Reagan to the Presidency, African Americans saw a throwback to the days of yesteryear when we knew our places. It was no coincidence that Reagan began his campaign for the Presidency by talking about "States Rights" in Philadelphia, Mississippi. Such a code word sent a signal to the American people that it was all right to retrogress on the issue of race. His lasting dastardly contribution to African Americans is that he turned up the volume on overt racism that had been somewhat covert because of the Civil Rights legislation of the 1960's. No wonder he was so popular.

Once you have a good thing going, why change? The race card was also used by George Bush in his campaign for the Presidency in 1988. The chairman of the Republican Party, the late Lee Atwater, used rapist Willie Horton to appeal to the worst in Whites and was able to defeat a weak Michael Dukakis, Governor of the State of Massachusetts. To his credit Lee Atwater gave several deathbed apologies for his part in the rise of George Bush to the Presidency through racist politics.

This race baiting was also demonstrated by Senator Jesse Helms of North Carolina as he ran against his African American opponent, Harvey Gantt in 1990. Many of the polls had Gantt leading the incumbent until Helms convinced the White voters of North Carolina that if Gantt was elected, the jobs based on quotas would go to the African American community. Because of this ploy, Jesse Helms finally pulled victory from the jaws of certain defeat. He was supported in this ungodly tactic not only by White Christians, but by religio-political conservatives of African American descent, who really feel no real kinship to their brothers and sisters. And, of course, within the context of White American Christianity, Jesse Helms is a Christian. No wonder Madalyn Murray O'Hair is an atheist. The Senator needs to learn that far more people die from the products of his tobacco producing state than from Affirmative Action.

The Clarence Thomas, Anita Hill fiasco in 1991 was a continuation of the racist strategy of pitting an African American woman against an African American male. Thomas, who was later confirmed by a 52 to 48 vote to become the second African American to serve on U.S. Supreme Court, was accused by law professor Anita Hill of sexual harassment, actions which transpired ten years earlier. While I do not question the veracity of either, I do question the strategy of two African Americans (highly skilled) performing for twelve White men (the Senate Confirmation Committee). If any good came out of this racist setup, it may be that Thomas came to the realization that those African Americans who become political surrogates of Barry Goldwater, Ronald Reagan, Pat Buchanan, et al. are still given their traditional "places" even if he has a White wife on his arm. Thomas referred to his ordeal as a "high tech lynching of an uppity Black." We all wondered if this was a breakthrough, or was it simply the playing of the race card in order to get confirmed? Regardless, the man was damaged because for millions, in spite of his future juridical contributions, he will always be known as Clarence "Long Dong Silver" Thomas, Justice of the United States Supreme Court. But Professor Hill was also damaged in that her ordeal continues to underscore the hostility between our men and women. Beyond this, America was once again seen as a racist nation.

As the 1992 Presidential election came into focus, there was a lot of side-stepping in regard to the Presidential candidacy of David Duke, former Grand Wizard of the Ku Klux Klan and reputed Nazi sympathizer. But Duke is a representative of that which has never changed in America. Policywise, there was not much difference between him and George Bush except Bush believed in a "kinder, gentler" crucifixion for the oppressed, while we bleed to death surrounded by "a thousand points of light." After Reagan, Helms, Lee Atwater, et al., Duke is a natural consequence. He is also a "born again" Christian.

Beyond this, the treatment of our Haitian brothers and sisters by the United States Immigration and Naturalization Society is immoral and criminal. Cubans, because they are looked upon as political refugees, are welcomed as a propaganda ploy against Castro and his communist Cuba, while Haitians are classified as economic refugees and sent back to their homeland. Even a blind mule can see the racism involved in this policy. But, on the other hand, the Cuban exile community keeps the pressure on, while African Americans by and large are not involved in the Haitian ordeal. This also has to do with our stupid voting habits where we always vote for the Democratic Party. In spite of this, we have had only one Democrat to occupy the White House between 1968-1992. Since most Republicans are not interested in Haiti, and since most African Americans don't vote Republican, the Republicans don't feel that they owe us anything. We must rise from our sleep or die in our sleep!

The Politics of Patriotism

Webster's Dictionary defines patriotism as "devotion to one's country." In the same vein a patriot is "a person who loves his/her country, zealously supporting and defending it and its interests." In every society it is a litmus test in determining the character of one's citizenship. It is designed to question loyalty, create guilt, and whip dissenters into line.

Because of perpetual racism in America, both personal and structural, race relations (authentic) will not radically change. For this, I blame a dysfunctional White Church that still does not take incarnational theology seriously. I wish I were in error, but the fact is, Whites en masse have always resented forced desegregation and really do not want to be associated with African Americans. In light of such a context, is patriotism to be expected of our people? Can an African American be patriotic? I would answer that it is impossible for Moses, the African-Hebrew, to be patriotic to the Egyptian government that wills his destruction, unless he separates himself from the liberation struggle of his people. If he continues to bask in the benefits of the palace, he can be insanely patriotic, but then he ceases to be a Hebrew; he is now an Egyptian pure and simple. For the issue again is not pigmentation, but identification. In this same vein, one could ask in what sense is General Colin Powell, Chairman of the Joint Chiefs of Staff, patriotic? Can one be patriotic and still be race conscious? Can one such as General Powell be an inspiration for his brothers and sisters in the brickyard? This is not a character evaluation of General Powell; it is an assessment of his position vis-a-vis the palace and the field. Can an African American who works for the Justice Department, such as the F.B.I. or the C.I.A., really be for their brothers and sisters in the field? Black police officers in South Africa- whose side are they on?

Another pertinent concern connected with the issue is the pledge of allegiance to the flag. Can one who takes the Biblical Christ seriously pledge allegiance to anyone other than Jesus? Even though we are part of the kingdom of this world and the Kingdom of God (Basilea Theos), we can be good citizens only in this world's kingdom. However, we owe our lives to the Kingdom of God. When we take a look at the pledge, it mirrors the ideal rather than the real. This is not "one nation under God," which, incidentally, was not added until 1954. The Pledge was first recited around 1892. Again, it is arrogant to say we can't be divided, because we are a divided nation. And there is no "liberty and justice for all." In this statement, in no way do I advocate an overthrow of this government or any other political system. This will happen when the Kingdom of God finally comes into power.

On the issue of patriotism, no smear tactic was as effective as being called a communist at the close of World War II, or shortly after the Cold War began between the former Soviet Union and the United States. This would last for forty years while the "military-industrial complex" really gave direction to the foreign policy of this nation. Multiple billions were spent by both countries on weaponry that was never used against the other, and hopefully it never will be. But when one looks back on it, it all appeared to have been a game engineered by the Establishment on both sides. In the 1950's Senator Joseph McCarthy became the chief propagandist as he accused many people of being communists. Such African Americans as Dr. Martin Luther King, Jr.; Eartha Kitt; and Paul Robeson, one of the most gifted minds of the twentieth century, were also accused. One wonders, now that communism seems to be an ideology of the past throughout Europe, what will be the next smear tactic to keep one in line.

Patriotism, as is often the case, can be an excuse for violence. In regard to African American people we have been taught to be non-violent towards the oppressor, but violent towards ourselves, and others, especially in war. General Arnold Schwarzkopf was the hero of the Persian Gulf War, but any thug on any street corner in America with forty-eight months of academics at West Point could achieve something similar. A military academy only provides the intellectual-technological medium for human extermination on a mass scale. So, as a Christian, I will give Uncle Sam no citizenship problems, unless he is in conflict with our Elder Brother (Jesus Christ). Since He was crucified by the religious Establishment (Jews) and the political Establishment (Roman Empire), in what sense was Jesus patriotic?

The Politics of Numbers

The frightening thing about a hostile democratic system is that the majority rules malevolently. On the other hand, if it is not hostile, an authentic democracy can be a blessing. The truth is, Whites exercise power because they are in the majority. In specific cities and towns, African Americans also demonstrate power though this is not always the case. In reality our political power, particularly in large urban areas, is based on White flight. The reason many of our largest metropolitan cities have a majority of African descent is that Whites moved to the suburbs and took their money with them. I wonder what would happen if they moved back? Since African Americans are not as numerically strong as Whites, can there ever be justice for our people? It is said that by the year 2056 A.D. Hispanics, Asians, and African Americans will outnumber Whites. However, unless there are radical changes in terms of race relations and coalition building between these groups, the "Rainbow Coalition" of Jesse Jackson will continue to be just a dream. At this time neither of the other two groups feels any kinship to us whatsoever, because it is not in the best interest of the Establishment for smaller ethnic groups to get together.

In 1979, while vacationing in the state of Virginia and the city of Washington, D.C., my wife Pat and I had an eye-opening experience while touring Capitol Hill. Of the 100 seats in the Senate Chamber only one had been occupied by an African American since Reconstruction. Of the 435 seats in the House of Representatives less than 30 were held by African Americans. The President was White. The Vice President was White. The Speaker of the House was White. And only one African American was on the United States Supreme Court, Thurgood Marshall. It was a chilling and a sobering reality.

Politically, African Americans vote for white candidates, but whites do not vote for African Americans en masse. In some instances, coalition building involving an African American politician, e.g. Tom Bradley (Mayor of Los Angeles), David Dinkins (Mayor of New York City), and Doug Wilder (Governor of the State of Virginia) can be a blessing to all citizens involved. However, in many instances, candidates who win an election this way, end up representing the concerns of the majority community, but, on the other hand, we must become politically astute enough to realize that a politician who wins by coalition cannot represent just the concerns of our people only. But our concerns must be represented.

The Politics of Divide and Conquer

One of the chief means that the Establishment uses to control the oppressed is that of divide and conquer. Since 1619, African Americans have been a pawn on the chess board of racist American politics. We have been divided and continue to be so. In slavery this was done by the elevation of a field slave to be a house slave. Once this was done, the house slave became as big an enemy to the field slave as the master. He/she had certain privileges granted to him/her by the master that were not given to the field slave. This created a spirit of arrogance on the part of the house slave and an attitude of resentment on the part of the field slave. In other words, the house slave literally became more of a non-being than the field slave, because he/she was still an animal to the master; and he/she was less than that in the scorning eye of his/her counterpart in the field. This tactic is still used today as a means of dividing the community. Some are given "big house" status, while others are left in the field. But all are the same in the eyes of the oppressor.

Politically, terms trouble us because the connotations keep changing. It is stupid for an oppressed people to identify themselves as liberal or conservative. What does it mean in the context of disenfranchisement? In the African American community vis-a-vis the White community, a liberal is one who advocates justice without love, and a conservative is one who advocates love without justice. Neither desires for us to be liberated. While we argue over who is conservative or liberal, the Establishment remains in power. Very few African Americans would vote for Utah's Senator Orrin Hatch in a national election. Yet, most would vote for Senator Ted Kennedy of Massachusetts. The irony is that the two of them are the best of friends.

We are also divided along the lines of political parties. Since most African Americans have voted for Democrats since the election of Franklin Delano Roosevelt in 1932, any person who votes for the Republican party in 1991, is almost looked upon as a pariah. It is interesting that, historically, African Americans who had the vote after the death of Abraham Lincoln in 1865 voted for the Republican candidate until the election of F.D.R. Since 1932, to use Tony Brown's description of our situation, we have been on the "Democrat plantation." Because of this we are taken for granted. With the election of Ronald Reagan in 1980 some started leaving the "Democrat plantation" and started going over to the "Republican plantation." Strategically this was a sound move, if we continue to understand that we are still on the "plantation." However, my racial pride will not allow me to believe that those of our people who voted for Reagan were insane enough to believe that he would be a blessing to our community. In retrospect he was a bane. Syndicated columnist Carl Rowan said:

> Under voodoo economics, "fiscal conservative" Reagan had tripled the national debt, saddling each American family with an obligation of $48,000 as of 1990, transforming the United States from a creditor to a debtor nation. The annual interest on that debt equaled $2,400 for every American child... During his eight years in office Reagan made 360 lifetime appointments to the federal bench, including the appointment of three Supreme Court Justices (Sandra Day O'Conner, Antonin Scalia, and Anthony M. Kennedy), the elevation of William H. Rehnquist to Chief Justice, and the appointment of nearly half the full-time appeals court judges... The rightward shift in the courts started slowly, picked up steam as Reagan appointees filled the federal bench, and reached a high point after Reagan left office. One of the most obvious areas of its impact was civil rights.[6]

But if we are to be fair, not only must we scrutinize conservative Republicans, but Democrats as well. The label does not mean a thing; the issue is commitment to freedom. We must remember that John Adams was a Federalist; Zachary Taylor a Whig; Abraham Lincoln was a Republican; and Woodrow Wilson was a Democrat, but all believed in our inferiority. It is reputed that former Democratic Governor of Alabama George Wallace said, "There is not a dime's worth of difference between a Democrat and a Republican." Usually American politics from an African American perspective is characterized by men and women sitting around arguing about which plantation will best serve the African American community. We even have the audacity to become enemies. This is the ultimate in powerlessness. Politically we must forget partisan politics and focus on who produces for our people. For example, the late Dr. Martin Luther King, Sr., who was a friend of mine, always voted for the Republican party until then Senator John Fitzgerald Kennedy was instrumental in getting the late Dr. Martin Luther King, Jr. out of jail in Reidsville, Georgia. Because of this, in the election of 1960, Dr. King, Sr. voted for J.F.K.[7] This was a wise strategy, and it still is. There is an unconscious feeling in our community which believes that we owe the Democratic party for its effort in getting the civil rights legislation of the 1960's passed. Many Democrats also feel this way. This explains President Lyndon B. Johnson's attitude when Dr. King opposed him on the Vietnamese War. He felt that because of what he had done in the area of civil rights, Dr. King should have been grateful, and therefore should have kept his mouth shut. Incidentally, many African Americans in the civil rights movement felt the same as President Johnson. But none really understood Dr. King's prophetic genius. Even today most Americans fail to understand the man, the mind, and the message. Likewise, the phenomenon of Reverend Jesse Louis Jackson is a study in tension between the political and the prophetic. A prophet cannot be President. Reverend Jackson must inevitably decide, in spite of his charisma, that while he is an erudite social critic, there is no harmony between Establishment politics and a prophet.

This ploy of divisiveness was also used for years by the masters of apartheid in South Africa. In 1991 it was irrefutably disclosed that the government was using Chief Mangosothu Buthelezi of the Inkatha Freedom Party as a tool against the African National Congress, which was led by Nelson Mandela who had been released from prison after serving almost three decades. It is criminal that our community allowed Martin King and Malcolm X to be divided by Establishment politics. The only meeting of Malcolm and Martin took place on March 26, 1964, at the U.S. Capitol. Both were attending the Senate debate of the Civil Rights Bill. This was significant in that this meeting took place two weeks after Malcolm broke with the Nation of Islam.[8] It is also ironic that two days after the assassination of Malcolm X on February 21, 1965, he and Dr. King would have had their first sit down strategy session, two days too late!

Global Politics and the African American Community

In the past, the consensus thinking of White America has been that the African American community has nothing to do with international politics. The truth is, we are constantly drawn into international politics through war, the paying of taxes that help to keep much of the world oppressed, and through silence. Thirty million African Americans must raise their collective voices wherever injustices are found; and we must not fail to criticize African leaders who oppress their people as well as other oppressors. It is a sin that African Americans out of ignorance are guilty of supporting the selfish greed of this nation as we have ripped off much of the world, particularly the Third World nations.

> There is little doubt that the advanced capitalistic nations are using up the world's resources in order to gratify the artificially created wants of their middle-class populations. For instance, vast amounts of land in Latin American nations are being used to grow cash crops for people in the more affluent Western nations. Land that is desperately needed to grow food for Latin American people is being used to grow sugar, coffee, and tobacco for people in the United States, Western Europe, and Japan. It is more profitable to grow and sell sugar, coffee, and tobacco among the middle classes of rich countries than to produce essential food for malnourished indigenous people. And in capitalistic systems, what is most profitable is what is done.[9]

The collective church community has never brought its weight to bear upon the evils of capitalism. During the Cold War between the former Soviet Union and the United States, Communism became a propaganda tool that was used to mitigate our guilt for exploiting much of the world. The collapse of Communism in Europe is a signal to America that God is no respecter of ideologies.

America is next unless she repents. It is not the role of the church to defend America. Her role is prophetic.

Therefore, the African American kerygmatic-political community must lead the way in sensitizing our people in terms of the evils that our ignorance continues to perpetuate. No wonder Martin Luther King, Jr. was ostracized when he dared to criticize America's involvement in the War in Vietnam. In spite of the fact that thousands of African Americans were involved in that disastrous conflict and thousands were killed, America felt that nobody but the Establishment and its executors had a right to deal with international politics. We have too many people to continue to lose valuable resources to the economic-political intrigues of the Establishment. This is why the kerygmatic-political community must keep a constant dialogue going on. We must be conversant when it comes to our foreign policy as it impacts other nations. And we must require our politicians to inform us as to how our tax dollars are being used. The Christians must refuse any complicity in the future oppression of any nation in order that the Establishment may continue to control us and the world.

Since we are always expendable, particularly in wars, we demand the right to know what the war or government policy is all about. There is still a debate going after the Persian Gulf War (1990) between the American-Allied Forces and Iraq, a country of about 17 million people, as to what the war was all about. Such stupidity must end. This debate should have preceded the war. As I said in an earlier chapter, if Iraq with 17 million can fight the American-Allied forces, certainly 30 million of us ought to be able to exercise more power in the economic-political arena, beginning right now.

The Politics of Illusion

The politics of illusion serves the purpose of keeping the oppressed ever striving to be happily oppressed, and the executors of oppression moving between the polarities of covert and overt racism. The White majority, the executors of oppression, are also under the control of the Establishment, and they also live under the illusion that they are in control. Therefore, racism is an important strategy to keep African Americans and Whites fighting while both are controlled by the Establishment.

Beginning with the enactment of the United States Constitution, African Americans lived with the illusion of freedom. The Constitution made it clear that we were inferior to Whites and were therefore free to be oppressed. This era of slavery continued for 244 years, and then came the Emancipation Proclamation which was delivered by Abraham Lincoln on January 1, 1863, which really only declared free, those slaves that were in states in rebellion against the Union. The others were still slaves. Therefore, even to this day we continue to live with the lie that we were freed as a people by the Emancipation Proclamation. Around this illusion was created the myth of Abraham Lincoln as the Liberator of the Slaves. While we often speak of the ambivalence of "Father Abraham" one thing is abundantly clear; he was not a liberator of African Americans.

> The Emancipation Proclamation was not an Emancipation Proclamation at all. The document was drafted in such a way that it freed few, if any slaves. It did not apply to slaves in the Border States and areas under Federal Control in the South. In other words, Lincoln "freed" slaves where he had no power and left them in chains where he had power. The theory behind the proclamation, an English paper noted, "is not that a human being can't own another, but that he cannot own him unless he is loyal to the United States."[10]

The real attitude of Abraham Lincoln is shown by his pre-Emancipation behavior. Lincoln, beyond a doubt, wanted to get rid of the slaves by sending them to South America or Africa.

> On August 14, 1862, he called a hand-picked group of black men to the White House and proposed a black exodus. Lincoln told the black men that it was their

> duty to leave America. "You and we," he said, "are different races. We have between us a broader difference than exists between almost any other two races. Whether it is right or wrong I need not discuss, but this physical difference is a great disadvantage to us both, as I think your race suffers very greatly, many of them by living among us, while ours suffers from your presence."[11]

Even on the brink of his assassination on April 14, 1865-actually he was shot on April 14th and died on April 15th-Lincoln was still trying to resettle the slaves.

> It seems that Lincoln never reconciled himself to the implications of emancipation. Shortly before his death, Lincoln summoned General Benjamin F. Butler to inquire about the possibilities of "sending the blacks away." According to Butler, he said, "I wish you would examine the question and give me your views upon it and go into figures as you did before in some degree as to show whether the Negroes can be exported." Butler went away and came back two days later with a sad story. "Mr. President," he said, "I have gone very carefully over my calculation as to the power of the country to export the Negroes of the South and I assure you that, using all your naval vessels and all the merchant marine fit to cross the seas with safety, it will be impossible for you to transport to the nearest place fit for them... half as fast as Negro children will be born here."[12]

This theme of recolonization would be picked up once again but this time in the twentieth century by Marcus Garvey, an African of Jamaican descent. Garvey's movement also failed, whether by logistics or sabotaging, but it still raises the question as to whether Whites and African Americans en masse will ever get along. But why was Lincoln so ambivalent? Some say it was because of his own Negroidal ancestry as well as that of his Vice President, Hannibal Hamlin, Senator from the State of Maine.[13]

> Lincoln was said to be the illegitimate son of a Negro by Nancy Hanks. In his campaign for the Presidency he was often referred to as a Negro by his opponents. He was even depicted as a Negro. He was called Abraham Africanus The First. What gave strength to this was that his hair was more Negroid than Caucasian. So was his color. Of his father, he said, "his face was round, his complexion swarthy, hair, black and coarse, eyes brown." Of himself, "of dark complexion with coarse black hair and dark eyes." William Herndon, his closest friend and law partner, said he had "very dark skin."[14]

Can we believe this as historically true? Interestingly someone has said that "history is a set of lies agreed upon." Whether it is true or not, White America's history of miscegenation is a fact. But it raises again the question of what makes a White person white and a Black person black. Was Ralph Bunche an African American, or was he White? Was Walter White, former Assistant Secretary of the N.A.A.C.P., White, or was he an African American? Both of them were as white as George Bush, yet they are called African Americans. So what the ruling majority says is what determines one's race. Therefore, Abraham Lincoln was White because White power says he was. If he was of African descent, we should not be proud because he would have been the father of ethnic treason. Yet the illusion has continued in many quarters since 1865. And many African Americans helped to perpetuate the myth. "Lincoln's assassination and the aggressive dissemination of the 'Massa Linkun myth' pushed the real Lincoln with his real limitations into the background. And black people were soon pooling their pennies to erect a monument to the mythical emancipator."[15] When on April 14, 1876, this monument was unveiled, with President U.S. Grant and other high officials in attendance, Frederick Douglass punctured the myths and looked frankly at the man and said:

> Truth is proper and beautiful at all times and in all places, and it is never more proper and beautiful in any case than when speaking of a great public man whose example is likely to be commended for honor and imitation long after his departure to the solemn shades, the silent continent of eternity. It must be admitted, truth compels me to admit, even here in the presence of the monument we have erected to his memory, Abraham Lincoln was not, in the fullest sense of the word, either our man or our model. In his interests, in his associations, in his habits, in his thought, and in his prejudices, he was a White man. He was pre-eminently the White man's President, entirely devoted to the welfare of White men...In all his education and feeling he was an American of the Americans.[16]

The whole affair of the post-Lincoln era as well as the pre-Lincoln era has been one giant illusion for African Americans, beginning with the Thirteenth Amendment that abolished slavery, the Fourteenth Amendment which made the former slaves citizens of the United States, and the Fifteenth Amendment which gave former slaves the right to vote. Then along came the grand illusion of all, which was Reconstruction between 1867-1877. Lest we forget, Plessy vs Ferguson of 1896, which advocated the doctrine of separate but equal, was also an illusion. The point is, when the Establishment is in control, legislation does not mean very much because they who have the power to make the laws can change them again. This was seen in the Presidency of Ronald Reagan. This administration made a frontal assault upon much of the Civil Rights gains of the 1960's. His administration was a reincarnation of the Presidency of Rutherford B. Hayes, the 19th President of the United States. Carl Rowan said:

> My worst political fears began in 1980 when Ronald Wilson Reagan assumed the presidency. Here was a man with great acting skills with which to cover up his ignorance about vital issues; a man who was so

> lacking in meaningful contact with black or poor people or women who had to work for a living, that no scheme to reward the rich and punish the poor provoked objections from his conscience.[17]

Again Rowan said:

> Reagan had said in the autumn of 1965 that he favored the Civil Rights Act of 1964, but eight months later he declared that he would have voted against this "bad piece of legislation." He opposed the 1965 Voting Rights Act, arguing that it was "humiliating to the South." After California's legislature passed the Rumford Act, which prohibited owners from offering property for sale or rent and then withdrawing it for racial or religious reasons, Reagan wanted to repeal this law. He once said to blacks that the Rumford Act was a "form of fascism," asking the blacks: "You wouldn't want to sell your house to a redheaded Kiwanian if you didn't want to, would you?" In 1967 Reagan opposed the federal fair housing law that was passed in 1968. I remember how, in 1966, Reagan used his radio program to fan the flames of white fear and hatred over black demonstrations and violence in the streets. In one of those programs he said: "Every day the jungle draws a little closer...Our city streets are jungle paths after dark, with more crimes of violence." Even in those days Reagan had a reputation for talking without the facts.[18]

It is one of the greatest moral failures of American Christianity that the Conservative White Church saw Ronald Reagan as a savior who would take America back to the halcyon days when the Founding Fathers were men of moral rectitude.

This political illusion was demonstrated in the two visions of Martin Luther King, Jr. and Malcolm X. Dr. King had a "dream," and

Malcolm X had a "nightmare." Dr. King said on August 28, 1963, in the March on Washington:

> I have a dream that one day this nation will rise up and live out the true meaning of its creed, "We hold these truths to be self-evident, that all men are created equal." I have a dream that one day...sons of former slaves and sons of former slave owners will be able to sit down together at the table of brotherhood...This is our hope... With this faith we will be able to work together, to pray together, to struggle together, to go to jail together, to stand up for freedom together, knowing that we will be free one day...This will be the day when all God's children will be able to sing with new meaning, "My country 'tis of thee, sweet land of liberty, of thee I sing."[19]

On the other hand, Malcolm X said on April 3, 1964, while speaking at Cory Methodist Church in Cleveland, Ohio:

> No, I am not an American. I am one of the 22 million black people who are victims of Americanism. One of the...victims of democracy, nothing but disguised hypocrisy. So, I am not standing here speaking to you as an American, or a patriot, or a flag-saluter, or a flag-waver, no, not I. I am speaking as a victim of this American system. And I see America through the eyes of the victim. I don't see any American dream; I see an American nightmare.[20]

And the dream remains alongside a seeming never-ending nightmare. In 1991 many young African Americans were choosing Malcolm instead of Martin as a symbol of liberation. This is just as ludicrous as those who chose Martin instead of Malcolm. Truth is never found in extremes. It is to be discovered in the center. Those who choose between the two play right into the hands of the oppressor. The fact of the matter is that usually our choosing merely underscores our ignorance of both of their philosophies and their tactical evolutionary changes. For African Americans it must be Martin and Malcolm, rather than Martin or Malcolm.

Politics At The Grassroot Level

African Americans must become politically astute or continue to perish at the hands of White politicians. And if we are going to continue to remain in this country we must know how the game is played. And those who favor an emerging nationalism will have to decide their level of political involvement.

In America, in general there is a great deal of political apathy. People by and large are basically cynical about the political institution. Very few even bother to vote. This lethargy is also quite apparent in the African American community. Some of the reasons are as follows:

1. The attitude which says, "It does not matter. Whites have the power, and they will always do those things which will keep them in power."

2. A deep sense of worthlessness.

3. A psychopathic notion that if Whites get the bread, that some has to trickle down to the African American community. This is the same nonsense that Ronald Reagan embraced. A rising tide usually raises all boats, but we have discovered that the American tide is prejudiced. Usually the White boats are lifted while our boats are left to flounder in the shallow waters of defeatism.

4. Many African Americans feel they have it made because they have a few of the social accoutrements such as cars, large houses in a White neighborhood, and solid financial investments. Therefore, they do not need to vote.

5. Many do not vote because of the disillusionment with partisan politics. While living in the city of Louisville, a radio talk show host asked a man who he was going to vote for, Ronald Reagan or Jimmy Carter, to which he replied, "Neither. If God wanted me to vote, He would have given us a candidate."

6. Many do not vote because of the retrogressive propensity of American politics in regard to African Americans. What Uncle Sam gives today, he takes away tomorrow.

Bruce Wright said:

> If blacks are ever to have more than symbolic recognition, black voters must express the power of their numbers. Persuading black voters to exercise the ballot has thus far been a lost cause in New York, as elsewhere other than the South, since the 1960's. When asked why he is reluctant to vote, the black man in the street will generally say that it only helps the so-called middle-class blacks to get token positions after which they move out of the ghetto and forget who helped them realize their ambitions. Consequently, tokenism will continue to be the rule.[21]

What are some practical principles that will help us to deal with the political institution?

1. Theologically we must come to grips with a holistic Gospel. While the Gospel is personal and social, it is not a dichotomy.

2. Through our churches, mosques, fraternities, and sororities we must make sure that every eligible person in our communities is registered to vote.

3. We must maintain or begin Political Awareness Committees which will serve as watchdogs for the political scene.

4. We must create political science departments in our religio-social organizations. The purpose of such a move is the education of our people in regard to the science of politics. It is a sad affair when people are encouraged to vote without knowing the intricacies and strategies of partisan politics. Our strategy must be to educate, registrate, and participate.

5. We must be astute enough to set an agenda for the wants and needs of the African American community. Ofttimes we argue about what we are not getting, but we have voted without demanding anything of our politicians.

6. We must interview political candidates before voting in order to discover how they stand on the issues and how our community will be impacted.

7. We must keep political report cards. If a candidate has not lived up to his/her commitment to our community, he/she will flunk and will not receive our vote next time. On the other hand, if the candidate has responded well, he/she will be supported.

8. We must overcome the ignorant habit of voting for the Democratic party without questioning the impact it will have on our community. We must have African Americans on both plantations.

9. We must master the art of local politics, because it is here that we can make a true difference.

10. We must reexamine the need for multiple organizations in our community such as: the N.A.A.C.P., the Urban League, S.C.L.C., et al. If there is a need for all of them, then we need to be able to convey to the community how each one fulfills its task of helping to liberate our people. And we, in turn, must give liberal financial support.

References - Chapter Seven

[1] Pat Robertson, The New World Order, Word Publishing Co., Dallas, Texas, 1991, 95.
[2] Ibid., 96.
[3] Ibid.
[4] Ibid.
[5] Anthony Campolo, We Have Met The Enemy and They Are Partly Right, Word Books, Waco, Texas, 1985, 156-157.
[6] Carl T. Rowan, Breaking Barriers: A Memoir, Little, Brown and Company, Boston, 1991, 327-328.
[7] Taylor Branch, Parting the Waters, America in the King Years 1954-63, New York, 1988, 369-370.
[8] James Cone, Martin and Malcolm and America: A Dream Or A Nightmare, Orbis Press, Maryknoll, New York, 1991 (pictures).
[9] Anthony Campolo, We Have Met the Enemy, And They Are Partly Right, Word Book Publishers, Waco, Texas, 1985, 163.
[10] Lerone Bennett, The Challenge of Blackness, Johnson Publishing Co., Chicago, Illinois, 1972, 171.
[11] Ibid., 167.
[12] Ibid., 174.
[13] J.A. Rogers, The Five Negro Presidents, U.S.A. MacMillan Company, Riverside, New Jersey, 1965, 8-11.
[14] Ibid., 8.
[15] Bennett, 174.
[16] Ibid., 174-175.
[17] Rowan, 309.
[18] Ibid., 309-310.
[19] Cone, Martin and Malcolm: A Dream or a Nightmare, 1.
[20] Ibid.
[21] Bruce Wright, Black Robes, White Justice, Carol Publishing Co., New York, 1987, 80.

Chapter Eight

Challenges Facing The African American Church In the Twenty- First Century

To Provide An Alternative Consciousness

How long will African Americans continue to sing "We Shall Overcome"? And what is it that we hope to overcome? Are we trying to be White? Or are we hoping to be accepted by Whites? How long will we continue to believe in the American Dream? In the year 2050 A.D. will the socioeconomic situation of our people be different? Is our ordeal almost over? Or is ours a longer captivity?

In light of these questions, what must be the role of the African American church? First of all the African American church must disengage itself from pursuing a deeper enslavement called the American Way of Life. We must be about developing our own people. As a church, we must no longer take our theological-kerygmatic cue from the White church, because the White church, by and large, is an instrument of the Establishment, which is synonymous with the "principalities and powers" that the Apostle Paul talks about in Ephesians 6:12. Therefore, we must not be overwhelmed by the numerical, academic, or the economic strength of the White church, because it is a colleague in oppression.

The African American church basically has three choices: (1)to continue to be the bastard offspring of a racist ecclesiastical system, (2)to become primarily a social organization that seeks the same things that Caesar has, without providing the moral restraints to keep us from becoming like him, (3)to become an alternative consciousness. For this term I am indebted to Old Testament Scholar, Walter Brueggemann. He said:

> The task of prophetic ministry is to nurture, nourish, and evoke a consciousness and perception alternative to the consciousness and perception of the dominant culture around us...The alternative consciousness to be nurtured, on the one hand, serves to criticize in dismantling the dominant consciousness. To that extent, it attempts to do what the liberal tendency has done, engage in a rejection and delegitimatizing of the present ordering of things. On the other hand, that alternative consciousness to be nurtured serves to energize persons and communities by its promise of another time and situation toward which the community of faith may move.[1]

For the church to become an alternative community is to invite danger and depression, because the model for our countercultural character will be based upon the biblical Christ. To take the biblical Christ seriously in regard to speaking and practicing truth, will get one killed in any nation. The only reason the church has not been persecuted in America, is that the church is a vanguard of culture, a protector, and a promoter of institutional racism. This is the price the White church pays in order to be left alone. Yet, I am the first to admit that the African American church, as well as the White church, will reject its task of being the alternative community. It is hard to be like Jesus of Nazareth when I am busy trying to be White!

Therefore, I believe that while individual African Americans may continue to pursue the American Dream of success, the African American church must take the path of creative servanthood, where our ultimate loyalty is to Jesus of Nazareth.

To take such a position automatically puts the church in an anti-Establishment position. This will in turn bring persecution. One of the greatest flim-flams in church history was the supposed conversion of Constantine, the Emperor of Rome, to the Christian faith in 312 A.D. The truth of the matter is, it was the church that was converted. Instead of the church remaining as the possession of Christ, it became the possession of the state.

> Constantine's adoption of Christianity was more of a political than a religious decision. The Roman Empire was fast declining. Its greatest need was a strong, internal unity that could both engender loyalty within and beat off attacks from without. . . It is hardly conceivable that Constantine really became a Christian. His considerable crimes, including murder, long after his alleged vision, could hardly have been the acts of a Christian. Thinking that baptism washed away sins, he delayed receiving this rite until he was at the point of death.[2]

The church does not need the protection of the empire at the expense of watering down its message. Because this has generally been the policy of the White church historically, the African American church must reclaim the suffering motif which is at the heart of biblical faith. It was the great African theologian, Tertullian from Carthage in North Africa, who said, "The blood of the martyrs is the seed of the church." In retrospect the church today is conspicuous because of the absence of blood. A skeptical world wonders how the Apostle Paul and Martin Luther King, Jr. got killed, and Billy Graham has a star in Hollywood's "Walk of Fame." This is not the Carpenter's faith. It is Establishment religion, pure and simple.

The church as alternative consciousness is not a world-denying movement, nor is it a move towards monasticism. It is about the church being in the world, but not of the world. It is about being completely loyal to Christ, rather than culture and the Establishment.

This alternative consciousness is what the Exodus experience was all about in Hebrew tradition.

> The radical break of Moses and Israel from imperial reality is a two-dimensional break from both the religion of static triumphalism and the politics of oppression and exploitation. Moses dismantled the religion of static-triumphalism by exposing the gods and showing that in fact they had no power and were not gods... In place of the gods of Egypt, creatures of the imperial consciousness, Moses discloses Yahweh the sovereign, one who acts in His lordly freedom, is extrapolated from no social reality, and is captive to no social perception, but who acts from His own person toward His own purposes.[3]

We must not kid ourselves. Most African Americans want a piece of the empire and are lured by the fatal stability that it offers. Therefore, this group will have to be converted unless more of them become neo-conservatives in support of the empire's evil system. However, the church must be converted first because it is also mesmerized by the offerings of the empire. Therefore, the countercultural message must be proclaimed, taught, and pragmatized before it can be sold in the marketplace. What the church will be offering will be the opposite of what the empire (America) offers.

> Moses dismantles the politics of oppression and exploitation by countering it with a politics of justice and compassion. The reality emerging out of the Exodus is not just a new religion or a new religious idea or a vision of freedom but the emergence of a new social community in history, a community that has historical body, that had to devise laws, patterns of governance and order, norms of right and wrong, and sanctions of accountability. The participants in the Exodus found themselves, undoubtedly surprising to them, involved in the intentional formation of a new social community to match the vision of God's freedom. That new social reality, which is utterly discontinuous with Egypt, lasted in its alternative way for 250 years.[4]

Again Brueggemann says:

> The program of Moses is not the freeing of a little band of slaves as an escape from the empire, though that is important enough, especially if you happen to be in the little band. Rather his work is nothing less than an assault on the consciousness of the empire, aimed at nothing less than the dismantling of the empire both in its social practices and in its mythic pretensions. Israel emerged not by Moses' hand, although not without Moses' hand, as a genuine alternative community.[5]

While we clamor for our places at Pharaoh's table through various judicial and legislative means, maybe the answer for us is a movement outside the palace, which confronts the empire in regard to oppression and ultimately brings the empire down. Such a movement was concretized by Moses and Aaron in Exodus 5:1. In regard to freedom, the choice is not about two kinds of freedoms, but about slavery and freedom. Anthropocentric (man-centered) freedom is really enslavement. And theocentric freedom (God-centered) is the only kind that brings authentic liberation. However, I am not naive enough to believe that the African American church en masse will take this, the only path to freedom, seriously. Only a remnant will accept and demonstrate freedom. Someone asked, "What about Whites who want to be free of the empire?" To the question I reply, "As I stated in an earlier chapter, the issue is not pigmentation; it is about identification. If Whites join, they cease to be White (oppressor, empire). And if a remnant from the camps of the oppressed and the oppressor comes together, no longer looking to the empire for solutions, then maybe we will have what Moses had, a mixed multitude (Exodus 12:38). This is also symbolic of what the Church is as the Body of Christ (Soma Christos)." This movement will be a rainbow coalition of all converted oppressed and converted oppressors, that will no longer define themselves by what Pharaoh has. But it will continue to speak prophetically against the evils of oppression and economic exploitation, which are an intrinsic part of empire politics. It will advocate a new lifestyle both privately and publicly based on the freedom in Christ Jesus, our liberator.

> Moses and Aaron now know that serious intervention and intercession must be made to Yahweh the God of freedom and not to the no-gods of Egypt. In Exodus 5:8 and 15 there is still a cry to Pharaoh, still a looking to the empire for help and relief: "Therefore they cry, let us go and offer sacrifice to our God . . . Then the foremen of the people of Israel came and cried to Pharaoh..." By the middle of the plague cycle Israel had disengaged from the empire, cried no more to it, expected nothing of it, acknowledged it in no way, knows it could not keep its promises, and knew that nothing is either owed it or expected of it. That is the ultimate criticism which leads to dismantling.[6]

When the African American church ceases to be the frustrated derivative of White American Christianity, then we will be free to be the beneficiaries of God's freedom which was incarnate in Jesus of Nazareth.

> Thus the history of Israel begins on the day when its people no longer address the Egyptian gods who will not listen and cannot answer. The life of freedom and justice comes when they risk the freedom of the free God against the regime.[7]

To me the choice is between perpetual frustration or freedom which is both imminent and eternal.

To Support Education

In the African American church we must overcome our "letter versus the spirit" mentality. This unnecessary schism grows out of a fallacious exegesis of Second Corinthians 3:6 which says, "who has also made us able ministers of the New Testament; not of the letter, but of the spirit: for the letter kills, but the spirit gives life."

This passage does not argue for ignorance over intelligence. It is referring to the minutiae of the law which finds its fulfillment in Christ, as the ultimate in life, freedom, and liberation. So such shoddy interpretation is a great argument for the importance of education. Since we have discussed public education in Chapter Five, we will not discuss it in detail again.

However, the African American church must lead the way in encouraging and giving public support to our schools. Each pastor has the responsibility to mobilize his/her membership in regard to taking action against the intellectual crucifixion that is taking place in our schools. Desegregation has hurt African Americans tremendously, and its deleterious impact will really come to fruition in the 21st century. I declare we must take another look at being educated in Pharaoh's public schools. The curriculum does not encourage thinking or liberation. Once I get my education, I am trained to work for him. While Moses may be captured by the Zeitgeist, there is a dangerous group of neo-conservatives in the community of the oppressed who believe that what Pharaoh has to offer is far superior to any exodus-wilderness education.

> *And all the congregation lifted up their voice, and cried; and the people wept that night. And all the children of Israel murmured against Moses and against Aaron And the whole congregation said unto them, would God that we had died in the land of Egypt! Or would God we had died in the wilderness! And wherefore has the Lord brought us into this land, to fall by the sword, that our wives and our children should be a prey? Were it not better for us to return into Egypt? And they said one to another, let us make a captain, and let us return into Egypt. Then Moses and Aaron fell on their faces before all the assembly, of the congregation of the children of Israel.*[8]

Even though the people rebel against Moses and Aaron, Moses, who is imbued with an education for certification - liberation, is the only qualified leader in the community of the oppressed. Those who wanted to go back to Egypt were defying the alternative consciousness of Yahweh. The limited certification training that they had received only served to enhance their feelings of serfdom. The only way they could receive liberation training was through the alternative community. This will be the role of the African American church in the twenty-first century. Whether the church supports private or public education, the fact is, she must fill in the gaps. All agree that education in America lags behind some of the other leading countries in the world. However, I will support private education only if we can keep up with the megatrends in education, have superior faculty and monies enough to pay quality salaries, have parental participation, and have a disciplined student body. Otherwise, it is a costly and frustrating exercise in futility.

Beyond public education, the African American church must be involved in supporting our Black colleges. It is a crime that Bishop College in Dallas, Texas, for all practical purposes, folded in 1988, while the National Baptist Convention U.S.A. Inc. (with 8 million members) was holding its annual session in Dallas in September 1988. While this group was meeting in Dallas, the National Baptist Convention of America was meeting in Fort Worth, Texas. This group has approximately 4 million members and it suffered a split during its session, and another convention was formed. So while two conventions representing above 33% of all African Americans in this country were meeting within 25 miles of each other, a college folded, and another schism occurred, and maybe 60 to 70 million dollars was left in the local economy. We must hurry and overcome this sadistic insanity. In the earlier years our foreparents with meager resources and little education built schools of higher learning and our generation cannot foster enough resources to keep them repaired. According to Carter G. Woodson, in the post Civil-War years the attitudes of the freed slaves in regard to education were radically different from our day:

> The Baptists established Shaw University at Raleigh in 1865; Roger Williams at Nashville and Morehouse at Atlanta in 1867; Leland at New Orleans and Benedict at Columbia in 1871. The Freewill Baptists

> founded Storer College at Harper's Ferry in 1867. The Methodists, who were no less active, established Walden at Nashville in 1865, Rust in Holly Springs in 1866, Morgan at Baltimore in 1867, Haven Academy at Waynesboro in 1868, Claflin at Orangeburg in 1869, and Clark in Atlanta in 1870. The Presbyterians who could not compete with the Baptists and Methodists in proselytizing Negroes, largely restricted their efforts to the establishment of Biddle at Charlotte in 1867 and to the promotion of the work begun at Lincoln University in Pennsylvania in 1854. The Episcopal Church established Saint Augustine at Raleigh in 1867...et al.[9]

These are just a few of the colleges and universities which were established by the African American church in the past. The Church, then, must continue to carry the torch for education through certification (Eurocentrism) and liberation (Afrocentrism). Not only must we continue to support our Black Colleges with students and monies, African Americans must endow their colleges. We could take the 20 billion dollars that we spend on drugs and have an endowment for all our colleges which would free them from White control, and free them to form a partnership with the church in liberating our people. Many of our Black Colleges are controlled by Whites. Many of them were founded by Whites for the purpose of controlling the minds of our people. In this they have been most successful. When one White person can write a check for one million dollars, and one million African American Church persons won't give $100,000, our extinction draweth nigh. All African Americans must support the United Negro College Fund of which former Congressman William H. Gray, III is the chairman. Dr. Gray who is also the pastor of Bright Hope Baptist Church in Philadelphia, Pennsylvania has a long history in the field of education. His father the late Dr. William H. Gray, II was the former president of Florida Memorial College and Florida A & M University. While his father was president of Florida Memorial, my mother-in-law who was a student at that time, was also former Congressman William H. Gray's babysitter. From the lap of a great woman leaped a great man. In the twenty-first century we must come up with an agenda whereby the ecclesiastical and the academic communities will be wedded, in order that we might become an alternative social reality in the face of the recalcitrance of Pharaoh's palace.

Beyond our colleges we must support theological education. As of this writing we have only three fully accredited theological institutions. They are Howard University Divinity School in Washington, D.C.; the Interdenominational Theological Center in Atlanta, Georgia; and Virginia Union University School of Religion in Richmond, Virginia. The pitiful plight is not that we have only three, but that not one is fully supported across the board by the African American churches. It is ironic that parents who would send their children to the best institution of higher learning in this country could care less about theological education. And I do not see this attitude changing as we go into the twenty-first century.

The standards for the clergy will not be high if we do not value theological education. The church still operates under the notion that if one opens his or her mouth, even without preparation, God will speak for that person. Empty heads and open mouths are dangerous. In spite of our oral-dialogical approach to preaching, we must be able to give substance to our ecstasy. There is no authentic inspiration without information. In the twenty-first century every pastor and staff person should have no less than an accredited undergraduate degree and a Master's degree in theology from an accredited seminary. A good policy would be to grant a temporary license to practice ministry after one enrolls in college and a permanent license upon graduation. Ordination would come either while one is enrolled in seminary or preferably after one finishes seminary. No longer must light be dismissed from our hallowed assemblies while darkness is exalted. We must overcome our romance with ignorance.

A consecrated heart and an educated head are a powerful combination.

> If we were asked to make a single policy recommendation that we consider critical for the future of black churches, it would be the need for more, better-trained, and better-educated black clergy. Although this need has been raised before by Woodson, Mays and Nicholson, and countless other denominational leaders, seminary presidents, and professors, there is but meager evidence that it has been taken seriously by the Black Church as a whole... The ministry of the Black Church is the only profession where one out of every four or five practitioners has graduated from professional school. Professional education could help enhance the skills and effectiveness of black clergy not only in the areas of spiritual nurture, theological understanding, biblical interpretation, preaching, and counseling, but also in financial accountability and economic development, record keeping, and political awareness and moral responsibility.[10]

Since freedom is a derivative of truth, we must learn to practice the same. We must be honest enough to admit that our theological education, as well as our secular education, has been Eurocentric and therefore oppressive. We have drunk from the fountains of Aquinas, Schleiermacher, Ritschl, Harnack, Barth, Brunner, the Niebuhrs, Rauschenbusch, Moltmann, Bultmann, and Tillich, only to reject our African American theologians such as James Cone, J. Deotis Roberts, C. Eric Lincoln, Clarice Martin, Renita Weems, Jacquelyn Grant, Gayraud Wilmore, et al. However, in spite of the theological education that we have received in Pharaoh's divinity school, we must make it lose its oppressive power by correcting it with the liberation theology that can be found only in the brickyard.

A trained clergy should mean that the pew is trained "to do the work of ministry" as it proclaims a gospel of liberation. However, the sad plight of our churches is that ofttimes there is no markable difference in terms of biblical knowledge between a church with a trained pastor and a church whose pastor is not trained. Our people simply do not know the content of their faith. The church is the only organization that one can join dumb, work in it dumb , and die dumb. The saints traditionally have been classified as the "glorified illiterates." This can be attributed to several things: (1) an oral tradition that is anti-intellectual, (2) a confusion in regard to what preaching is and what teaching is, (3) a satanic attraction to ignorance, (4) low expectations and standards for church membership. In all of our churches a simple Bible quiz would be flunked by an overwhelming majority of our parishioners. This was underscored in James Smart's book entitled <u>The Strange Silence Of The Bible In The Church.</u> Even if the pastor is trained he/she is guaranteed to have officers who know absolutely nothing about the content of their faith. The sad part is that most leaders in our congregations view the church as a sanctified extension of his/her fraternity or sorority. This crowd will never grasp the meaning of alternative consciousness.

Personally, I believe in pre-membership and pre-baptismal training. In the early church the gospel was initially preached to the Jewish community. However, as the gospel moved out into the Greco-Roman world, paganism started infiltrating the church. So there was a move towards pre-membership training through the catechetical schools. In some schools this training lasted from three to six years. One such school was founded by an African by the name of Pantaenus. This catechetical school which was located in Alexandria, Egypt was a great center for Christian scholarship.[11] In the Great Commission in Matthew 28:19-20, Jesus underscores the need for discipline prior to baptism; then after baptizing them He insists that we must keep on teaching them. And all of this discipline had to do with teaching one to buy into an alternative consciousness in order that he/she could make disciples to the same. Unless the church proclaims a costly discipleship, we will be well-organized clubs without power. Our church in Fort Lauderdale, the Mount Olive Baptist Church, has a pre-membership catechetical program, which has been, and is, a tremendous blessing to the thousands in our congregation. I recommend this kind of training if we are going to have integrity in our memberships. On this one, we must go back to the example that was set by the early church.

> Catechetical instruction basically centered around ethics, and Christian doctrine. The post-apostolic church was interested in a balance between right belief and right conduct. J.G. Davies says: "The ethical teaching common to many of the New Testament epistles derived from an early pattern of catechetical teaching. . . Not only was the church interested in ethical conduct, it was also interested in intellectual comprehension."[12]

To Mobilize the Laity

If the African American Church is going to lead the way in the transformation of our people in the twenty-first century, we must equip and empower the laity. Findley B. Edge said:

> One of the major attacks of the Reformation was centered at the point of recapturing the ministry of the laity. . . In the churches today the laity in the main has the attitude that the primary responsibility for ministry rests in the hands of the clergy. The layman feels that he should support the ministry and the church with his money, by attending the services, and by doing some work, primarily for and in the church. Still the layman feels that the major responsibility for carrying out the ministry of God in the world rests with the clergy. . . The sharp distinction that exists today in the churches between the clergy and the laity finds no basis in the New Testament.[13]

We must recapture the power of the laity in order that they will become equipped to propagate this alternative consciousness which is the Kingdom of God. The pastor must be removed from his/her perch of ineffectiveness, by allowing him/her time to equip the saints, who are supposed to get the job done. One of the reasons the trained pastor does not teach his congregation effectively, is that he/she is being burned out doing things that the congregation ought to be doing.

While the theology of the Jehovah's Witnesses is considered heretical to many mainline Christians, their methodology in mobilizing the laity is correct. The action is not in the pulpit, except as it trains. The action is in the pew, where those who are being trained will go forth with a gospel of transformation. Everybody heads for the pulpit, but no one should go up there until he/she has been trained to "equip the saints." Otherwise, he/she should remain in the pew in order to be trained to be on the firing line for Christ. In a technical sense Jesus and His disciples were laymen rather than professional clerics. So let us get our example from the Carpenter.

To Overcome Our Frustrations Which Lead To Schisms

As African Americans become more and more disenfranchised, the church will have to help us to overcome our socioeconomic, political, and sexual frustrations. As Dr. James Washington said in his book, we are "A Frustrated Fellowship." African Americans are angry with the oppressor. However, the anger is expressed in our community. We often hear that African Americans really love Whites, but it is not so much that we love Whites, it is that we hate ourselves. The frustration of our people will be expressed in the home, the school, the streets, or in the church. Unless there is a radical change in the socioeconomic conditions of our people, even the church will not be a safe haven. As the frustration level increases, much of our inner strife will be directed towards the pastor upon whom we will transfer our hostility. In the twenty-first century the pastor will be challenged more than ever in the area of authority. I predict that pastorates will be shorter in duration. The pressure will be too great. Churches will be investing more and more in security not only for church funds but for pastors as well.

On this same issue the church must find ways to free its pastor from having to deal with pettiness and marginal issues. He/she who is trained in the alternative consciousness must spend his/her time preparing our people for freedom.

Again freedom-liberation will be defined as the antithesis of Pharaoh's Palace. Pharaoh is not going to give up the Palace without a fight. Those who crave the benefits of being with Pharaoh are the frustrated ones. It is interesting that Moses did not stir up the folk in the brickyard to overthrow the government of Egypt. They wanted out, pure and simple. To make such a choice in America is to go a long way towards our liberation. Granted, there are frustrations to be experienced in the wilderness, but if our alternative consciousness is maintained, we shall be free. If not, we will continue to be oppressed.

All of our anger ought not be wasted on Whites, and especially not on ourselves. Our anger and our frustrations are to be sublimated in helping us to become another social reality where Christ becomes our Liberator, rather than Uncle Sam. In spite of the efforts of Abraham Lincoln and Marcus Garvey, our people en masse are not going to return to Africa except to visit. Therefore, the challenge is to remain in Egypt physically, but not spiritually. We must be in Egypt, but not of Egypt.

To Protest and To Produce

The role of the African American Church in the twenty- first century will be to continue to sound the trumpet against the Establishment that oppresses our people. Moses ceased in his protestation against Egypt once the Exodus took place (Exodus 12:50-51). But since most African Americans at this time do not have emigration on their minds, we then will continue to confront this evil empire. The church must continue to sound the alarm that all is not well. Not only must we speak against the evils that are ever present in our community, but we must broaden our scope in speaking and acting against evils done to any oppressed people anywhere on the planet.

However, we cannot be the alternative consciousness that our people so desperately need if we can bring only heat but no light to our situation. In one of his addresses delivered before the National Baptist Convention U.S.A., Inc., the late President Dr. Joseph Harrison Jackson told us that we must move from "protest to productivity." In spite of his enormous gift for preaching, many considered him an arch-conservative. The truth of the matter is, the only way we can move from protest is to move from America. Since we are staying, we must protest and produce. It is healthy to blame the empire. It is unhealthy when that becomes our daily bread. The twenty-first century will be a make or break century for our people. As I stated in Chapter Six, we must overcome our sensate spending habits with other people and must instead focus on ownership of businesses, banks, and properties, etc., in our communities.

To Blend the Priestly And The Prophetic

It is often said that the White church is priestly, and that the African American church is prophetic. The White church primarily supports the status quo, while the African American church speaks against the status quo. The White church is like Amaziah, the priest of Bethel (Amos 7:10-13), and the African American church is like the prophet Amos (Amos 7:14-17). But in dealing with this issue, we do not have to be either/or, because in Jesus of Nazareth the priestly and the prophetic blend, for He is Prophet, Priest, and King. So the church does not choose one above another to the exclusion of the other. Both are indispensable in the authentic church. Not only must the African American church speak against what is wrong in "Bethel", but it must also speak against the evils done where "the sycamore fruit is gathered" (Amos 7:14-15).

In our priestly function, we must be public defenders for the disenfranchised, the dispossessed, and the disinherited. We must have compassion for homosexuals, AIDS patients, the homeless, drug addicts, alcoholics, cigarette addicts, those who suffer as a result of sexism, unwed mothers and fathers, et al. By compassion, I do not mean any condescending air of superiority, but genuine concern and helpfulness to the best of our abilities. The best definition of compassion that I ever heard was from the lips of pop singer, Gladys Knight, in her hit song, "Love Overboard." That's what Jesus meant by compassion, love overboard. Only as the church moves from maintenance to missions can this be realized. To carry out this function of ministry is both costly and risky. In Jesus' parable of the Good Samaritan (Luke 10:30-37) this hated half-breed risked: his time; being rejected by the victim of the crime, who could have said, "Nigger, leave me alone"; being rejected by his own people if they found out that he had helped a "honkey"; being beaten up by the Jews if they caught him; his reputation; being killed by the man who had been robbed — suppose the victim was only faking it? Once the Jew got well, he might not have been grateful. The story is told of a White man who had been rescued from a car crash by an African American. When he finally came out of his coma he wanted to meet the man who had saved his life. The doctor, knowing that he had been saved by an African American, tried to put him off, but to no avail. Finally, the man who had saved his life showed up, and the White man said, "I wish I had died"; [and finally he risked his resources]. Such is the task of the church. The church must stop hoarding monies that ought be used for helping humanity. In our priestly function we must not only give water, food, clothing, shelter, and visit the incarcerated, but we must minister to the point where the naked can buy his/her own clothes, etc. In our prophetic function, we must not only speak against the evils done to us by others, but we must also rail against those things done to us, by us. We must give water to the thirsty, but we must put them in position to get their own water. We must visit the prisoner, but we must proclaim the liberating power of the alternative consciousness which keeps our people out of prison. Not only must we love the homosexual, AIDS patient, et al., but we must proclaim the biblical view of sexuality. In our prophetic role we must tell the truth to others and to our people. This is no time for moral relativism; it is the time to opt either for further oppression or for liberation through the principles of the Kingdom of God.

To Orient Our Conventions To Programs Rather Than to Personalities

Millions of African Americans are members of various religious organizations such as conventions and conferences. So much could be done for our people through this medium, if we were not so personality conscious. Usually Southern Baptists split over theological-biblical issues which are often undergirded by power. But National Baptist Conventions split for sociological reasons. Who is going to be president? Or who owns the publishing board? The National Baptist Convention U.S.A., Inc., which was founded in 1880, merged with other groups in 1895 to form the National Baptist Convention, U.S.A., Inc. This group under the leadership of then President, Dr. E.C. Morris, suffered a split in 1915 over who owned the publishing board. The R.H. Boyd family said that the Publishing Board was family property, and so he pulled out with his publishing board, and the National Baptist Convention of America was formed. This group became known as the "Boyd Convention." These two groups remained the principal Baptist groups until 1961.

In 1961 the National Baptist Convention U.S.A., Inc. suffered its second split in less than fifty years. The issue this time was over tenure. Dr. Joseph Harrison Jackson was elected president in Miami, Florida in 1953, supposedly with the understanding that he would vacate the office when the Convention met in Louisville, Kentucky in 1957. When this did not take place, his challenger Dr. Gardner C. Taylor, of the Concord Baptist Church of Christ in Brooklyn, New York, opposed his continuation as president. Supporting Dr. Taylor were such well-known pulpit giants as Dr. Martin Luther King, Jr., Dr. Martin Luther King, Sr., Dr. William Holmes Borders, et al. However, the next year, 1958, the courts sustained Dr. Jackson as president because of a constitutional oversight on the part of the convention. But in 1961, the showdown finally came in Kansas City, where such a tumult arose that Rev. A.G. Wright of Detroit, Michigan was killed as he fell from the platform while a shoving match was taking place between the followers of Drs. Jackson and Taylor. As a result of this day, which lives in infamy in National Baptist history, the Progressive National Baptist Convention was formed. These three conventions continued to exist as the three major National Baptist ecclesiastical voices. In 1982 in Miami, Florida, where he had been elected twenty-nine years earlier, Dr. Joseph Harrison Jackson, of the

Olivet Baptist Church of Chicago, Illinois finally came to the end of his tenure, and Dr. Theodore Judson Jemison of Mt.Zion Baptist Church of Baton Rouge, Louisiana was elected to succeed Dr. Jackson as president. As of this writing the issue is still a potentially explosive issue. Since African American religious groups tend to multiply by dividing, another schism could happen in the future if someone is overcome by a serious presidential itch. True to form in 1988, the National Baptist Convention of America which held its annual session in Fort Worth, Texas suffered a split involving the same family (The Boyd Family) which was also involved in the split of 1915. So now we have another convention, and another president, and the oppressed masses say, "so what?" This tradition of fighting and divisiveness is going to be very difficult to sell to a younger generation of African Americans who will be coming to flower in the twenty-first century.

First of all, to say that tenure is not "Baptistic" is to insult the intelligence of our people. If we have only one individual who can lead out of millions, then we need to close the convention down. We, as the Body of Christ, must overcome our lust for power. The Alternative Consciousness is the very opposite of this craving for prestige and power. While preaching at the Olivet Baptist Church for the late Dr. J.H. Jackson, I said to him, "The greatest mistake we ever made, Dr. Jackson, was to elect you president of the National Baptist Convention." He responded instantly and quizzically by saying, "What did you say?" To answer I clarified my statement by saying, "Sir, I mean no disrespect, but you were too great a preacher-prophet to be tied down by the Machiavellian pragmatism of convention politics. You should have been incarcerated six days and let out on Sundays to proclaim the "Unsearchable Riches of the Carpenter." He then smiled in resignation that the words had not been spoken by an enemy, but by a friend who was a great admirer of a great preacher-theologian. We must never again allow another preacher of the magnitude of Dr. Jackson to become president of the National Baptist Convention. The same can be said for many who seek the bishopric. It is easier to prophesy against Bethel when you are not on the king's payroll.

Beyond this, we need to take the financial profit out of being president. Since we follow White church polity anyway, why not move to a full time executive-secretary, who will be responsible for running the Convention. All of our Conventions can afford to pay such a person a starting salary of $75,000 to $100,000, plus benefits. If the work of our Conventions is important, then we should be willing to pay for quality. Therefore, the Convention president's office would be one of ceremony, and one where he/she would represent us at various ecclesiastical-political functions. I would personally recommend a two-year tenure for the presidency. Also, we need a commission on convention leaders. Before anyone is elected to office he/she should meet criteria in regard to doctrine, the New Birth experience, education, previous support of the convention's agencies, personality, thinking ability, listening ability, morality, and a programmatic agenda for the empowerment of our people. In the future we ought to commit ourselves to keeping great pastor-teachers in the pulpit and let Godly, trained non-pastors be the executive-secretary. Before one even runs for a two-year term as president, he/she should be examined by the Commission on Convention Leadership, and their findings should be presented to the body. And again, whoever is elected as executive-secretary should face the same process.

To Establish Corporate And Transdenominational Goals

Initially, since I am a member of the National Baptist Convention, U.S.A. Inc., we need to strategize with our 8 million followers in regard to the liberation of our people. Then we need to work with all National Baptist groups in terms of corporate efforts in lifting our people. There may even need to be a return to unification or reunification. Foolishness divided us; maybe oppression will force us to join forces as we help our people. However, I am not naive; until we can take the prestige, power, and possession syndrome out of our office holding, we will not be effective. If National Baptists would merge, we would be almost as large or as large as the Southern Baptist Convention. What a powerful group we would be if we would only exercise wisdom. If we don't, our right to exist is going to be severely questioned in the coming years.

But beyond this, we must not allow our denominational prejudices that we inherited from the oppressor to keep us divided and weak. We must work with Methodists, Pentecostals, Catholics, et al., in the liberation of our people. The African Methodist Episcopal's church history of liberation must be a model for all church persons. Theirs is a rich history of protest and productivity. Some will raise the issue of working with the community of Islam. My position is that theologically we shall have problems, because I believe in the uniqueness of the Christ. However, sociologically, whoever can add a gem of wisdom to our cause, must be heard.

> *And when Jesus was entered into Capernaum, there came unto him a centurion, beseeching him, and saying, Lord, my servant lies at home sick of the palsy, grievously tormented. And Jesus said unto him, I will come and heal him. The centurion answered and said, Lord, I am not worthy that you should come under my roof: but speak the word only, and my servant shall be healed. . . When Jesus heard it, he marvelled, and said to them that followed, verily I say unto you, I have not found so great faith, no, not in Israel.*[14]

Here was a pagan and an executor of oppression who received one of the highest verbal rewards that the Carpenter could give. If Jesus' vision was so penetrating that he could look beyond a pagan and see the good, we must do no less in our quest for freedom.

In the future we need regular summits between the religious leaders of the African American church community. The meetings will have a two-fold agenda which will be God and our people. Hopefully these meetings will not be designed for the displaying of egos. These will be strategy sessions which will result in mandates for action.

Beyond this we must move ahead in a more profound and deeper sense. The ideas presented in this book have not been written as the answer for our dilemma. They have been penned with the hope that the reader-thinkers of our community will come up with new ideas and strategies whereby we can become an empowered people. As a joint mission effort we can all pool our resources in order to connect African Americans with the Continent of Africa, socioeconomically, educationally, and culturally in the twenty-first century. Dr. Leon Sullivan is moving in this direction with the International Foundation for Education and Self Help (IFESH). If we pull this off, the Establishment will be upset, because it has been in its best interest to keep us divided.

Also at home we can build businesses, start banks, foster certification-liberation education, and, in general, meet the needs of our people. Again, our Convention and Conferences can agree not to meet so often, because it tends to leave us, as Tennessee Ernie Ford said, "Another day older and deeper in debt." When we are leaving multiple millions in the hands of the oppressor, we are getting deeper in oppression. For example, why couldn't all Baptists pool their resources and pledge to build a major luxury hotel or hotels in Nashville, Tennessee which could be used by all of the conventions. Since Nashville is headquarters for most of our National Baptist work, why couldn't there be a Convention Center-hotel complex. Three or four of our conventions could build a 20-thousand seat arena. We could even change our meeting times in order not to conflict with another convention's meeting time. And all the conventions would have people on the convention complex staff. We could even lose our minds and reunify. It could work if we got mad enough with Pharaoh to take our destiny into our own hands. Our conventions and conferences could also create powerful media ministries such as radio, television, etc., to tell our story. If Paul and Jan Crouch, Jim and Tammy Faye Bakker, Pat Robertson, Jimmy Swaggart, Robert Schuller, and D. James Kennedy could build powerful media ministries, certainly millions of us could do the same. The tragedy is, that for the last twenty years, the whole world has been listening to men who had meager training. Such men as Jim Bakker, who was sent to prison for fraudulent religious schemes, and Jimmy Swaggart whose sexual indiscretions with prostitutes brought his religious empire down, were not well trained. So African Americans do not have a monopoly on ignorance. Whites, too, have fallen prey to the syndrome which believes that the dumber one is, the better he/she can be used by God. If education is not important for the clergy, then we need to close down our seminaries, and let us all die from a terminal case of dumbness.

If television is to be used effectively, it needs to be transformed ecclesiastically, from a medium of entertainment, to a medium of liberation. In order to do this, we must put our best consecrated minds forward. This could go a long way towards breaking down the barriers that exist between theologians, pastors, and people. Our theologians will be required to transform the theology that they learned in Pharaoh's palace into the language of the brickyard. The majority of African American church members at the grass roots level have never heard of James Cone, J. Deotis Roberts, C.Eric Lincoln, Gayraud Wilmore, Cain Hope Felder, Clarice Martin, Renita Weems, William H. Myers, Charles B. Copher, James Washington, and other outstanding African American theologians. They deserve to be heard. They must be heard, provided they speak the language of the masses. The purpose of coming to the masses is not for monologue but for dialogue. Such a dialogue can be a source of enlightenment for our race.

There will also be a mandate for our college and seminary presidents to speak to our people. We need to close the gap between our colleges and our people. The people need to know the purpose, programs, problems, and potentials of our colleges, seminaries, and universities. This could also be a forum for the head of the United Negro College Fund to push our people and our church communions to endow our schools for liberation. The people could then prod our schools toward education for certification-liberation. What a powerful tool this would be for authors and other artists. Leading pulpiteers could be featured sermonizing, yes, but also leading discussions about the power, problems, and potential of the African American church. Our people need to know the history of our church. Nobody is better equipped to tell our story than we. Our people need to know about the great preachers of yesterday and today such as, Black Harry, John Jasper, C.T. Walker, L.K. Williams, C.A. Tindlay, Henry McNeil Turner, Henry Highland Garnett, Howard Thurman, Gardner C. Taylor, J.H. Jackson, Vernon Johns, Samuel Proctor, William A. Jones, Sandy F. Ray, et al. We also need trans-denominational forums for discussing differences which divide, but also ties that bind.

Again, we need to discuss biblical, theological, historical issues as they impact society and our people specifically. In the twenty-first century we must interpret the Bible through the eyes of the biblical Christ. In other words, we must interpret the Bible for ourselves. But in a technical sense this will not be easy. Since we have been prisoners of a Eurocentric hermeneutic, we must look for ways whereby as a people we can get back to Jesus, the early church, and the church fathers, without the socioeconomic undergirding of Eurocentric theology.

On the issue of biblical interpretation my friend Dr. William H. Myers, Professor of New Testament at Ashland Theological Seminary in Ashland, Ohio said:

> It should be evident that the Eurocentric approach to biblical interpretation is under siege in diverse parts of the church. The data suggest that the Eurocentric way of doing theological hermeneutics is inadequate in Third World cultures and minority cultures within oppressive Western cultures. In fact, African American theologians, historians, and biblical scholars alike have argued that the African American's usage and understanding of the text as well as appropriation of Christian constructs developed in an altogether unique manner. Furthermore, the manner in which the African American approach developed and is presently utilized is not incorporated in the Eurocentric method. It is omitted in all major works on hermeneutical methodology.[15]

We will not develop our independence from a Eurocentric biblical interpretation until we have a proliferation of certification-liberation trained scholars, who will emphasize alternative consciousness and will make Afrocentricity an indispensable part of our biblical-theological journey. The research done by Dr. Charles Copher is critical in identifying the Black presence in the Old Testament,[16] and Dr. Cain Hope Felder can help us with the presence of Blacks in the New Testament.[17]

The African American church and community must be introduced to the truth, that after the Apostles died, the theology of Christianity was formulated and shaped by the great theologians from the continent of Africa. We need to know such African theologians as:

1. Augustine, the Bishop of Hippo, which is now the country of Algeria. After Paul, he was probably the greatest mind in Christian history.

2. Tertullian of Carthage. He was first to use the term "trinity." Carthage is present day Tunisia.

3. Cyprian of Carthage.

4. Cyril of Alexandria, Egypt.

5. Clement of Alexandria, Egypt.

6. Origen of Alexandria, Egypt.

7. Athanasius of Alexandria, Egypt. He is remembered not only for his incredible genius, but on Easter Sunday, 367 A.D., he basically had the last word in declaring our present 27 books of the New Testament to be canonical.

Such knowledge as this is liberating within itself.

To Empower The Small Church

I am a firm believer that we have too many churches in the African American community, and many of them really lack the resources to make a substantive difference in our community. Because of doctrinal, class, economic, and personality differences we have ten churches or more in every block in our communities.

Literally we have more churches than businesses. But not only are smaller churches at fault, in many instances our larger churches fail miserably. The problem is that the smaller church, or storefront, lacks the educational, financial, and the numerical resources to make a lasting impact. On the other hand, the larger church may have all of the above resources and yet fail to be a liberating factor in our community. Why, then, is there failure in both instances? The answer is that both see their chief goal to be that of maintaining the local church. They feel that as long as they can raise enough money to pay the pastor, the janitors, and the musicians, they "have done as the Lord has commanded." Secondly, neither the smaller, nor the larger church, understands the mission of the church in the world. So the issue is not about quantity. It should be not how many we can count, but how many we can count on. I believe many smaller churches ought to merge in the next century. However, this possibility is a long shot. This does not have to be a smaller church merging with a larger church, but maybe three or four smaller churches merging for effectiveness, rather than playing the numbers game.

In the twenty-first century a church of 200 members with a trained pastor, educational, and financial resources can be more effective or as effective as the larger church. In all of our churches, stewardship giving (tithes, offerings, sacrificial giving) is a problem. Our churches are still supported by Jesus' crowd, the common people. The Black Bourgeoisie primarily views the church as an extension of its social strivings. Most times in churches that have multi-million dollar budgets, less than 15% of the congregation are supporting the church. My church, has a budget of well over a million dollars, and less than 40% support the church. This is to say that if I had a church of about 200 tithing members who had salaries between 30 to 50 thousand dollars a year, I could accomplish what I am doing now with 5,000 names on the computer.

Personally, I favor the smaller church, because it provides the best opportunity for authentic discipleship. The larger church has more social prestige in the community. Its budgets, buildings, and baptisms give them great social eminence, but at the level of equipping the saints, sometimes they fall short. Our model should be Jesus of Nazareth who took twelve men and taught them the principles of Alternative Consciousness, and a revolution took place 2000 years ago, that still has the power to transform. Everybody who is discipled in the principles of the Kingdom of God (Alternative Consciousness) is not going to be steadfast in the implementation of the Kingdom. The character of Judas Iscariot is a classic example of the individual who receives the teaching of Jesus of Nazareth and still reverts to the solutions of the oppressor. And yet Jesus took eleven Jewish peasants, minus Judas, and trained them to be executors of freedom, and that became a revolution. What the African American community needs in the twenty-first century is a revolution of substance rather than rhetoric.

In terms of structure maybe it would be a good idea to study the history of the Church of The Savior in Washington, D.C. This small congregation of multi-racial groups is on target in terms of its understanding of Christology as it impacts sociology. It is a church founded by Gordon and Mary Cosby, who graduated from Southern Baptist Theological Seminary in Louisville, Kentucky. The major theme is to take the biblical Christ seriously. I am not saying that we need to copy what they have done, but there is a need for the African American church to renew itself through small groups rather than prestigious institutionalism.

Before this will happen the smaller church must overcome its inferiority complex. The smaller church feels that it cannot do what the larger church can do. As a result, it usually attracts people with the same negative attitudes. It also attracts preachers who are interested only in maintenance. Therefore, pastor and congregation spend their whole ecclesiastical lives, being envious and ineffective. Ofttimes the pastor of the smaller church is not well trained and is bi-vocational. Because the congregation does not make the commitment to a trained full-time clergy and an evolving full-time staff, there is a certain low level of expectation. If the smaller church is to be empowered, we must develop the attitude that God's people deserve the best. In light of this we must also be concerned about the rural congregation. In most instances its pastor is also bi-vocational. Yet we must give thanks to God for their unfailing dedication, who, down through the years, have given great service in the face of overwhelming odds. They have not had great salaries or other benefits, but they have been faithful. On the other hand, a skeptic might wonder why most of the trained pastors are in our towns and cities. Is God behind a metropolitan conspiracy? The irony is, most rural pastors want to be in town, whether they are trained or not. And those who are trained are merely waiting to move to a city church. But why? Is it because the benefits are better? If all the trained pastors go to the city, then what should the rural congregants do? And if God's action is really in town, then everyone either needs to move to the city or be willing to be bused to a city church that has a trained pastor. If this strange scenario seems to be puzzling, it is, if you think about it. An individual who pastors a church of 100 members would find it difficult to become president of a Baptist convention or become Bishop of a major denomination. The truth of this matter should challenge all Christians to try and square this mentality with a Carpenter who experienced capital punishment.

To Accept Women Into Ministry

I use the term women in ministry only because many see this as a problem. This is not the problem. The problem, in a nutshell, has to do with a female standing behind the pulpit desk sermonizing. Very few pastors and churches would object to a woman serving as a staff person or going out into the streets sharing the gospel. The same message that the pastor delivered on Sunday morning, including introduction, three points, and a conclusion, would not be objected to, if a woman took this same message out into the streets word for word. So then what is the problem? First of all the problem is one of biblical hermeneutics. How does one interpret the Bible? Most male/female church persons reject the idea of "women preachers" based on their understanding of a Bible that appears to be chauvinistic. God is usually addressed in the third person masculine. Adam is the first created (Genesis 2:7). The Patriarchs (Abraham, Isaac, Jacob) are all men (Genesis 12-50). Moses was a male (Exodus 2:2), as well as his successor, Joshua (Deuteronomy 34:9). With the exception of Deborah all of the Judges were males (Judges 4-5). During the reign of the kings of Israel and Judah, only Athaliah reigned in Judah (Second Kings 11:1-20). Even here there is overwhelming male domination, though not exclusively. The prophetic ministry was also overwhelmingly male, but again women were also known as prophetesses: (1) Miriam, the sister of Moses (Exodus 15:20); (2) Deborah (Judges 4:4); (3) Huldah (Second Kings 22:14); (4) Isaiah's wife (Isaiah 8:3); (5) Noadiah, a false prophetess (Nehemiah 6:14); (6) Anna (Luke 2:36); (7) Philip the evangelist's daughters (Acts 21:8); (8) Jezebel, also a false prophetess (Revelation 2:20). And, of course, in the New Testament the Word became flesh as a Jewish male (John 1:14). During His ministry Jesus chose twelve men to be the foundation for His church (Matthew 10:1-4). Of these twelve, eleven were commissioned to make disciples of all nations (Matthew 28:18-20). And then we have the Pauline passages that seem to teach the preeminence of a Patriarchy:

> *Let the woman learn in all silence with all subjection. But I suffer not a woman to teach, nor to usurp authority over the man but to be in silence. For Adam was first formed, then Eve. And Adam was not deceived, but the woman being deceived was in the transgression. Notwithstanding she shall be saved in childbearing, if they continue in faith and charity and holiness with sobriety.*[18]

We also have Paul saying:

> *Let your women keep silence in the churches: for it is not permitted unto them to speak; but they are commanded to be under obedience, as also saith the law. And if they will learn anything, let them ask their husbands at home: for it is a shame for women to speak in church.*[19]

Boy, have we been breaking that rule! If this injunction is pragmatized, some feel that our churches would approximate a mausoleum. Another passage for many is also confusing:

> *And a certain Jew named Apollos, born at Alexandria, an eloquent man, and mighty in the scriptures, came to Ephesus. This man was instructed in the way of the Lord; and being fervent in the spirit, he spoke and taught diligently the things of the Lord, knowing only the baptism of John. And he began to speak boldly in the synagogue: whom when Aquila and Priscilla had heard, they took him unto them, and expounded unto him, the way of God more perfectly.*[20]

In light of Paul's previous injunctions, was Priscilla, the wife of Aquila, breaking the rule by joining with her husband in teaching a male preacher (Apollos)? Will God forgive such a sin, especially if such training results in Apollos getting his facts together? What about men being taught by women in theological seminaries? Others point to Galatians 3:28 to be the passage of ultimate concern on this issue: "There is neither Jew nor Greek, there is neither bond nor free, there is neither male nor female: for you are all one in Christ Jesus." No matter how one interprets the Bible in regard to the role of women in ministry, we need to hear from our women theologians on this issue. It is not the time for hostile confrontation nor boring monologue. It is the time for dialogue. Our sisters have light to share.

Another problem in dealing with this issue, is that of understanding the Call. In the Christian church we suffer from a failure to communicate. On this issue of the call, White women, African

American men, and African American women are confused because White men are confused. I believe that everybody is called to salvation, and everyone that accepts the call to salvation is called to preach the gospel (Acts 8:1-4). For example, I used to say that I was called to preach in 1966, and I was saved in 1953. There is a thirteen year gap, which raises the question of what I was doing between 1953-1966, if I were not preaching? I would have communicated better if I had said, "I was saved and called to preach in 1953, and I became a pastor-teacher or an equipper of preachers in 1966. I am convinced that the confusion would be diminished, if we made a distinction between New Testament preaching (Acts 2:14-38; Acts 8:1-4) and sermonizing, which is a cultural phenomenon. While the kergyma can and should be transmitted through the sermon, this is not the only medium. As a cultural phenomenon, many African Americans define preaching within the context of intonation, while one stands behind a pulpit. The men are confused, sisters, and so are you. Everybody preaches in the New Testament (Acts 8:1-4). Culturally, the one who delivers the sermon will have to be settled by local church polity. I am convinced that the sermon as an icon stands in the way of evangelism.

Again, the Jehovah's Witness model approximates the New Testament model on this issue although they have their own problems. In their communion, everybody is a minister, and everyone is a preacher. In most of our churches, whoever sits on the pulpit platform, are the preachers. No wonder we are flunking evangelism. But the Witnesses have a "Minister" of the kingdom hall who is the pastor-teacher, whose job it is to equip the other minister-preachers to go out, and preach, and bring them to the kingdom hall, to be taught, baptized, and sent out. The issue is not women preachers or women in ministry. It is about who gets to stand on the platform and deliver the sermon. I believe that if the platform and the pulpit desk were taken out of our sanctuaries, 85-90% of the aspirants to the ministry would be dissuaded. It is an issue of esteem in many instances. If a woman stands on the floor and does not use the term preach, but yet uses a text, subject, and points, she would not be condemned. The problem is a matter of inches from the floor to the platform. Another item to be considered is that of the call to ministry. Here again, all Christians are called into the ministry (diaconia). Ministry is about the implementation of one's Faith. It is the concretization of the invisible. So all persons, male and female, who accept Jesus of Nazareth, are called to action. While everyone who is saved is called to ministry in general, one's specific gifts, coupled with his/her training qualifies one to do a particular ministry. I tell you, what we are fighting over is not the issue.

If our women continue to outnumber our men in our theological seminaries, what are we going to do with them once they graduate? Invariably, the women are often better students than our male seminarians. As we go into the twenty-first century, some of our greatest minds will be females. Will we choose a man of meager training above a highly skilled female? Will biology take precedence over theology? I trust we can have the sense that Apollos had in accepting the input of Priscilla along with Aquila (Acts 18:24-26). I suppose an adequate paradigm for dealing with this issue would be to ask the following questions:

1. What was the role of men and women in creation?

2. What was the role of men and women in the Fall?

3. What is the role of men and women in Christ?

4. What will be the value of sexuality in the eschaton?

To Transform The Institutional Church

In a positive sense, from an ecclesiological perspective (doctrine of the church), the institution is the organizational structure through which the organism (Body of Christ) expresses itself. On the positive side, the institutional church has built hospitals, colleges, universities, seminaries, nursing homes, homes for the homeless, homes for the aged, drug rehabilitation centers and has established community programs, etc. The problem with all of this is the question of whether it was done for the glory of God or for the institution's sake. Particularly in the case of the White institutional church, sometimes one wonders if what has been done is the result of divine intervention or White power with all of its stolen resources. On the negative side, institutionalism in the African American church is characterized by the following:

1. Non acceptance of Jesus as Lord.
2. Non acceptance of the Bible as authoritative.
3. Non acceptance of the Holy Spirit as regnant.
4. Biblical illiteracy.
5. An anti-teaching mentality which grows out of the confusion between preaching and teaching.
6. A Madison Avenue form of church administration where maintaining the organization with a profit in mind takes preeminence over the church's mission in the world.
7. Tradition, which chokes the adventurous spirit. (Peter would have found it difficult to operate in the institutional church. -Matthew 14:28-29.)
8. Segregation at the eleven o'clock worship hour. (As we go into the twenty-first century, some African Americans will still be looking for a White church to join. But few Whites will be looking for an African American church.)
9. A lack of discipline. (Most of our mainline churches have little or no ethical restrictions that are enforced. Therefore, immorality sometimes gets out of hand.)
10. The practice of stewardship by the few.
11. Rebellion against the authority of the pastor. (In years past, this was true only in the White church. But as African Americans have become more educated, or "miseducated," they have a problem with the pastor not only as an autocrat, but also as a democrat. As the frustration level crescendos, there will be a decrescendo of pastoral authority, except in family heirlooms or cults. Pastoral influence will be further curtailed by the church oligarchies who have institutional

agendas, but who have no knowledge or understanding of the kingdom of God.)

12. Majoring in circumferential issues. (Usually when the church assembles to discuss matters, it is basically "much ado about nothing." The only thing that raises the ire of the congregation is primarily monies to be spent in regard to the institution.)
13. Competitiveness within and without. (This is especially true in regard to local religious institutions.) Eugene H. Peterson said, "The pastors of America have metamorphosed into a company of shopkeepers, and the shops they keep are churches. They are preoccupied with shopkeeper's concerns - how to keep the customers happy, how to lure customers away from competitors down the street, how to package the goods so that the customers will lay out more money. Some of them are very good shopkeepers. They attract a lot of customers, pull in great sums of money, develop splendid reputations. Yet, it is still shopkeeping; religious shopkeeping to be sure, but shopkeeping all the same."[21]

The greatest enemies that Christ has in any town are a great institutional church and a great institutional preacher. Since institutional religion was a conspirator in the death of Jesus of Nazareth two millenia ago, the present day institutional church "crucifies the Son of God afresh, and puts Him to an open shame" (Hebrews 6:6). If the institutional church in the African American community cannot be transformed, then it, too, must be condemned, along with its White counterpart, to the place where there are perpetual summers and the wind never blows.

To Define Nationalism Accurately

Let me begin by saying what I do not mean by nationalism. First of all, nationalism does not mean massive emigration to the Motherland. Secondly, it is not the quest for acquiring several Southern states in which African Americans can settle. For years this was high on the agenda of the Black Muslim movement, under the late Elijah Muhammad. Thirdly, nationalism is not about the violent overthrow of the United States or any other country. Fourthly, it is not a call for legal resegregation. Fifthly, it is not a call for the exclusion of all others who might be kamikazes for our cause.

If we are to be successful, we must deal with reality rather than fantasy. As was stated earlier, most African Americans are not going to emigrate to Africa. Unlike the ancient Hebrews, who emigrated from Egypt to Canaan, the overwhelming majority of our people will live and die in America. We have too much tied up here to leave en masse. Too many tears have been shed. Too many lashes have been laid across the naked backs of our foreparents. We can't leave because we have not been paid. The paradox of our situation is that while W.E.B. Dubois died in Ghana on August 28, 1963, Paul Robeson, another kamikaze, died in America on January 23, 1976. This has been and will continue to be our plight.

Beyond the recolonizing plans of Abraham Lincoln, some African Americans supported an emigration strategy, though not for the same reason as Abraham Lincoln. Lincoln recognized after the Civil War that the purpose for which the slaves were brought to America no longer existed. So why keep them? Such African Americans in the 19th and 20th centuries as Martin R. Delany, Alexander Crummell, Edward W. Blyden, Bishop Henry McNeil Turner, and Marcus Garvey supported a return to Africa. They believed that there was no hope for persons of African descent in this country. The only way that we would ever experience justice would be in Africa.

With no disrespect intended for the legacy of the Black Muslims under the late Elijah Muhammad, African Americans are not going to move from New York to live in a Southern state for the purpose of separation. And neither will Whites move from Mississippi to Pennsylvania in order that African Americans can relocate. Nationalism must not be based on moving to Nigeria or Natchez, Mississippi, unless that is a personal choice. We must strategize for a people who will not accept forced or voluntary recolonization. While the Hebrews left Egypt never to return (Exodus 14:13), there is no existential evidence that our liberation will be the result of physical separation from the oppressor. Yet, there will always be a lingering question as to whether such a liberation is possible without leaving the presence of the oppressor. Although Moses' liberation was one of physical separation, Jesus' liberation was not physical, but rather it was spiritual and mental, which was an alternative consciousness, or a whole new Way of Life. As I stated earlier in this chapter, the more I see of oppression, the more I am convinced that an authentic embracing and appropriation of the Kingdom of God is the only hope for our people. Some will see this as a cop-out, but it is a result of the realization that what the oppressor serves up as freedom is enslavement indeed.

The moral implications of violence have been debated down through the years by many theologians and ethicists. Our purpose here is not to discuss the theology of violence, but to deal with the practicality of violence. In the United States violence is not a major option in our liberation. Here is where Jesus, Gandhi, and King will continue to inform us and challenge us in the twenty-first century. When irrationality takes over, one is sobered by the reality that hunting rifles, AK-47's, and UZI's cannot defeat stealth bombers. What confused the British Empire in regard to Mahatma Gandhi, was his emphasis on satyagraha (soul force) which defeats the oppressor without firing a shot. Dr. King's reliance upon non-violence was a strategy that caught this violent nation completely off guard. This nation was founded on violence. And it is sustained by violence. We must remember that the Pentagon is not a prayer chapel.

> This is not to imply that the Negro is a saint who abhors violence. Unfortunately, a check of the hospitals in any Negro community on any Saturday night will make you painfully aware of the violence within the Negro community. By turning his hostility and frustration with the larger society inward, the Negro often inflicts violence on his own black brother. This tragic problem must be solved.

> But I would not advise Negroes to solve the problem by turning these inner hostilities outward through the murdering of Whites. This would substitute one evil for another.[22]

As African Americans become increasingly frustrated, Dr. King will still be a sobering force in the twenty-first century. Aggressive non-violence will continue to be a strategy both practically and as a by-product of the alternative consciousness.

> Of course you may say, this is not practical; life is a matter of getting even, of hitting back, of dog eat dog. Maybe in some distant Utopia, you say, that idea will work, but not in the hard, cold world in which we live. My only answer is that mankind has followed the so-called practical way for a long time now, and it has led inexorably to deeper confusion and chaos. Time is cluttered with the wreckage of individuals and communities that surrendered to hatred and violence. For the salvation of our nation and the salvation of mankind, we must follow another way. This does not mean that we abandon our militant efforts. With every ounce of our energy we must continue to rid our nation of the incubus of racial injustice. But we need not in the process relinquish our privilege and obligation to love.[23]

In the twenty-first century, I predict that there may be a call for voluntary segregation. Legalized segregation as of now is defunct, but there is great despair in both the African American and the larger community in regard to forced desegregation. Those of us who grew up prior to, and during the 1960's, can testify that we have been hoodwinked. This is why both Martin and Malcolm must be properly interpreted, lest we end up exalting one above the other as we have done in the past. It is our concern that ill-informed people will not accuse Dr. King and other Civil Rights leaders of setting us up for failure and deeper frustration. There is no integration in America, and desegregation was choreographed for failure. However, we will die before we accept forced segregation again. The blood of our mothers and fathers inspires us from the blood-soaked grounds of this country and the battlefields of the world. We will never endure what we suffered before. But we are no fools; desegregation is not working , and because it is not, America still has not solved its race problem. No wonder this country has been slow to enforce sanctions against South Africa. America is not that far removed from its own apartheid. But the problem again, at a deeper level, has to do with a derelict White institutional church that has failed to liberate White people from their racism. This is why I say that the White church's task is not to try to liberate (save) African Americans because Pharaoh's evangelism is poisonous. The task of the White church is to renounce its triumphalism and its racist arrogance and become a part of the alternative consciousness.

Nationalism, undergirded by the Kingdom of God, simply means African Americans taking the responsibility for themselves and their own. The fact that there are thirty million of us ought to be the foundation for sanity in the twenty-first century. We are larger than many countries in the world and should think of ourselves as a powerful reservoir of potentiality. Since we are not going to leave America en masse, nationalism will be Afrocentrically focused. We will build ourselves. Yet, there are those in the African American community who advocate separation, and others favor assimilation. Philosopher Cornel West said:

> Narrow black nationalism is unjustifiable, simply because it cannot deliver what it promises to achieve: black enhancement, especially of the black working poor and underclass. The black community does not possess the necessary wealth and power, nor will it possess them in the future to alleviate the deplorable plight of the black working poor and underclass. Indeed, black America can do much better with its economic and cultural resources than it is presently doing. But the notion that the destiny of black America can be set right by means of black economic develop-

> ment (as argued by black conservatives) or racial political strategies (as argued by black liberals) can only lead black people into a political cul-de-sac. As the great Martin Luther King, Jr., repeatedly noted, the destiny of black America is inextricably bound with that of America.[24]

Such a statement coming from Cornel West must not be ignored if we plan to stay in America. I have no problem with the term "America" if that means all the White people who are not a part of the Establishment. As I said earlier, Whites, as well as other groups, are victims of the Establishment. However, the game of racism became a strategy to perpetuate polarization. This is why, early on, Martin King was a far greater threat than Malcolm X because Martin's strategy was racially inclusive, and Malcolm's was racially exclusive. However, when Malcolm left the Nation of Islam, he broadened his vision of liberation to that of inclusion, rather than exclusion. Therefore, he and Martin became candidates for assassination.

As we strategize in regard to our situation in America some will see the term "Nationalism" as a call for the disunification of the United States. For me this is not the case at all. Again, what is nationalism?

1. It is 30 million African Americans no longer looking to the empire for solutions that will only end up in a deeper enslavement for our people.
2. It is about 30 million people thinking for themselves. This will result in the creation of think tanks, rather than talk tanks. All facets of the African American community will be represented, if they have something to offer. It will be male/female, liberals, conservatives, and radicals in the community, as well as the poor. The purpose is not to see who can generate the most heat, but how to collectively give light to our situation.

3. It is about 30 million people participating in the political system, but not without agendarizing for all of our people. Such a person as Reverend Jesse Jackson would be far more effective being a worker-strategist for African Americans, than being President of the United States. I think our efforts in the twenty-first century should be focused on our people, and what we can do collectively to extricate ourselves from the perfidious stratagems of the Establishment. I still believe theoretically in Reverend Jackson's Rainbow Coalition. As I stated earlier, it was possibly a rainbow coalition that came up out of Egypt (Exodus 12:38). However, we will only coalesce with those who will our liberation.
4. It is about 30 million people voting as a moral mandate.
5. It is about 30 million people accepting their own scholars. This will be the concerted efforts of our greatest minds coming together to move us to verifiable productivity. Unless we can start producing rather than consuming, we have no great future.
6. It is about 30 million people reclaiming and redeveloping our neighborhoods. We will not give an inch to those who would turn our neighborhoods into jungles. We will be vigilant and victorious.
7. It is about 30 million people strategizing for the development of strong families. This will begin in the formative years of a child's life.
8. It is about 30 million people creating and supporting their own financial institutions. However, this will not happen until we extricate ourselves from our miseducation.
9. It is about 30 million people creating and supporting their own businesses. As I stated in Chapter Six, this will not be easy because of the brainwashing that we have received over the years.
10. It is about 30 million people controlling the education of their children. They who feed the mind control the

body. Therefore, as I stated in Chapter Five, our education must be for certification and liberation.

11. It is about the reclamation of the African American mind. In this we will create conditions for self-esteem, which is critically needed in our community.
12. It is about controlling the media insofar as 30 million people are concerned. They who control the media control the arena of perception from which society forms its opinions and its behavior.
13. It is about 30 million people keeping up with the megatrends of society without losing our Alternative Consciousness. We must not allow social isolationism to factor us out of existence.
14. It is about 30 million people coming up with preventive strategies in order to keep our young men and women out of prison. This will also include continuing to minister to those in prison and the newly released.
15. It is about 30 million African Americans working creatively to reach those who are considered the under class. Since the death of Dr. King these have been affected very little by Civil Rights legislation. These are indeed the "wretched of the Earth."
16. It is about 30 million African Americans getting acquainted with other Africans of the Diaspora, for the purpose of dialogue, cultural exchange, mutual trade, and economic development. The new foundation started by the Reverend Dr. Leon Sullivan, which is called the International Foundation for Education and Self Help, is a most important move in that direction. Although its emphasis at this time is primarily centered on the continent of Africa, we must not forget that there are millions of Africans all over the world. And such a movement will meet with hostility from the Establishment.
17. It is about 30 million African Americans taking their intellectual resources seriously. We must read our own scholars, as well as the scholars of the larger

community. Both Malcolm and Martin must be read cautiously and critically through our own eyes.

18. It is about 30 million African Americans defining what the Promised Land is. This is critical for any discussion of liberation. What is success? How will I know it once I get it? Do I have it without being aware of it?
19. It is about 30 million people becoming vigilant and educated about the tactics used by the oppressor to control the threatening demographics of the African American people, such as AIDS, drugs, and easily obtained handguns. There is a paranoia in the African American community, particularly in regard to AIDS, after the "Tuskegee Experiment" in the 1930's in which innocent and unlearned African American men were used as guinea pigs in the testing of syphilis. These men were infected with the disease by the scientific-medical profession. Such past actions encourage healthy paranoia. We must educate our people in order to remain a people.
20. It is about 30 million people controlling the meaning of words, terms, and names used for sociopolitical classification. "It is time for Blacks to stop being the pawns in the word games of others. Our youth are wasting away in imitation schools, overloading the few drug programs available, filling up the prisons, being forgotten in mental institutions and dying faster than the statistics can record their forgotten bodies. The Black testing time has passed."[25] We have been troubled too long about the political implication of our Blackness. We have been called: Nigras, Niggers, colored, Negroes, Afro-Americans, Blacks, and African Americans. White has represented the good, and Black has represented the evil. Even the late A.M.E. Bishop Henry McNeil Turner refused to use scriptures or hymns that underscored the goodness of Whiteness. The truth of the matter is that our people are a rainbow of colors, and it is erroneous to

continue to call Whites by that term, when in reality they are Beige, rather than White. So as of now, I refer to Whites as Beige people.

21. It is about 30 million people supporting their religious institutions. The church, though confused and frustrated, will continue to be our only hope. This means that my nationalistic aspirations will be informed by Jesus of Nazareth.

Am I a pessimist? No. I am a weather reporter. "The dark clouds are rising. Let's go home. Can't you see the lightning flashing? Can't you hear the thunder roaring? The dark clouds are rising. Let's go home."[26] For it is only in returning home, that we can see the light.

> So every bondman in his own hand bears
> The power to cancel his captivity.
>
> William Shakespeare
> Julius Caesar
> I, iii, 101

References – Chapter Eight

[1] Walter Brueggemann, The Prophetic Imagination, Fortress Press, Philadelphia, PA, 1978, 13.
[2] Robert A. Baker, A Summary of Christian History, Broadman Press, Nashville, Tennessee, 1959, 24.
[3] Brueggemann, 16.
[4] Ibid., 16-17.
[5] Ibid., 18-19.
[6] Ibid., 21-22.
[7] Ibid., 21.
[8] Numbers 14:1-5.
[9] Carter G. Woodson, The History of the Negro Church, The Associated Publishers, Washington, D.C., 1921, 180-182.
[10] C. Eric Lincoln and Lawrence H. Mamiya, The Black Church in the African American Experience, Duke University Press, Durham, North Carolina, 1990, 399-400.
[11] J.A. Rogers, World's Great Men of Color, Vol. 2, Collier MacMillan Publishers, New York, 1972, 4.
[12] Mack King Carter, Establishing A Program for Catechumens at the Green Castle Baptist Church, of Prospect, Kentucky (Doctoral Thesis) Southern Baptist Theological Seminary, Louisville, Kentucky, 1978, 28.
[13] Findley B. Edge, A Quest for Vitality in Religion, Broadman Press, Nashville, Tennessee, 1963, 100.
[14] Matthew 8:5-8, 10.
[15] Cain Hope Felder, Editor, Stony The Road We Trod, Fortress Press, Minneapolis, Minnesota, 1991, 47. Article by, Dr. William H. Myers.
[16] Ibid., 146-164.
[17] Cain Hope Felder, Troubling Biblical Waters, Orbis Books, Maryknoll, New York, 1989, 46-48.
[18] First Timothy 2:11-15.
[19] First Corinthians 14:34-35.
[20] Acts 18:24-26.
[21] Eugene H. Peterson, Working the Angles: The Shape of Pastoral Integrity, William B. Eerdmans Publishing Company, Grand Rapids, Michigan, 1987, 1
[22] Dr. Martin Luther King, Jr., Where Do We Go From Here: Chaos or Community?, Beacon Press, Boston, Massachusetts, 1968, 64.
[23] Ibid., 65.
[24] Cornel West, Prophetic Fragments, William B. Eerdmans Publishing Company, Grand Rapids, Michigan, 1988, 140.
[25] Haki R. Madhubuti, Black Men: Obsolete, Single, Dangerous? The African American Family in Transition, Third World Press, Chicago, Illinois, 1990, p. 247.
[26] Negro Spiritual.

Bibliography

Akbar, Na'Im. Chains and Images of Psychological Slavery. Jersey City, NJ: New Mind Productions, 1984.

Andrews, William L., ed. My Bondage and My Freedom by Frederick Douglass. Urbana: University of Illinois Press, 1987.

Baker, Robert A. A Summary of Christian History. Nashville, TN: Broadman Press, 1959.

Bennett, Lerone. Before the Mayflower. Chicago: Johnson Publishing Company, 1982.

——-The Challenge of Blackness. Chicago: Johnson Publishing Company, 1972.

Berton, Pierre. The Comfortable Pew. Philadelphia: J.B. Lippincott Company, 1965.

Billingsley, Andrew. Black Families in White America. New York: Simon and Schuster, 1968.

Binkin, Martin, Mark J. Eitelberg, Alvin J. Schexnider, and Marvin M. Smith. Blacks and the Military. Washington, DC: The Brookings Institute 1982.

Blasinggame, John W. Frederick Douglass: The Clarion Voice. Washington, DC: Division of Publications, National Park Service, U.S. Department of the Interior, 1976.

Boddie, Charles E. God's Bad Boys. Valley Forge, PA: Judson Press, 1972.

Branch, Taylor. Parting the Waters: America in the King Years, 1954-63. New York: Simon and Schuster, 1988.

Brueggemann, Walter. The Prophetic Imagination. Philadelphia: Fortress Press, 1978.

Buttrick, George A. Christ and Man's Dilemma. Nashville, TN: Abingdon Press, 1945.

——Ed. Interpreters Bible Commentary. Vol. 3, 1954.

Campolo, Anthony. We Have Met The Enemy and They Are Partly Right. Dallas, TX: Word Publishing, 1985.

Carter, Harold A., Waytt T. Walker, William A. Jones. The African American Church, Past, Present and Future. New York: Martin Luther King Fellows Press, 1991.

Carter, Mack King. Establishing A Program for Catechumens at the Green Castle Baptist Church of Prospect, Kentucky (Doctoral Thesis), Southern Baptist Theological Seminary, Louisville, KY, 1978.

Cone, James H. God of the Oppressed. New York: Seabury Press, 1975.

—— Martin and Malcolm in America: A Dream and Or A Nightmare. Maryknoll, NY: Orbis Press, 1991.

Davis, Anne and Lucien Coleman. Review and Expositor. "The Single Person in Contemporary Society," 74:1 (1977).

Dostoyevshy, Fyodor. The Brothers Karamazov. translated by Constance Garnett. New York: New American Library, 1957.

Dubois, W.E.B., The Philadelphia Negro, Philadelphia: University of Pennsylvania, 1899.

Ebsen, Akpan, "The Care Syndrome: A Resource for Counseling in Africa," Journal of Negro Education. 42:205-211.

Edge, Findley, B. A Quest for Vitality in Religion. Nashville, TN: Broadman Press, 1963.

Ellison, Ralph. Invisible Man. New York: Random House, 1952.

Ellul, Jacques. The Subversion of Christianity. Grand Rapids, MI: Eerdmans Publishing Co.

Fant, Clyde, E., Jr., and William M. Pinson, Jr. Twenty Centuries of Great Preaching, Vol. X. Waco TX: Word Books.

Felder, Cain Hope, ed. Stony The Road We Trod. Minneapolis, MN: Fortress Press, 1991.

——-Troubling Biblical Waters. Maryknoll, NY: Orbis Books, 1989.

Frazier, E. Franklin. The Negro in the United States. New York: MacMillan Company, 1957.

——Black Bourgeoisie. New York; MacMillan Company, 1957.

Freire, Paulo. Pedagogy of the Oppressed. New York: Continuum Publishing Corporation, 1985.

Gladstone, W.E., Speech delivered in Liverpool, England, June 28, 1886.

Hale-Benson, Janice E. Black Children: Their Roots, Culture and Learning Styles. Baltimore: Johns Hopkins University Press, 1986.

Haley, Alex. The Autobiography of Malcolm X. New York: Grove Press, 1965.

Hewlett, Sylvia Ann. "A Wilting Generation," The Fort Lauderdale Sun Sentinel. July 14, 1992.

Hughes, Langston and Arna Bontemps, ed. The Book of Negro Folklore. New York: Dodd, Mead Publishers, 1958.

Jacob, John E. (Article) Westside Gazette, Fort Lauderdale, Florida, October 3, 1991.

Jones, Major J. Christian Ethics for Black Theology. Nashville, TN: Abingdon Press, 1974.

King, Martin Luther, Jr. Where Do We Go From Here: Chaos or Community? Boston: Beacon Press, 1967.

Koestler, Arthur. The Thirteenth Tribe. New York: Random House, 1967.

Kunjufau, Jawanza. Countering the Conspiracy to Destroy Black Boys. Chicago: African American Images, 1982.

Lincoln, C. Eric. The Black Muslim in America. Boston: Beacon Press, Boston, MA, 1961.

——"The Black Church," Christianity and Crisis, 30:18 (1970) 226.

Lincoln, C. Eric and Lawrence H. Mamiya. The Black Church in the African American Experience. Durham, NC: Duke University Press, 1990.

Madhubuti, Haki, R. Black Men: Obsolete, Single, Dangerous? Chicago: Third World Press, 1990.

Peterson, Eugene H. Working the Angles: The Shape of Pastoral Integrity. Grand Rapid: Eerdmans Publishing Company, 1987.

Roberts, J. Deotis. Liberation and Reconciliation: A Black Theology. Philadelphia: Westminster Press, 1971.

——-The Roots of a Black Future: Family and Church. Philadelphia: Westminister Press, 1980.

Robertson, Pat. The New World Order. Dallas, TX: Word Publishing Company, 1991.

Rogers, J. A. The Five Negro Presidents of the U.S.A.. Riverside, NJ: MacMillan Company, 1965.

——-The World's Great Men of Color, Volume 2. New York: Collier MacMillan Publishers, 1972.

Rowan, Carl T. Breaking Barriers: A Memoir. Boston: Little, Brown and Company, 1991.

Salley, Columbus, and Ronald Behm. What Color is Your God? Black Consciousness and the Christian Faith. Downers Grove, IL: Intervarsity Press, 1987.

"The Search for Adam and Eve," Newsweek, January 1988: 46-52.

Spero, Sterling, D. and Abram L. Harris. The Black Worker. New York, Columbia University Press, 1931.

Toppin, Edgar, A. A Biographical History of Blacks in America Since 1528. New York: David McKay Company, 1969.

Vance, Rupert B. "Racial Competion for the Land," in: Race Relations and the Race Problem. Durham, NC: Duke University Press, 1939.

West, Cornel. Prophetic Fragments. Grand Rapids: Eerdmans Publishing Company, 1988.

Williams, Richard. They Stole It, But You Must Return It. Rochester, NY: Hema Publishing Company, 1990.

Wilmore, Gayraud S., and James Cone. Black Theology: A Documentary History: 1966-1979. New York: Orbis Books, 1979.

Winter, Gibson. The Suburban Captivity of the Churches. New York: Macmillan Company, 1932.

Woodbury, Pickney, ed. The Struggle for Survival: A Partial History of Negroes of Marion County: 1865-1976. Central Florida Community College Press, 1976.

Woodson, Carter G. The History of the Negro Church. Washington, DC: The Associated Publishers, 1921.

——-The Miseducation of the Negro. Philadelphia: Hakim's Publications, 1988.

Wright, Bruce. Black Robes, White Justice. New York: Carol Publishing Company, 1987.

Wright, Richard. Native Son. New York: Harper and Row Company, 1966.

Biography

Dr. Mack King Carter is a native of Ocala, Florida, where he became a slave for Jesus Christ in 1953. He earned the following degrees: the A.A. from Central Florida Community College; the B.A. from the University of Florida; and the Master of Divinity and the Doctor of Ministry from Southern Baptist Theological Seminary of Louisville, Kentucky.

He served as pastor of three churches in Florida and of the Green Castle Baptist Church in Prospect, Kentucky before being called to his current position. Presently, Dr. Carter is Senior Pastor of the 5,000 member Mt. Olive Baptist Church in Fort Lauderdale, Florida.

In addition to his pastoral ministry, Dr. Carter has been guest preacher in many church pulpits and at denominational meetings and conferences. He has served as Professor of Theology, Church History, Homiletics, and New Testament at Simmons Bible College. He has also been Visiting Professor of Pastoral Theology and African American Studies at Southern Baptist Seminary. Further, he has lectured extensively on many college and seminary campuses throughout the country.

Besides preaching, teaching and lecturing, Dr. Carter has authored two other books, To Calvary and Beyond: Nineteen Lenten Sermons (1990), and A Catechism for Baptists (1989).

He is married to the former Patricia Thomas of Ocala, Florida.